CW01189657

Arctic Convoy PQ18

For Sophie

Contents

Preface viii
Acknowledgements xii
Glossary xiv
Maps xvii
Prologue xxii

Chapter 1   2–5 September 1942   1

Chapter 2   6–8 September   12

Chapter 3   9–10 September   22

Chapter 4   11–12 September   32

Chapter 5   13 September – Early Morning   43

Chapter 6   13 September – Late Morning   54

Chapter 7   13 September – Afternoon   68

Chapter 8   14 September   79

Chapter 9   15–16 September   103

Chapter 10   17–18 September   116

Chapter 11   19–20 September   126

Chapter 12   21–22 September   142

Chapter 13   23–27 September   153

Epilogue 158
Appendix I 166
Appendix II 168
Bibliography 169
Index 170

Preface

There are many images of the Second World War that have become ingrained in the modern psyche. British soldiers forming lines on the Dunkirk beaches as they wait patiently to be evacuated; American and British troops storming the Normandy beaches on D-Day; and Japanese bombers destroying the US Pacific fleet at Pearl Harbor: these are probably some of the first that come to mind.

However, one of the most important operations that directly led to the success of the Allies in ridding Europe of the Nazi scourge has never had the recognition it deserves. There have been no films made, and very few books written, about those brave men who sailed on the Russian convoys. This lack of acknowledgement and appreciation of those who fought and died in the bleakest of environments rankled with the men who saw action there, long after the guns fell silent and the ships in which they sailed were broken up for scrap. The Russian convoys accounted for 20 per cent of all the equipment and supplies used by the Soviets on the Eastern Front during the war. Therefore the importance and sacrifice of the men who got them there should never be underestimated.

When the Germans invaded Russia in June 1941, Stalin appealed directly to Churchill for aid to repel the Nazis. This assistance was immediately forthcoming, and over the course of the war, seventy-eight convoys made the horrendous journey to and from Russia to deliver that aid. Sailing from Loch Ewe in Scotland, the route took the convoys around Iceland and then across the Norwegian Sea, north of Bear Island, to the Barents Sea, then on to the Russian ports of Murmansk and Archangelsk. This brought the ships within range of Luftwaffe bases in northern Norway and also put them at the mercy of the U-boat wolf-packs and Kriegsmarine surface ships that operated in that area.

Added to the dangers of the German war machine was the savage Arctic weather. Operating in temperatures of around -30°C, sailors had go out on frozen decks, between attacks, to remove ice from weapons and superstructures in order to stop the ships becoming top-heavy and capsizing. Storms, appearing from nowhere, would throw men around as though they were toys, and any unfortunate soul falling into the sea would have around two minutes before he froze to death. It was possibly the harshest place on earth to conduct a war, and it led to Churchill describing the Arctic convoys as 'the worst journey in the world'.

My own interest in these voyages began quite by chance. In October 2015 I was contacted by my ex-high school English teacher, Joyce Holden who, knowing of my interest in the Second World War, thought I might like to attend a talk at my local museum she had arranged for a group of schoolchildren. This was to be a presentation given by a gentleman named Bill Halliwell, an ex-Royal Navy telegraphist who had sailed on the last Arctic convoy to Russia in May 1945 on the frigate HMS *Bazely*. The talk was to be about his time in the Royal Navy.

At the time, I was working for Wigan Council, and the museum was just across the road from my office. After rescheduling a couple of meetings, I managed to attend the talk, and my interest in the convoys was subsequently roused by Bill's enthusiasm, charm and humility. I met up with him a couple of times afterward and, upon reading a number of books on the subject, I decided to write a novel based on these voyages. This book I entitled 'The Worst Journey in the World', after Churchill's description. This book has since won a literary award and has been renamed *Hell and High Water*.

This led to my meeting another veteran, Charlie Erswell. Charlie had read the book and in December 2019 got in touch via email to commend the accuracy of my portrayal of the convoys. This was high praise indeed, as Charlie himself had been on many of those journeys to Russia during the war as a seaman/gunner on two destroyers, HMS *Milne* and HMS *Savage*. If anyone knew what those voyages were like, then it was surely him.

Charlie and I rapidly became firm friends and, upon listening to his stories, my interest in the Arctic convoys was once again brought to the fore. To prevent his story becoming lost in the mists of time, we decided to collaborate on writing his wartime memoir, which was published in June 2021 by Pen & Sword (*Surviving The Arctic Convoys – The Wartime Memoir of Leading Seaman Charlie Erswell*). Sadly, Charlie was to pass away in October 2021 after a short illness, just two months short of his ninety-eighth birthday.

Charlie's first ever voyage was on the newly commissioned destroyer and flotilla leader HMS *Milne*, in convoy PQ18 that sailed in September 1942. Of all Charlie's stories, it was his account of PQ18 that interested me the most, partly because not only was it his first voyage at the tender age of eighteen, it was also the first for 70 per cent of his ship's crew. He also told me that this convoy was the most heavily attacked of the whole war, and I became interested in finding out why this was so. Why did the Germans assault it in such great numbers? What was so important about this convoy that set it above the others that had gone before?

The more I read about and researched PQ18, the clearer it became to me that this was possibly the most important convoy of the whole war, and it is sad that it, along with the Arctic convoys in general, has not had the recognition it so richly deserves. Make no mistake about it, had Britain not supplied the Soviets with the materiel they needed, particularly in the early stages of the war, then they might very well not have had the resources to repel the Nazis, and the European map might look very different today. The bravery shown by the men of the Royal and Merchant Navies in getting those supplies to Russia should not have been ignored by successive governments, and the literary and film industries, for so many years.

PQ18 came hot on the heels of the ill-fated PQ17; the majority of the ships that sailed in that convoy were sunk by the Germans after a major mistake was made by the Admiralty. Fearing the huge German battleship *Tirpitz* was on her way to engage with the convoy, the order was given for the merchant ships to scatter and the Royal Navy covering force to be withdrawn; the idea was to avoid an attack by the German surface fleet, a battle the Admiralty feared could not be won. However, the consequences of this order were huge. It effectively left the merchant ships unprotected, and over the following few days, twenty-four of the thirty-five ships that had set out on the journey were sunk by the Luftwaffe and U-boat wolf-packs. It was a complete and utter disaster.

The Germans now saw an opportunity. Should PQ18 suffer the same fate, then the whole Arctic route might very well become untenable for the Allies. With Stalin unable to comprehend the disaster that was PQ17 and accusing the British of lying about just how many ships had set out, Churchill was keen to restore relations and at the same time prove that the route was still viable.

PQ18 therefore needed to be bigger and better protected than any of the Arctic convoys that had gone before it. The loss of so much materiel on PQ17 had to be rectified, and so as much cargo as was possible had to be crammed onto the ships, supplies that were crucial to Russia at that time, as the Battle of Stalingrad was raging in the south. At the time of PQ18 this battle was hanging in the balance; its outcome would determine who would be victorious on the Eastern Front and, consequently, in the Second World War in Europe as a whole. It was therefore essential for the Allies that PQ18 was a success. Equally, it was essential for the Germans that PQ18 be stopped.

What followed was one of the most dangerous voyages for any mariner in any area of operations during the Second World War. Under constant attack from the air, U-boat wolf-packs and extreme weather, the twenty-five days it took to escort PQ18 to Archangelsk and the returning QP14 back to Iceland became the most important of the whole Arctic theatre.

I hope the following pages have done justice to the heroism and sacrifice of the men who sailed on it.

John R. McKay
Wigan, 2023

Acknowledgements

There are so many people I would like to thank for their contribution and support in the process of writing this book. I apologize now to any I may have missed. If I have done so, please accept my apologies, for it is not intentional.

Firstly, I should like to thank all at Pen & Sword Maritime, notably Henry Wilson, Matt Jones, George Chamier, Matthew Potts and Charles Hewitt. Working with you all on this project has been an absolute pleasure.

My next thank you is to Adrian Wait, for all his support and advice and for reading an early draft of the manuscript. Adrian is the administrator of the Facebook group 'Arctic Convoys, Forgotten Heroes', and I am glad to have him as a friend. I would like to add my thanks to other members of the group who have provided me with information and support and for keeping the memory of those who sailed on the convoys alive. This includes Jos Odijk, who gave me some excellent research material on the sinking of SS *Stalingrad* and MV *Atheltemplar* – I would not have been able to write those sections without the information provided, so a massive thank you for that.

Thanks also to my good friends Joyce and John Holden for reading an early draft of the manuscript and for the support they have given me in all my writing endeavours. It was Joyce who put me in touch with Bill Halliwell, a veteran of the Arctic convoys (no longer with us, sadly), who sparked my interest in this little known theatre of the Second World War.

I would also like to give thanks to Leona Thomas, author of *Through Ice and Fire* (Fonthill), again for her support and advice and for allowing me to use information from her father's memoir. Thanks, too, to Pam Ingram, whose father sailed on the SS *Temple Arch* in PQ18, for kindly providing me with his account of the convoy.

Thanks to Paul Gill, author of *Armageddon in the Arctic Ocean*, his father's memoir of his time on SS *Nathanael Greene*, for allowing me to use a scene from his book and providing me with an accompanying photograph of his father, a very brave man.

Thanks to Valentina Golysheva, ex-curator at the Archangelsk Museum in Russia, for her help and support in all my writings about the Arctic convoys.

Acknowledgements xiii

I would like to thank my brother Paul, my niece Leanne Worsley, Bill and Trish Halsall and Phil Patterson for reading an early draft of the manuscript and giving me their critiques. Again, this has been invaluable in the process of getting the final draft right.

I would also like to give a big thank you to Andrew Strang for putting me in touch with Chris King. Chris was a wireless operator on the corvette HMS *Bluebell* and sailed on PQ18 back in September 1942. Chris was kind enough to read the (almost) final draft. His input has been absolutely invaluable. Who better to have read it than someone who was actually there? Thank you so much, Chris.

I would also like to give another huge thank you to best-selling author and historian Damien Lewis for all his support and advice over the last couple of years. Having him as a friend and mentor has spurred me on to get this book right, and inspired me to continue with my writing.

Thanks also to Pamela Brown for her support in my writings on the convoys, and to Dave Roberts of the Western Approaches Museum in Liverpool. Dave was kind enough to invite me to give a presentation on PQ18 at the museum last summer and to contribute to the production of their permanent Arctic Convoys exhibition, which opened in February 2022. Although my contribution was rather small in comparison to others', it was an honour and privilege to have been asked for my input. The museum is well worth a visit if you are ever in Liverpool.

This leads on nicely to a shout out to the Russian Arctic Convoy Museum Project based at Loch Ewe in northern Scotland. The museum does great work in keeping alive the memory of those who sailed on the Arctic convoys. Their website can be found at www.racmp.co.uk.

Thanks to my family for all their support in my writing; to my daughters Jessica and Sophie, but mostly to my wife Dawn, who has had to put up with me leaving books about the convoys strewn around the house for many months and listening to me waffle on about warships, U-boats and Arctic storms. Those books can now finally be put away in the bookcase!

Finally, it was my late friend Charlie Erswell who first made me aware of PQ18 and its importance to the war in the Arctic and the Eastern Front. He sailed in the convoy on HMS *Milne* at the very young age of eighteen. His memories of the journey were as clear at the age of ninety-seven as they were the day he arrived safely back at Scapa Flow following the escorting of QP14 back to Iceland. Sadly, Charlie is no longer with us, but hopefully his memory will live on in these pages, and in his wartime memoir, on which we collaborated before he 'crossed the bar' in October 2021.

Glossary

Arrestor hook – hook underneath an aircraft used to connect with arrestor cables on an aircraft carrier to assist with landing

Asdic – a form of sonar used to detect submarines

Athwartship beam – a sideways beam going across a ship to give it support

Bofors – Anti-aircraft weapon with 40mm calibre

Bow – the front of a ship/boat

CAM ship – Catapult Aircraft Merchant ship with a single fighter aircraft on its bow that could be catapulted into the sky to defend shipping but had no way of landing back on board

Catalina – flying boat operated by RAF Coastal Command for reconnaissance and anti-submarine operations. Had a crew of nine

Coastal Command – RAF Command responsible for the protection of Allied shipping from attacks by the Kriegsmarine and Luftwaffe

Commodore – senior commanding officer of a merchant convoy

DEMS – Defensively Equipped Merchant Ship, i.e. a merchant ship that possessed a degree of weaponry to protect itself

Depth charge – an anti-submarine weapon. Dropped into the water nearby and detonating, it subjected the target to a powerful and destructive hydraulic shock. Could be set to explode at various depths

Director – unit above the bridge on a warship that targeted aircraft and controlled main armaments. Normally would have a watch of four/five people

Dog tags – identification tags worn by military personnel

Fairway buoy – a buoy indicating the water to either side of it is unobstructed and safe to sail

Fireman – naval firemen were responsible for the running of the ship's boilers and engines

Glossary xv

Galley – ship's kitchen

Hampden bomber – British twin-engine medium bomber operated by the Royal Air Force

Hawser line – a thick cable or rope used for mooring or towing a ship, also used by sailors to attach themselves to when carrying out duties on deck to prevent them falling overboard

Heads – ship's toilets

Heinkel He-111 – twin-engined German torpedo-bomber with crew of five

HMS – His/Her Majesty's Ship

Hudson bomber – a light twin-engined bomber used for reconnaissance by RAF Coastal Command

Jerkin – a sleeveless wool-lined leather overcoat

Junkers Ju–88 – Twin-engined German torpedo-bomber with crew of four

Knot – unit of speed equal to one nautical mile per hour – equates to 1.15 miles per hour

Kola Run – informal name given to the Arctic Convoys, particularly from Britain/Iceland to Murmansk (the Kola Inlet)

Kriegsmarine – German Navy

Kye – a thick chocolate drink enjoyed by sailors

Lammy coat – sheepskin-lined overcoat

Lend-Lease Agreement – an agreement between the USA and its allies that allowed the USA to lend or lease war supplies to any nation deemed 'vital to the defence of the United States'. This included ships loaned to the Royal Navy

Liberty Ship – mass-produced cargo ship constructed in USA

Luftwaffe – German Air Force

Matelot – informal name for a sailor

MV – Motor Vessel

Oerlikon – Anti-aircraft weapon of 20mm calibre

Operation EV (or EVY) – the Royal Navy undertaking to protect merchant ships travelling on convoys PQ18 and QP14

Pom-pom – four-barrelled quick-firing 40mm anti-aircraft weapon

Port – the left hand side of a ship/aircraft

PRU – Photographic Reconnaissance Unit

Quartermaster – assistant to officers of the deck and navigators. They serve as helmsmen and perform ship control, navigation and bridge watch duties

RAF – Royal Air Force

RFA – Royal Fleet Auxiliary

RNAS – Royal Naval Air Service

SS – Steam Ship or Screw Steamer

Starboard – the right hand side of a ship/aircraft

Stern – the rear of a ship/boat

Stoker – another name for a fireman

Stringbag – nickname of the Swordfish aircraft (due to its ability to carry all kinds of equipment)

U-boat – German submarine, often referred to as just 'boat'

Vichy/Vichy France – area of southern France not occupied by German forces until November 1942, overseen by puppet government in Vichy who collaborated with the Nazis

Western Approaches – area of Atlantic Ocean west of Britain and Ireland, often patrolled by wolf-packs to attack supply ships coming from America

Wolf-pack – Group of U-boats operating together

Maps

Loch Ewe
Loch Ewe, Wester Ross, Scotland, the mustering point for the Arctic convoys from early 1942.

Royal Navy Bases in Scotland
Scapa Flow and Arctic convoys' mustering point, Loch Ewe.

PQ18 Convoy Set-Up
Merchant ships in the centre, surrounded by escort of warships.

PQ18 Route

Operation Orator

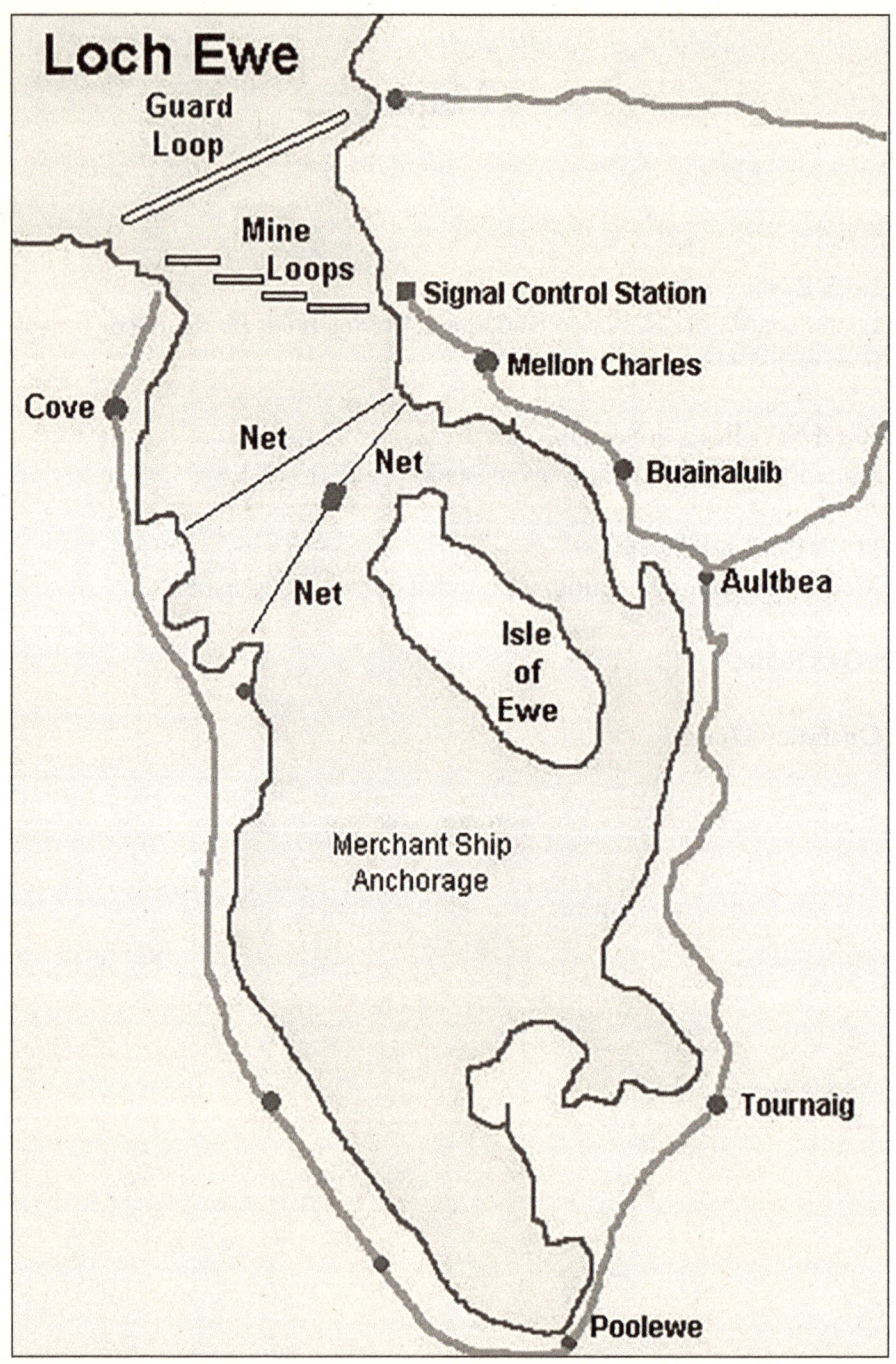

Loch Ewe, Wester Ross, Scotland, the mustering point for the Arctic convoys from early 1942.

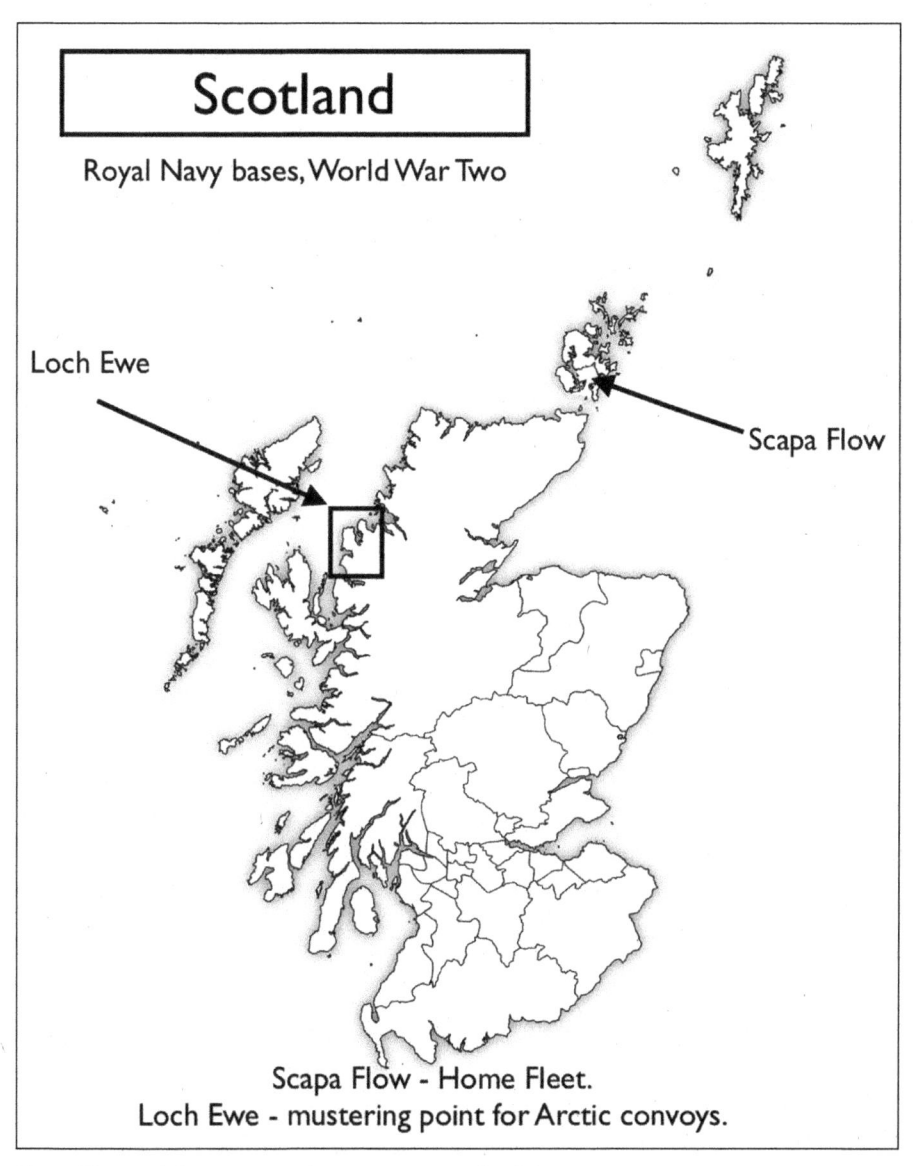

Scapa Flow and Arctic convoys' mustering point, Loch Ewe.

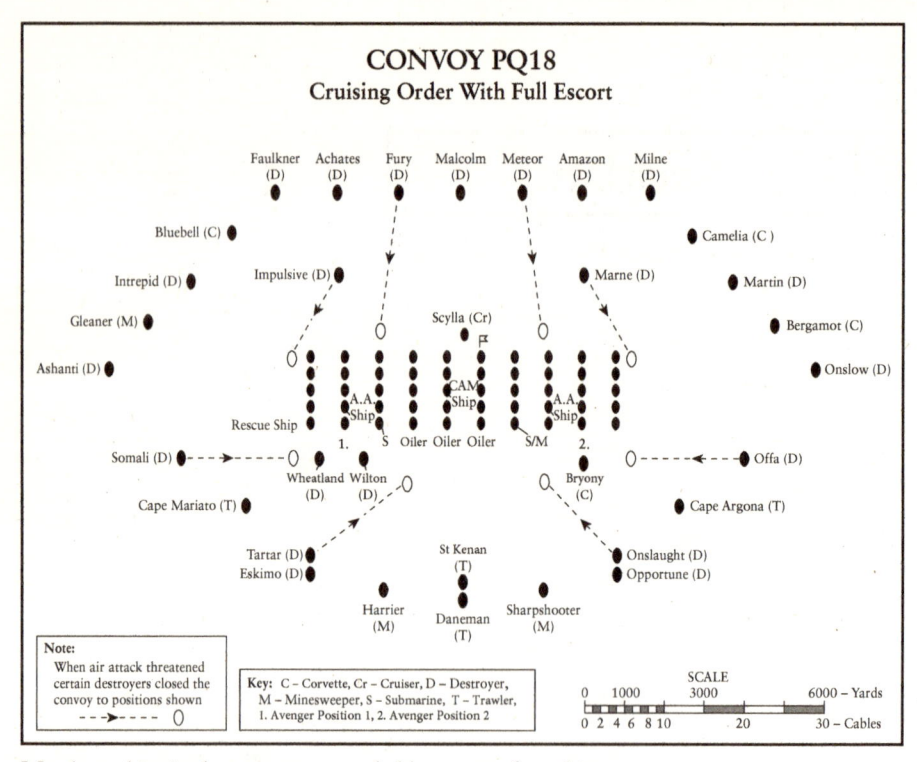

Merchant ships in the centre, surrounded by escort of warships.

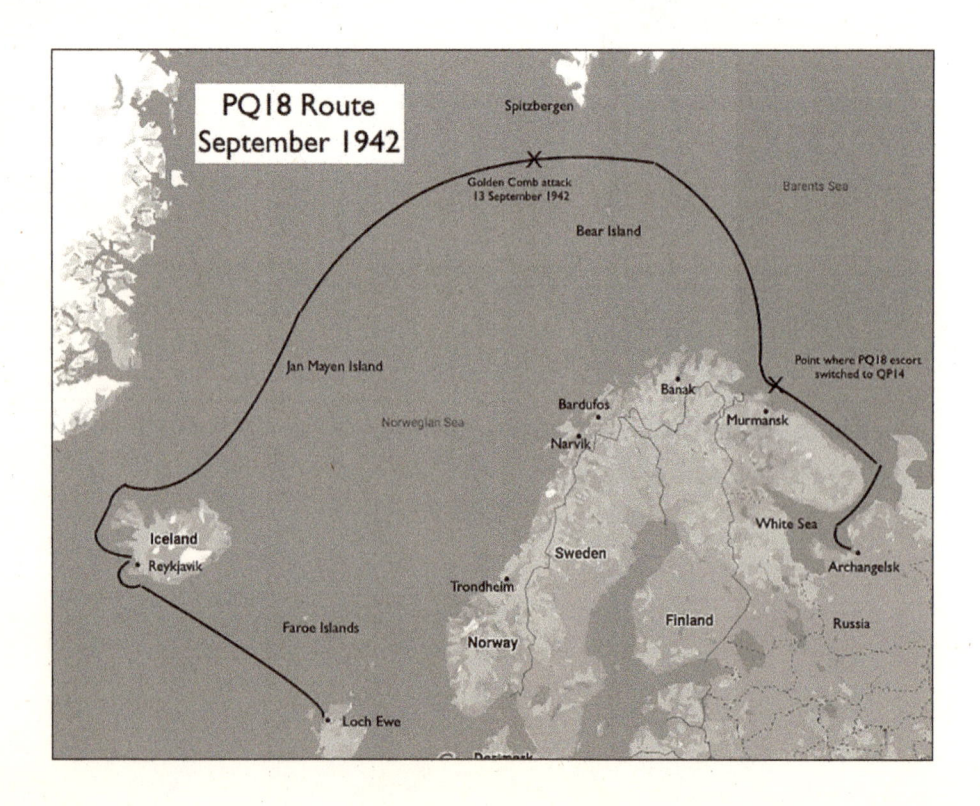

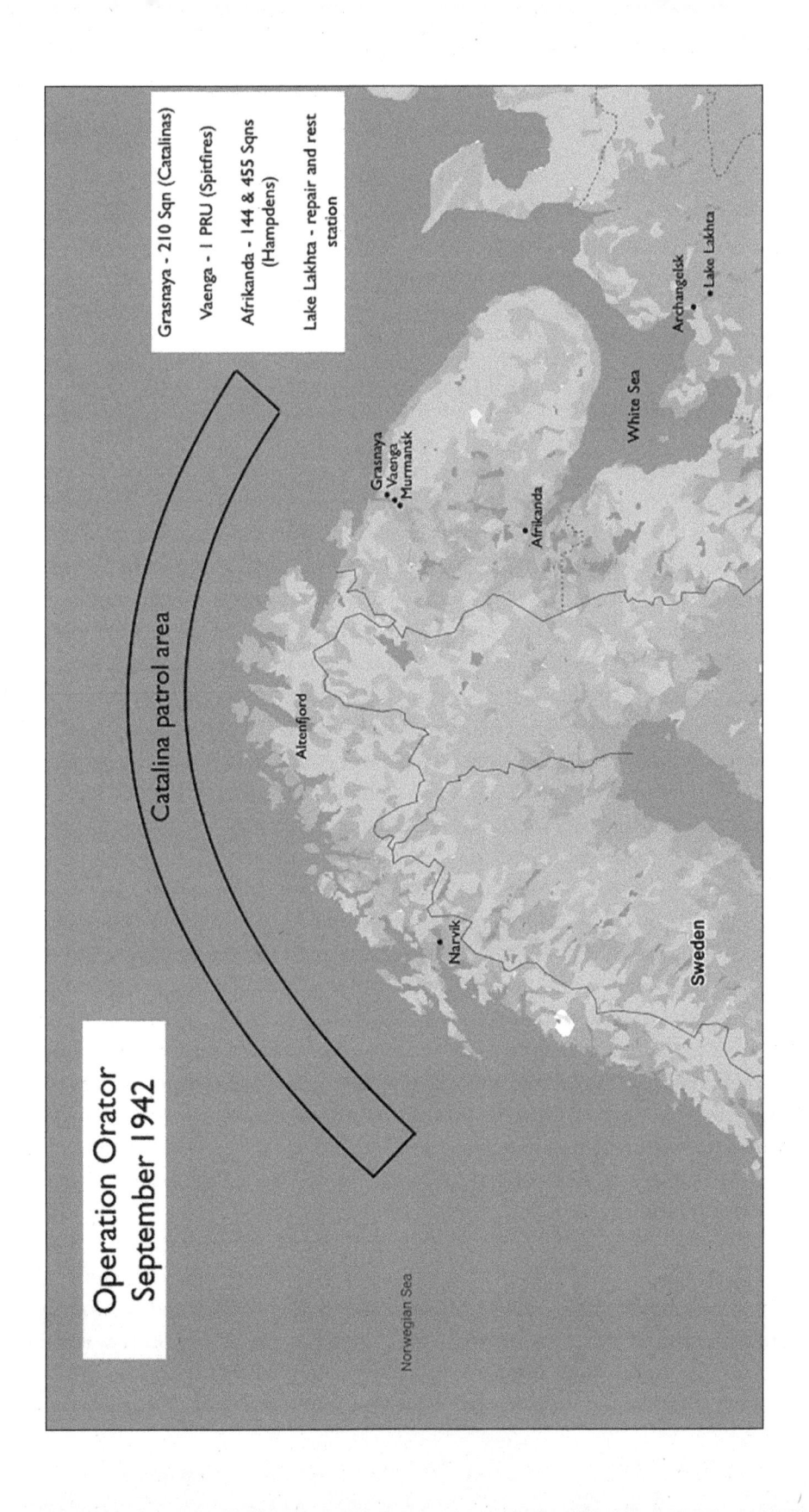

Operation Orator
September 1942

Grasnaya - 210 Sqn (Catalinas)

Vaenga - 1 PRU (Spitfires)

Afrikanda - 144 & 455 Sqns (Hampdens)

Lake Lakhta - repair and rest station

Catalina patrol area

Norwegian Sea

Narvik

Altenfjord

Sweden

Afrikanda

Grasnaya
Vaenga
Murmansk

White Sea

Archangelsk
Lake Lakhta

Prologue

Luftwaffe Airbase, Bardufoss, northern Norway, 1300 hrs, 13 September 1942

Thirty-one year-old Major Werner Klümper threw his cigarette butt to the ground, zipped his flight jacket to his throat, thrust his hands deep into his jacket pockets and shivered against the cold. He knew, as far as the weather was concerned, that things were not going to get any better. It was approaching the time of year when temperatures were only going to drop a lot further and become increasingly uncomfortable. The thought of having to operate in such conditions did not appeal to him in the slightest.

Bardufoss, in the far north of Norway, was a far cry from the warmth he had enjoyed when the squadron had been based in the Tuscan city of Grosseto, 120 miles north of Rome. There he had been chief instructor at the torpedo-bomber school, teaching low-level bombing runs using Heinkel He-111 aircraft, before the recent transfer to Bardufoss, where his newly trained pilots would put into practice the skills he had taught them. Grosseto had been a wonderful place to be stationed; beautiful scenery, delicious food and wine, and almost constant sunshine next to a warm and bright blue Mediterranean Sea. In downtime he and his friends would drive to the golden beaches of the Tuscan coast and enjoy all the region had to offer. Yes, he thought, Bardufoss was very different to all that.

Prior to the transfer of the squadron to Norway, he had achieved promotion from Hauptmann to Major, and along with the burden of responsibility that the rise in rank had brought, he was filled with a sense of pride at the faith the Luftwaffe hierarchy had shown in him. The promotion was long overdue, for he was an excellent and very experienced pilot, and his abilities as a leader and instructor were equally impressive.

Bardufoss Airbase was one of the most important military sites in Norway. Close to the Arctic Circle, it was the perfect place from which to launch air attacks against the port cities of Murmansk and Archangelsk and the convoys that sailed from Iceland with war supplies for the Soviet Union. It was vital those ships were stopped, for they contained materiel that would be pitched against German forces currently fighting a fierce and bloody battle in the southern Russian city of Stalingrad, a battle that was apparently hanging in the balance.

And one such convoy was at that very moment north-west of Bear Island and steaming towards Russia – almost forty merchant ships with as many Royal Navy warships escorting them.

Hunching his shoulders against the wind, Klümper headed towards the row of aircraft lined up along the apron. All his pilots had been given their orders and knew exactly what was expected of them. Today was going to be extremely important. His squadron, *1 Kampfgeschwader 26*, (I/KG26), containing twenty-eight Henkel He-111s, along with sixteen Junkers Ju-88s of *Kampfgeschwader 30* out of Banak airbase, were to conduct a *Goldene Zange* (Golden Comb) operation, the first of its kind. Each aircraft carried two LT F5b torpedoes on its undercarriage, long, sleek, deadly missiles capable of causing sizeable damage to any ship they hit. Should the mission succeed, those vessels he was about to lead his squadron to attack would be annihilated. This would be the day when this Allied convoy would suffer the same fate as that which had sailed in July.

For some reason, he knew not why, that previous convoy had been ordered to disperse, scattering to leave the merchant ships without Royal Navy cover. Some had argued that this was due to the success of the air operations against them, but he was not so sure. It had, however, allowed the Luftwaffe and U-boat wolf-packs to pick the ships off one by one, and only a handful had made it through to Archangelsk. If the same result could be achieved again, then the British might think twice before dispatching any more convoys to Russia.

A small flight had set off half an hour ago. This was the first part of the plan; they were to reconnoitre and harass the ships, drawing their attention and paving the way for the larger attack that was to follow, the one Klümper himself was to lead. Flying low, in line abreast just above sea level, Klümper and his comrades would release their torpedoes together in one long line, effectively becoming the 'teeth' of the comb. If it went well, there was a strong chance that many of the merchant ships would be hit.

In theory, the plan seemed perfect, but Klümper was an experienced torpedo-bomber pilot and knew that the best-laid plans did not always go the way you wanted. Attacking at low altitude at 300mph, his planes would need to overshoot the outer screen of escort ships before their torpedoes could be released. Flying so low, with their undercarriages exposed, they would be vulnerable to the guns of the Royal Navy destroyers and the anti-aircraft ships that travelled with them. To avoid this, the strategy was to fly even lower still, along the bow or stern of the ships, thus avoiding the flak from the 4.7-inch turret guns that would struggle to depress their barrels that low. However, this would leave them closer to, and at the mercy of, the smaller calibre weaponry which he knew to be plentiful on the enemy's ships.

He was also aware that this time there was an aircraft carrier in the convoy and so had to assume the Sea Hurricanes she carried would be airborne as soon as I/KG26 was picked up on the enemy's radar and his commanders became aware of their approach. Sending the small flight beforehand was aimed at tempting the planes out early, hoping that they would need to refuel and re-arm as the Golden Comb aircraft came in to carry out the full attack.

Reichsmarschall Hermann Göring, the commander-in-chief of the Luftwaffe, had issued a directive that the aircraft carrier was to be the main target, and so the squadron were under orders that the attack against it should be 'so violent that this threat is removed'. Klümper, however, was not sure that this was the most important ship to focus on; surely the overall aim was to stop the delivery of the cargoes to the Soviets, making the merchant ships of much higher strategic importance. But he knew that no aircraft carrier had been sunk by the Luftwaffe in any theatre of war, and should they manage to sink it, this would be both a feather in Göring's cap and a boost to the morale of the German public.

Klümper did not expect all those he flew with today to return. He did not have to tell his crews this; they already knew. He had seen it in their faces at the final briefing, when he had informed them of the convoy's composition, course and speed, and explained to them the importance of the day's mission: the ships they were to attack contained supplies that would be used against their countrymen on the front line in Russia, and they needed to be stopped at all costs.

Climbing on board, he waved good luck to the other crews as they too stepped up into their aircraft. Settling into his seat next to his navigator he took a deep breath and exhaled. He flicked the ignition switches and started the twin Jumo 211F-1 engines. As the ground crews removed the chocks from the wheels, he waved at them, and a few moments later he pushed the throttle forward and taxied the Heinkel to the runway.

All around, the throbbing of aircraft engines filled the air as the planes of the squadron formed up alongside and behind him. Each aircraft carried a crew of five: pilot; navigator, who also acted as bombardier and nose gunner; waist gunner; ventral gunner, who was probably the most exposed of all the crew, operating the machine guns situated on the undercarriage; and dorsal gunner, who had the added responsibility of operating the radio.

Klümper set the throttle to maximum and pushed forward, sending the aircraft hurtling down the runway. A few moments later, he felt the ground fall away as he pulled back on the control column, lifting the Heinkel into the sky. He checked to his left and could see the others following him as their pilots did the same, expertly guiding their planes into the early afternoon sky. Now airborne, he set a northerly course, determined to fulfil his mission and stop this convoy.

Klümper had mixed emotions about wreaking such slaughter. He knew that should the *Goldene Zange* attack be a success, many people would die horribly this day. He would be consigning many unfortunate souls to the bottom of the ocean. His mind flashed back to five years previously, when he had been flying with *Seefliegerstaffel 88* as part of the Condor Legion during the Spanish Civil War. Seeing a defenceless enemy troopship en route to Cartagena, he had made the choice not to attack it. He could very easily have sunk the unarmed ship with 400 enemy combatants on board, but instead he told his Spanish translator to radio the ship's captain and tell him there was a U-boat in the water nearby on its way to sink her. The ship was then ordered to sail to Melilla and surrender to General Franco's troops. This was, of course, a bluff, but fearing that what Klümper had told him was true, the captain did as requested, thus saving the lives of all those on board and avoiding what would have been a massacre. This act of integrity had earned Klümper huge respect, not only from his comrades but also from those he was fighting.

With these thoughts still running around his head, he settled into the flight and tried to relax as best he could.

* * *

They had been in the air for two hours now, and Klümper looked out of the window to his left and right. The squadron was keeping formation, flying at a steady pace. Maintaining an altitude of around 200ft, above a choppy and restless sea, forty-four aircraft stretched out across the sky. It was an awesome sight.

The weather had been intermittently problematic. Flying conditions, although not the best, had become more bearable as they had progressed, the wind buffeting them occasionally and rain and sleet splashing hard against the front canopy. With visibility down to around six miles, he had been unable to locate the shadowing Ju-88 that was supposed to guide them in. Realizing that if he waited any longer for the missing aircraft he might have to turn back without conducting the attack, he had taken a chance and turned to the east, hoping his calculations were correct and he would soon spot the convoy.

And then he could see them, a huge fleet of ships heading in a north-easterly direction at a slow and ponderous pace.

It was like nothing he had seen before. They were so many that he didn't bother to try and count them; it was pointless, they were so large in number. He tried to seek out the aircraft carrier but understood that recognizing it among such a vast number of ships would be too difficult. There were ten long columns of merchant vessels, evenly spaced, with Royal Navy escorts around them and others flitting between the columns like shepherds keeping their flock in order, providing a protective screen to stop predators from attacking. The logistical operation in getting such a number loaded, formed up and kept in order was impressive, he had to admit; the sheer scale of the British operation had to be admired.

But then he was not there to sit in admiration of the brilliant organization of the Royal Navy. His orders were to smash this convoy, and he was going to do his level best to do just that. He was under no illusion that the destroyers would by now have picked the planes up on their radar and would know they were coming. He allowed himself a small smile. What must their commanders have thought on seeing so many aircraft headed their way?

Although so great in number, to Klümper the ships looked like sitting ducks; easy pickings should they get this attack right. He scanned the multitude of ships again for the aircraft carrier but could not make it out among them. He did not waste too much time trying to find it as he needed to concentrate on maintaining formation and getting on with the *Goldene Zange* attack. Göring might have to wait a little longer yet for his prize.

He knew the destroyers were armed to the teeth, with 4.7-inch turret guns, Bofors, Oerlikons and a myriad of other weapons that could be used against him and his crews. They were headed towards a maelstrom of fire, there was no doubt about it. He knew that success and survival was all about his pilots keeping their nerve.

He flicked open the mic and spoke to the other pilots, giving them words of encouragement as they settled into the attack formation; Ju-88s and He-111s, spread out across the skyline, like a soar of eagles going in for the kill. As one, the planes dropped to an altitude of 70m above the surface, and as they drew closer, a sudden burst of ack-ack exploded around them as the turret gunners on the destroyers tested their range. However, most of the shells burst above them, the big guns unable to get their trajectories quite so low.

Speeding past the destroyers of the outer screen, flak and small arms fire filling the air around them, Klümper was relieved to see no Sea Hurricanes in the sky. It appeared the diversionary attack earlier had done its job, the British planes being forced back to the aircraft carrier to re-arm and refuel.

His concentration was now total as they approached the optimum range for release and, when he judged them to be 600m away he gave the order to fire. At once torpedoes dropped from the long line of aircraft, splashing into the water as their wet heaters kicked in and they were propelled forward at 40 knots, a long line of death on a collision course with the convoy. His ordnance now released, Klümper pushed forward on the column to take the aircraft even lower.

And then he was upon them, banking sharply to avoid hitting one of the ships, flying his plane only a few metres from her stern. With machine-gun fire and Bofors shells bursting all around him, he pulled back on the control column to take the Heinkel higher and away from the immediate danger. He could now see the muzzle flashes of the guns below. The air began to fill with tracer and exploding shells, as the 4.7-inch turret guns started to pound the skies, throwing shrapnel and destruction all around, buffeting his aircraft and shaking him and his navigator violently. The airman in the dorsal gun turret let out an oath, but Klümper ignored him. He needed to focus just to keep airborne, clutching the control column hard, his feet working the pedals furiously. If they were hit and had to ditch in the sea, there would be little chance of survival.

He observed the ships turning as the order was given by the convoy commodore for them to move 45° to port, away from the approaching danger. By turning parallel to the tracks of the torpedoes as they came ever nearer, ships could reduce the target area and thereby the chances of being hit.

Klümper was now flying alongside the ships, almost at mast height, speeding through the lanes between the columns. The bursts of heavy enemy ordnance were now ever closer, mixing in with machine-gun fire, some of which thwacked terrifyingly into the side of the plane. He glanced to his left and saw another of his He-111s, flames bursting from the port engine as it was hit by anti-aircraft fire from one of the destroyers. Almost immediately it cartwheeled into the sea, its wings ripped from the fuselage as it hit the water. For a brief moment it settled on the surface before rolling onto its side and sinking beneath the waves.

Klümper knew there was no hope for the crew. If the enemy fire hadn't already killed them then, even if they managed to get out of the plane, the ice-cold water of the Arctic Ocean would do for them instead. They were gone. Time for mourning their loss would have to come later. For now, there was still a job to do.

A few minutes passed as the squadron tried to avoid the relentless barrage put up by the multitude of ships and attempted to drop more bombs onto them. He could see Hurricanes in the sky, having now taken off from the carrier HMS *Avenger*, harassing more of his planes. In his peripheral vision he saw another of the squadron go down, taking with it its crew of five airmen.

As more of his planes looked to be getting hit, he gave the order to turn for home and banked towards the south. Still the constant fire from the destroyers shook his aircraft, but, luckily, from what he could make out, the plane had not been seriously damaged.

It was only now that he was able to see how successful the attack had been. It appeared that the whole of the starboard column had taken hits, and he could see at least five ships burning, smoke rising in great plumes into the mid-afternoon sky. As he looked on, he witnessed one of the merchant ships disappearing beneath the waves, gone forever, taking her cargo and crew with her. However, despite so many ships having taken hits, he could see the majority still afloat, the quick reactions of their skippers to the turn order having saved them.

He tried to count the planes that were now following him and realized they were rather fewer than had set out earlier from Bardufoss. Smoke trailed from the engine of one, and he wondered if it would manage to hold out until it got back to land or would become another casualty of this horrendous war.

He knew that the crews of the planes that had now gone were almost certainly all dead. However, from what he could gather from his initial observations, it looked as if the attack had had at least limited success.

Had it been worth it? he asked himself. Was the loss of so many crews justifiable in the whole scheme of things? One thing was certain: he could not have asked for more from any of his men. They had performed impeccably.

As the remaining planes of I/K26 continued south, he checked his watch. From start to finish, the whole attack had taken no longer than fifteen minutes; so much death and destruction in such a short space of time. He only hoped they had done enough, but he knew there would be more of the same to come. More attacks like this were required if the convoy was to be destroyed. Maybe, if his pilots held their nerve and were not too disheartened by their losses, they could achieve the victory his superiors so craved.

Only time would tell.

Chapter 1

2–5 September 1942

Loch Ewe, in north-west Scotland, is a bucolic and tranquil place. Its banks are home to small crofting hamlets, with the village of Poolewe at the head of the loch to the south and the larger village of Aultbea nestling on its eastern shore. Facing Aultbea is the large, picturesque Isle of Ewe, which occupies the centre of the loch. The area is home to hundreds of varieties of flora as well as a wide diversity of wildlife, including red squirrels, pine martens, red deer and numerous species of birds. In the summer, otters and seals can occasionally be seen popping their heads out of the water to observe golden eagles swooping majestically over the loch's deep, calm waters.

In early 1942, Loch Ewe was to become home to more than just wild animals and interesting plant life. It was decided by the Admiralty that this peaceful and rather thinly-populated area was the perfect location to be the new mustering point for the ships that were to sail the Arctic convoy route. Previously, the ships of those convoys had travelled independently to Iceland from the ports at which they had been loaded, forming up in Faxa Bay at Hvalfjödur, near Reykjavik.

From these assembly points the ships sailed east towards Norway and then on to Russia to deliver their cargoes. The route took them partly along the Norwegian coast and then around the northern tip of Scandinavia, before heading east to the ports of Murmansk on the Barents Sea, just inside the Kola Inlet, and Archangelsk, further east on the White Sea at the mouth of the Dvina River. The route varied depending on the season, the frozen pack ice in winter making it impossible to sail too far north and forcing them closer to land and consequently nearer to the Luftwaffe bases in Norway.

However, with the threat of U-boat wolf-packs operating in the Western Approaches it was determined the ships needed to be afforded more protection in the early stages of the journey and so would travel in convoy from Loch Ewe to Iceland. There, they would rendezvous with other merchant ships coming from North America for the onward journey to Russia.

Over the course of only a few weeks, a number of anti-aircraft gun positions had been constructed, spaced strategically around the loch's shore; an anti-submarine boom had also been stretched across the mouth of the loch, from Mellon Charles on the east, via the small isle of Sgeir an Araig, to Firemore on the west. Sailors, administrators and staff of the Women's Royal Naval Service (WRNS or Wrens), along with civilian construction and maintenance workers, descended on the area in large numbers, bringing with them heavy machinery and all manner of military vehicles and hardware. Around 250 men of the Royal Artillery were also posted to the area to crew the air defences at places such as Boor and Rubha Nan Sasan. To add to this protection, barrage balloons were spaced out at different locations around the loch, with the building used to inflate them erected in Tournaig. At Poolewe, the stately home of Pool House was appropriated to act as Command Headquarters.

Almost overnight the population of the villages around Loch Ewe increased fourfold. To accommodate this influx of personnel, wooden dormitory huts, offices and equipment stores were constructed in Aultbea for over 1,000 workers, and a cinema was built in the village, which soon became the main social hub for locals and their new military neighbours.

As the ships arrived, laden with cargoes that had been loaded in such ports as Liverpool, Glasgow, Belfast and Hull, their captains and senior officers would meet at Pool House to receive orders and intelligence reports. If time permitted, their crews would be granted shore leave. Entertainment was often laid on by the locals; merchant sailors mixing with their Royal Navy counterparts to attend dances and the occasional movie screening; local pubs filled to bursting with sailors, Wrens and civilian workers from the shore bases making the most of the opportunity for one last blow-out before embarking on what Winston Churchill described as 'the worst journey in the world'. For they knew there was a very good chance they might not return from the voyage on which they were about to embark.

And so, in no time at all, Loch Ewe went from being a quiet, unassuming place, so far untouched by war, to one of the busiest naval locations in the whole of the British Isles.

* * *

At the end of August 1942, the largest Russian convoy yet began to assemble in the loch.

As each ship arrived, crews already present, seeing the huge number of vessels already at anchor, presumed this would be the last; yet still more kept appearing, filling every available berth the loch had to offer. Heavy cargo ships lying low in the water, their holds laden with essential war materiel for the Soviets; tanks, trucks, aircraft (broken down and packed in boxes), ammunition, food, fuel, medicines and raw materials. When their holds had been filled to bursting point and no more room could be found, more items were strapped and chained firmly to their decks, including armoured vehicles and trucks (there was even the odd locomotive). Every available space was utilized. The loss of so many ships and so much equipment on the disastrous convoy that had preceded this one meant that each ship embarking on this new journey was filled to the brim.

Mixed in with these merchant vessels was the 'Local Escort', a number of warships of the Royal Navy which would give them protection for the journey to Iceland; destroyers, minesweepers and corvettes, armed trawlers and bespoke anti-aircraft ships, all anchored alongside. Hundreds of matelots swarmed across their decks, carrying out drills and checking weapons and equipment, hoping for that last shore pass to allow them some fun before the serious work began.

For those on the ships there was a sense of apprehension, creating an atmosphere, for some, of quiet restlessness. Rumours abounded of what had happened to the previous convoy to Russia. Although the details were not yet clearly known, it was understood that convoy PQ17 had met a terrible fate, with most of its merchant ships ending up at the bottom of the sea. There was also gossip that the Royal Navy had abandoned them, leaving them to the mercy of the Luftwaffe and the U-boat wolf-packs. Nobody could believe this was true, but the rumours persisted nevertheless.

The sailors were right to feel nervous, since some of what they were hearing was quite true, albeit not the fault of the men who sailed on those ships. On 27 June 1942, convoy PQ17 had set sail heading for Archangelsk. As it closed on Norway, information from Allied agents arrived at the British Admiralty reporting that the 'Bismarck-class' battleship *Tirpitz* had left her base near Trondheim and was heading for waters which the convoy was approaching. Although this information proved in the end to be incorrect, it did not prevent panic erupting in the Admiralty; upon receiving this intelligence, the First Sea Lord, Admiral Sir Dudley Pound, gave the order for the convoy to 'scatter' and for the covering force to be withdrawn. To scatter meant the ships were to head off in any and all directions in an attempt to prevent the enemy from destroying them. Ironically, this order effectively led to exactly the opposite result. Over the next few days, with the merchant ships now unprotected, twenty-four of the thirty-five merchantmen that had left Iceland were sunk, with the loss of 153 lives and thousands of tonnes of cargo. It had been a complete disaster.

But the British were not to be put off. Now, a mere two months later, another convoy was about to embark on that very same journey. Churchill had made a personal promise of supplies to Stalin and nothing would stop that promise from being fulfilled. The supplies were crucial, since the pivotal battle of Stalingrad was raging in southern Russia, the outcome of which would probably decide the war on the Eastern Front and, therefore, the whole of the war in Europe.

This latest convoy, PQ18, would effectively be the last throw of the dice. The Admiralty could not allow another disaster to occur, and so it needed to be more heavily protected than any of its predecessors. The *Tirpitz* was still out there and still a very real threat, and every effort had to be made to ensure that threat was nullified. Should PQ18 suffer the same fate as PQ17, then any future Russian convoys would be unviable.

No matter the fears, no matter the dangers, PQ18 simply had to succeed.

Having retired from the Royal Navy in August 1939, after an illustrious naval career, 55-year-old Edye Kington Boddam-Whetham was recalled from that retirement to resume his service. He was to be the convoy commodore, and his ship, the SS *Temple Arch*, flying the commodore's pennant, would lead the thirty-nine cargo vessels that were to make up PQ18. Over the previous few days, as ships had gathered in the loch, their captains and officers headed to the Headquarters in Poolewe to receive their instructions and intelligence reports, and to discuss the formation the convoy was to assume. Each captain was given a pennant number which would determine his position in the convoy. They were informed the ships were due to leave Loch Ewe on 2 September, in two columns under local escort. Upon reaching Iceland they would be joined by the close-cover escort and assemble into ten columns before setting off on the 1,000-mile journey to Russia.

In charge of the close escort which would provide protection for the majority of the voyage was Rear-Admiral Robert (Bob) Burnett, who was to sail on the flagship, the cruiser HMS *Scylla*, which had only recently been commissioned. Convoy PQ18 would be her first voyage. In fact, many of the Royal Navy ships providing the close-cover escort were doing so for the very first time. Some, like the destroyer HMS *Milne* of the Fighting Destroyer Escort, with a crew made up of almost 70 per cent newly recruited sailors, had herself only recently been commissioned and was yet to go to sea.

Burnett had been in the Royal Navy for forty years. Born in Buchan, Aberdeenshire, he was educated at Eastman's Royal Naval Academy in Winchester and later at Bedford School before joining the Navy in 1902 at the tender age of fifteen. Serving on the China Station and then with the Atlantic and Mediterranean fleets, he became an instructor at the Navy Physical Training School. When the First World War broke out, he saw action at the Battles of Heligoland and Dogger Bank and was promoted to Lieutenant-Commander in April 1918. Between the wars, Burnett rose through the ranks, becoming a Rear-Admiral in January 1941. In March 1942 he was given the position of flag officer of the Destroyer Flotillas of the Home Fleet.

HMS *Scylla*, now anchored near to the mouth of Loch Ewe, was to steam ahead to Iceland to link up with the Fighting Destroyer Escort, currently anchored at the large naval base in Scapa Flow, Orkney, leaving the Local Escort to bring the merchants in. On board the ship was Sub-Lieutenant Robert Hughes, a young officer from Wales who worked in the ship's 'blue' director.

A few days previously, whilst *Scylla* had been at Scapa Flow, and along with his counterpart Sub-Lieutenant Rowland from the 'red' director, Hughes had been called to a meeting in the gunnery officer's wardroom with Lieutenant Wainwright. Hung over after a mix-up with a bottle of gin the previous day, it took his superior two attempts to explain to him and his fellow officer that the captain had finally received his orders to sail. They had spent the last few weeks since the ship had been commissioned carrying out drills and honing their gunnery skills off the island of Arran and had become restless to get out to sea.

Wainwright, or 'Guns' as he was affectionately known, laid out a map on the table and with his finger drew an arc from Iceland around to northern Russia passing over Jan Mayen, Bear and Hope Islands.

'Guns' went on to explain that the journey was well over 1,000 miles long and they would be travelling at no more than 8 knots (around 9mph), the route taking them along the Norwegian coast where the Germans had many Luftwaffe bases, the largest being at Banak, near Hammerfest. The two Lieutenants listened intently as their superior told them to expect many air attacks the closer they got to Bear Island, for as long as it was daylight; this would be many hours, since darkness lasts for only a fraction of the night that far north.

This, of course, was quite true. Daylight in the far northern hemisphere at this time of year could last well over twenty hours. In the winter months, the opposite would be the case, the days passing in almost perpetual darkness.

This did not make Hughes feel good at all. From what Wainwright had told him, as an officer in the director it was clear he would be kept very busy indeed.

'Guns' went on to tell them of the convoy configuration and that the *Scylla* would be at the head of one of the merchant columns, moving out ahead to engage the enemy should the convoy come under air attack.

Rowland asked about the *Tirpitz* and other heavy German surface ships known to be operating in the Norwegian fjords, the presence of which had led to the disaster of PQ17 only a few weeks previously. Wainwright reassured him there were substantial units of the Home Fleet patrolling the area and there was nothing for him to worry about.

Wainwright, however, was not 100 per cent correct. Although it was true there were patrols out in the Norwegian Sea, it was unclear whether they could provide sufficient protection should the German hierarchy decide to utilize the *Tirpitz*.

With so much riding on the success of PQ18, the planners had looked at how it could be better supported than the previous convoys. With Kriegsmarine surface ships, U-boat wolf-packs and the Luftwaffe bases in northern Norway all operating in the area, something had to be done to reduce their threat.

Just as with PQ17, the main surface danger was perceived to be that of the battleship *Tirpitz*, which was known to be temporarily docked in the northern port of Narvik, her usual base being Trondheim further south.

The *Tirpitz* was a formidable battleship and the second of the 'Bismarck' class. Her sister ship, the *Bismarck*, had, however, been sunk in the North Atlantic the previous year, but not before destroying the battleship HMS *Hood*, resulting in the deaths of 1,415 British sailors. The loss of the *Hood* was felt throughout Britain, and although the German ship had eventually been sunk after a combined operation between many ships and sixteen Swordfish aircraft, a repeat of the destruction these German battleships could inflict was something the Admiralty was keen to avoid.

The *Tirpitz* had armament which was far superior to any of the ships of the Royal Navy and could hit them at much longer range. With eight 15-inch guns located within four twin-turrets having a range of 41,500 yards (23.5 miles), they could devastate any formation well before any Allied ship could get within range to fight back. The *Tirpitz*'s firepower was enhanced by six more twin-turrets housing twelve 5.9-inch guns and a further sixteen twin-turrets with eight pairs of 4.1-inch and eight pairs of 1.5-inch guns to provide anti-aircraft protection. Another twelve 0.79-inch anti-aircraft guns were dotted around the ship. In all, the *Tirpitz* was the largest and most heavily armed battleship available to any fleet in the conflict. She was a floating killing machine.

Along with the *Tirpitz*, the cruisers *Admiral Hipper*, *Admiral Scheer* and *Köln*, together with eight destroyers, were also understood to be stationed in Altenfjord in northern Norway. They could set sail at any point to intercept the convoy. Should the Germans decide to utilize this force to its full ability, they could wreak havoc on any ships passing through their area of operations.

To counter this, a Distant Covering Force (DCF) commanded by Vice-Admiral Bruce Fraser, which included the battleships HMS *Duke of York* and HMS *Anson* and the cruiser HMS *Jamaica*, would sail from northern Iceland to patrol the area, and a total of nine Allied submarines would position themselves off the Lofoten Islands and in northern Norwegian waters.

Along with this, a Cruiser Covering Force (CCF) of six ships of the 18th Cruiser Squadron would provide a further distant cover, to engage enemy surface ships should they proceed to attack the convoy. However, its commander, Vice-Admiral Stuart Bonham-Carter, was not prepared to pit his force against the *Tirpitz* should she leave port to intercept. In a 'Most Secret' memorandum dated 4 September 1942, entitled 'Orders for Cruiser Covering Force during the passage of convoys PQ18 and QP14' (known as Operation EVY), he outlined what was expected of his captains, including the tactics they were to employ should they come under air attack or encounter enemy surface ships. Significantly, the memorandum stated, 'It is not my intention to engage any enemy which includes *Tirpitz*.' It is therefore not clear what the convoy was supposed to do should the *Tirpitz* leave port in order to attack it, as the cruiser cover escort provided by Bonham-Carter was likely to retreat from any action. The hope was that the German fleet would remain in port if it knew the Royal Navy covering forces were so numerous.

However, Hughes and his shipmates were unaware of Bonham-Carter's intentions, and now, as Hughes stood near the quarterdeck looking out at the vast gathering of merchant ships, his nerves were steadied by a growing quiet confidence. He knew he could do his job and could do it well, and from what he had so far seen of the performance of the officers and men on the *Scylla*, he knew they too would not let down their colleagues on the merchant ships when the time came.

Over the last few days there had been a constant coming and going of senior officers on board, the boatswains' pipes continually sounding as commanding officers arrived for conferences with Admiral Burnett. Now, late in the afternoon of the second day of September, the hustle and bustle had stopped; there was a general feeling that matters had come to a conclusion and the convoy was finally about to set sail.

Earlier in the afternoon, a number of aircraft from Coastal Command had flown over the loch to loud cheers and waves from the ships' crews. It gave them great comfort to know that not only would the convoy be protected by the ships of the Royal Navy, but the aircraft of the Royal Air Force and Fleet Air Arm would also contribute to keeping them safe.

A siren blasted out from somewhere in the centre of the mass of assembled vessels. Suddenly there was a movement of masts as one by one the ships started to weigh anchor and move slowly towards the mouth of the loch. At their head was SS *Temple Arch*, the commodore ship, with Rear-Admiral Boddam-Whetham on the bridge, followed by a long and seemingly endless line of cargo vessels all eager to be on the move. Hughes saw movement to his right and spied the *Scylla*'s skipper, Captain MacIntyre, and Admiral Burnett on the quarterdeck, coming out from their positions on the bridge to watch the first stage of convoy PQ18.

As the *Temple Arch* passed alongside *Scylla* she dipped her Red Ensign. At once the *Scylla*'s White Ensign was lowered in reply, acknowledging the salute. A siren shrieked as the ships moved on, passing the anti-submarine boom which had been opened to allow them out into the wider sea.

For the remainder of the afternoon, Hughes and a group of fellow officers stood near the quarterdeck watching on as this long procession of ships moved out, forming into two lines as they exited the loch and turned north towards Iceland, where they were to rendezvous with yet more cargo ships and the escorts that would take them on to Russia. As each ship passed the *Scylla*, Hughes observed them closely. These were ships flying the flags of an assortment of nations: Great Britain and America (such as the SS *Empire Beaumont* and SS *Meanticut*); a couple with Russian flags (including the SS *Sukhona*); and also a handful flying the flag of Panama (such as the SS *Africander*) – empire ships and Liberty ships, many of which had seen much better days. Old ships coming to the end of their useful service and newer ships beginning theirs. Huge oilers such as the MV *Atheltemplar* and SS *Black Ranger* that would provide fuel en route, the cold Scottish water splashing white against their grey and rusting hulls as they glided through the waves, their bilge pumps gushing out yellow water as they passed. As each ship sailed by she sounded her siren in salute, as though eager and excited to get out to sea and get on with the job, whatever it might bring.

On their decks, a handful of sailors waved in greeting as they passed. It was remarkable, Hughes mused, that such large vessels could be controlled by such small crews compared to the numbers that sailed on the naval ships. He had nothing but admiration for the seamen of the Merchant Navy. A lot of them had been sailing for many years, peacefully transporting goods around the world, when suddenly war broke out and their journeys became filled with the danger of being targeted by Nazi ships, planes and U-boats. For the men of the Royal Navy, this was an accepted hazard of the job, something they knew they were letting themselves in for when they signed on. For the merchant seamen, however, it was something fate had forced upon them.

On the opposite shore, a group of Wrens waved what looked like colourful pieces of material at the men on the ships. Someone quipped it was their underwear, but they were so far away that Hughes could not be sure if this was the case or if his colleague was trying to be witty. Maybe their sweethearts were setting off on the journey, he pondered. Sweethearts of maybe only a few days duration in some cases, brief opportune romances that only happen in times of war.

Hughes couldn't help but notice the lack of armaments on most of these ships. There appeared to be an odd assortment of weaponry spaced on their decks, decks covered in packing cases, tanks and trucks, giving the ships a somewhat grotesque and misshapen appearance. A mish-mash of weaponry that included what looked like ancient Great War 4-inch guns, Lewis guns and Marlin machine guns. Some were lucky enough to have been fitted with 20mm Oerlikons and 40mm Bofors, but these seemed few and far between. He was aware that on some, detachments of Royal Marines and US Navy Armed Guards had been posted to man the weapons. From what Hughes witnessed, it was clear just how much the men on these ships relied on the Royal Navy escorts to ensure their voyage to Russia passed safely.

The last to leave the loch was the Panamanian-registered freighter SS *MacBeth*.

First Lieutenant 'Mac' Mackean turned to Hughes and remarked, 'Very apt name, don't you think? Just one of the tragedies, that's all!'

As Hughes turned away to return to his cabin he frowned to himself. Had what Mac said been an omen of what was to come, he wondered. He sincerely hoped not.

That evening, HMS *Scylla* weighed anchor and sped north at full speed for Iceland, arriving at Hvalfjordur less than two days later.

* * *

Meanwhile, the two long lines of the convoy ploughed on at only 8 knots. In order to remain in convoy they had to travel at the speed of the slowest ship, which made them vulnerable to U-boat attack. To reduce the chances of this, their route took them to the north-west of Ireland to avoid U-boat wolf-packs known to be operating further east. With the ships so heavily laden, it would take almost five days to reach Iceland to form into the ten columns that would then carry on to Russia.

Sailing alongside the two columns was the Local Escort, under the co-ordination of Western Approaches Headquarters in Liverpool, which would provide cover as far as Iceland. These ships were then to await the returning QP14 and protect them on their return from Russia. However, this was some days away yet, as the ships of QP14 were still docked in Archangelsk.

QP14 consisted of Allied shipping that had carried cargoes to Archangelsk on previous Arctic convoys – some of them had survived the hell that was PQ17 – and were waiting to be escorted back to Britain. This returning convoy was to rendezvous with their escorts just north of the Kola Inlet, near the port of Murmansk. These escorts were to break off from PQ18, leaving the Russia-bound convoy to proceed to Archangelsk with reduced cover from that point.

Out of sight and ahead of the convoy, RAF Coastal Command were flying regular Catalina and Hudson sorties, hunting for U-boats in case any had travelled this far west. A strike on the convoy before it had properly set up would be disastrous, not only in terms of losing precious cargo but also for the morale of the crews, and so it was extremely important they made it to Iceland unmolested.

Although the only enemy faced on the journey up to Iceland was the increasingly bad weather, this did not stop the captain on each ship from testing his men. 'Action Stations' would regularly sound, no matter what time of day or night. Sailors hurried to their posts in increasingly inclement weather the further north they travelled, slipping and sliding on wet decks as seawater turned to foam when it splashed over the gunwales, before draining away through the scuppers as the foredeck rose against the movement of the heavy seas. Once at their stations they would remain there for the duration, often having to answer the call of nature over the side of the ship, not being allowed to return to their mess decks to go to the heads.

For those working below decks, things were quite different. Whereas those above could see what was happening and, to a degree, felt they had some control over their fate, those below felt quite disconnected. Within the boiler rooms (to some the most important part of the ship, for it kept the ship moving and, as well as providing drinking water, produced heat and hot water to the mess decks), crewmen would fret at any unfamiliar loud noise emanating from above. During Action Stations the boiler rooms would be locked shut, the firemen and stokers having to work in almost pitch darkness, completely oblivious to what was taking place above them. To some, it was like working 'in a can'. This was no job for the claustrophobic, that was for sure.

To conserve precious fresh water, the captains ordered there to be no showers or shaving. However, on some ships it was clearly evident that the officers did not comply with their own orders, as they were, in the main, freshly shaved and always looked quite clean. To most ratings, this was frustrating as it looked as if there was one rule for the officers and another for the lower deck. However, it was generally accepted as being part of navy life, and their gripes were rarely aired.

The following day, 3 September 1942, the convoy was joined by more destroyers out of Scapa Flow. Immediately, the crewmen of the merchants felt more at ease. Already it was clear that PQ18 was going to have more protection than any previous Russian convoy.

As the ships slogged on further north the weather became worse. On 4 September they were hit by gale-force winds and high seas. Those on deck were now getting a taste of just what it would be like for the remainder of the journey. They were under no illusions that things would improve when they entered the even harsher waters of the extreme north and the Barents Sea.

Ahead of them, anti-submarine sweeps were being carried out by four Hudson aircraft, flying from the United Kingdom and landing in Iceland once their sorties were completed. However, disaster struck on the morning of 5 September, when a Short Sunderland flying boat (call sign W4032), having completed its sweep, crashed into the sea near the Isle of Tiree in the Inner Hebrides, killing seven of its ten-man crew. Another crew member and the *Glasgow Herald* war reporter, Fred Nancarrow, who had been travelling with them, were listed as missing. There were only two survivors. These airmen were, effectively, the first casualties of PQ18.

The following day, flying an anti-submarine sortie approximately 160 miles south of Iceland, one of two United States Navy (USN) Catalinas noticed something in the water ahead of them. Immediately, the pilot headed to investigate. It was clearly the conning tower of a U-boat. On seeing the plane turn towards them, her skipper ordered the submarine to dive, and by the time the aircraft was over where she had been spotted, she had vanished beneath the waves. The Catalina made a couple more sweeps around the area before giving up and heading back to base.

The sighting of the U-boat was a warning to all the ships' captains. At no time whatsoever could they rest easy. The threat was out there. It was constant. And should a captain relax for one second, it could spell disaster for him and his ship.

The convoy steamed on.

Chapter 2

6–8 September

Owing to its geographical and strategic significance, control of Iceland was essential, to protect both convoys heading to Britain from America and convoys travelling to Russia. To ensure the safety of Allied shipping, British forces had hurriedly invaded what had been a neutral country on 10 May 1940. Churchill, who took over as Prime Minister on the same day, understood that should the island fall into German hands, then the Western Approaches could not be protected, meaning much-needed supplies from the United States to Britain would have been impossible to deliver. Additionally, the Arctic convoys that were to follow would have been a complete non-starter had not Iceland been in Allied hands.

With the Germans having invaded neutral Denmark only a few days previously, the new Prime Minister feared that should they realize the strategic importance of Iceland and mount an invasion, it would have huge repercussions on Britain's ability to protect vital shipping. And so, a hastily gathered force of nearly 750 men of the 2nd Royal Marine Battalion, under the command of Colonel Robert Sturges, were transported on the cruisers HMS *Berwick* and HMS *Glasgow* to Iceland, meeting little resistance when they arrived and quickly taking control of the capital, Reykjavik. Promising to remove all British forces at the end of the war, Britain occupied the country for the duration, supported by American troops once the USA entered hostilities in December 1941.

* * *

Sunday, 6 September 1942 awoke to a cold and crisp morning. The relentless high seas the ships had thus far endured continued with no sign of abatement. Still a few hundred miles short of the relative protection of Iceland, they lumbered slowly northwards, two long lines of huge cargo ships stretching back, snakelike, for miles. Although it had been only three days since they had left the sanctuary of Loch Ewe, to most the peace and calm of its waters felt a thousand years away.

For those on board the ships, life was becoming increasingly difficult. The temperature was now so low that breath was beginning to freeze on the stubble and beard of anyone working outside. Due to the sighting of the U-boat the previous day, lookouts on all the ships had been doubled, and the guns were permanently manned. Swaddled in as much clothing as possible, and with life jackets inflated to add a further degree of comfort, some slept at their action stations to ensure a quick response should an enemy plane or submarine be spotted. Working shifts of four hours on and four hours off, they could only manage at most three hours sleep at any one time. Toilet breaks were not allowed once in position, but officers turned a blind eye to those finding themselves caught short and attending to the call of nature over the side.

While battling against stormy seas, the provision of hot food became impossible. Unable to keep their pans on the stoves due to the violent motion of the ships, cooks in the galleys resorted to preparing endless corned beef sandwiches to feed the men. However, this was supplemented by hot, steamy drinks: tea, coffee and the sailors' favourite, 'kye', a hot, sweet chocolate drink, often served with a thick skin on top.

And so, as men pulled their balaclavas low and their scarves high, it was clear that the first battle of PQ18 was going to be against the elements, and this was one that would not stop until they were safely back in home ports. For those who had done this run before it was slightly more bearable. They'd known to expect this and they joked that this weather was almost tropical compared to what they would face when they hit the Barents Sea.

As they continued north all was not well aboard the Catapult Aircraft Merchant (CAM) ship SS *Empire Morn*. Only four days at sea, and she was already experiencing engine trouble. So much so that she was forced to drop back and eventually came to a dead stop whilst engineers on board hurriedly carried out repairs.

With the rest of the convoy continuing on to Iceland, the anti-submarine trawler HMS *Cape Argona* was detached to guard her whilst the repairs were undertaken.

As the crew of the *Empire Morn* waited patiently for the mechanics to complete their work, the two RAF pilots on board had to remain more resolute still. This was a journey on which the services of only one of them could be utilized, and then only if absolutely necessary. The decision to use them would ultimately rest with the convoy commander.

The role of a pilot on a CAM ship was possibly the most hazardous of them all. The *Empire Morn* had one Sea Hurricane attached to a catapult at the bow of the ship. Once launched, there was no chance of it returning. It was essential its launch be timed right and only carried out when absolutely necessary. With twelve Sea Hurricanes on the *Avenger*, the catapult was only likely to be used in the later stages of the journey, when the aircraft carrier was to leave them on the final approach to Archangelsk. If that happened, the pilot would have to do his best, most probably against a much superior enemy force, and then either ditch in the freezing waters of the Barents or White Sea and wait to be rescued, or, if fuel allowed, try to make it to land.

As the repairs were being carried out, the *Cape Argona* circled the much larger ship, carrying out an Asdic sweep (naval sonar, used for detecting submarines). Lying stationary, she presented an easy target, and any U-boat commander who might be in the vicinity would undoubtedly attack; it was a chance not to be missed. Like the other trawlers on the convoy, the *Cape Argona* was towing a Motor Minesweeper (MMS), which was to be delivered to the Russian Navy on arrival at Archangelsk. During the convoy these craft were to be used as additional rescue vessels should the need arise.

However, it wasn't the threat of U-boat attack that they needed to worry about. A couple of hours after the last ship of the convoy had disappeared over the horizon, leaving *Cape Argona* and *Empire Morn* alone on the open sea, Telegraphist Les Wightman on board the *Cape Argona* spotted something in the sky to the east. Heading directly towards them, at only a few feet above the waves, were six Blohm and Voss seaplanes of the Luftwaffe.

Immediately, 'Action Stations' sounded and gunners ran to man the single 4-inch gun on the bow. Before they had a chance to fire off a shot, each of the approaching planes opened up with their two MG 151 cannon, spraying bullets into both ships from bow to stern. As Wightman and his shipmates dived for cover, he realized they were sitting ducks. A sustained attack on the two largely unprotected ships would almost certainly result in their destruction.

Although still in the early stages of the voyage, Wightman thought this would be as good a time as any for the Sea Hurricane to be dispatched from the *Cape Argona* to protect them.

He took a quick look at the sky and saw that, thankfully, the German planes had overshot the ships and were not turning to come in for another attack. With mounting relief, he realized they were heading away, possibly due to a lack of fuel, and after a short while, just like the convoy earlier, they were gone from view.

Wightman could see that despite the attack, which had left the hull and deck riddled with bullet-holes, neither ship was in danger of sinking; the damage was merely superficial and could easily be repaired. As those who had thrown themselves to the deck or taken cover on seeing the approaching planes got back to their feet, he noticed one of the gunners holding his shoulder. He had been hit by a ricochet and was grimacing in pain.

Immediately, his colleagues took hold of him and led him off to the sick bay to have his wound attended to. The injury looked quite superficial, and the man would clearly be fine.

A short while later, the SS *Empire Morn*'s engine was repaired and they set off to catch up with the convoy, reaching them almost twenty-four hours later without further incident.

* * *

As the convoy battled the elements, heading toward the rendezvous at Hvalfjord, those already lying at anchor in Icelandic waters and awaiting them were enjoying quite spectacular views. All around, snow-capped mountains provided protection from the wind, their foothills sloping down towards the cold and choppy sea. Winding roads clung precariously to their sides, and the occasional glimmer of light and patch of cultivation advertised the fact that people actually lived in this desolate-looking landscape. Beyond the near summits, more peaks could be seen in the far distance, sunlight breaking occasionally through dark clouds and reflecting off the snow.

The ships' crews, waiting patiently for the others to arrive, shuddered as heavy squalls, appearing from nowhere, ripped down from the mountains, causing their vessels to bob and sway as the disturbed water crashed violently against their hulls. As the ships strained at their anchor cables, officers of the watch checked their anchor bearings for signs of dragging. It was with great relief that the captains had received their orders from Admiral Fraser the day before, advising them to be ready to sail within the next few days; it was the waiting around that frustrated them the most, enduring unnecessary discomfort when they would sooner be on the move. They knew the voyage was going ahead, and they would prefer to be getting on with it, although the time at anchor allowed them to give a number of their crew some brief shore leave.

On board one such ship, the Russian freighter SS *Stalingrad*, carrying among other things 500 tonnes of ammonal and other explosives, 36-year-old Anatoly Nikolayevich Sakharov, the ship's captain, looked out from the bridge onto Faxa Bay. He sighed to himself. The weather was getting no better. For him personally, this trip was no more than routine, something he had done many times before, but he worried about some of the people currently resting in the cabins and mess decks. For not all who travelled with him were crew, and not all of his cargo consisted of military supplies.

In the decks below were a number of passengers returning to Russia. These included diplomatic staff from the London embassy who had joined the ship that day, and sailors being repatriated following the loss of their vessels in the Atlantic, some of whom had been transferred from hospitals still recovering from the injuries they had sustained. Worryingly, included among the passengers were three women, one of whom was heavily pregnant, and also a group of children heading home.

For Sakharov himself, too, this journey was something of a homecoming, he being a native of Archangelsk; he was eager to return to his home city after spending so much time away. Spread out over 25 miles along both banks of the northern Dvina River, where it flows into the White Sea with many small islands in its delta, Archangelsk was a large and historic industrial city. Along the riverbank, large dockland areas, including the main unloading areas of Ekonomia and Bakharitsa, awaited the convoy's arrival, their cranes and hoists ready to take off its important cargo.

But, Sakharov thought, a cargo ship containing high explosives was no place for women and children, with Nazi U-boats, surface ships and aircraft on the prowl. However, he knew he had no choice in the matter. He just had to hope all would go well.

His instructions from the Admiral had contained the *Stalingrad*'s pennant number for the voyage to Russia. She was to sail in position 103, placing her as the third ship in the tenth column, with the Russian freighter SS *Sukhona* sailing behind and the Panamanian-registered SS *MacBeth* ahead. The *Stalingrad* was to be the centre ship in the outer starboard column, a position he was not altogether happy with. The starboard column would be the closest to land and, by default, the first merchant ships any enemy aircraft would encounter if the convoy came under attack, which Sakharov was sure it would. He would have felt more comfortable had he been allocated a slot somewhere within the centre of the convoy, closer to the anti-aircraft ships; but, he supposed, orders were orders, and he would just have to make do and hope for the best.

The arrival of the heavy cruiser HMS *Scylla* a couple of days previously had made him feel a little more comfortable. Royal Navy ships were starting to arrive in great numbers, and with more on the way he could see that the British were trying to ensure this convoy would be better protected than any that had made the journey previously. Nevertheless, he was still unhappy with the *Stalingrad*'s position. It was ironic that at that very moment a battle was raging in the very city after which the ship was named – and, from what he understood, it was a battle that could go either way. The supplies in his ship's holds were crucial to his countrymen's fight against the Nazi invader. It was extremely important that the materiel he was transporting made it to those on the front line.

For a moment he saw movement on the tank-laden deck; it was the second engineer, Mister Isaiah, talking with a small group of men. These he recognized as the newly arrived embassy couriers, Comrades Shmakov and Khromov. It looked as though they had come up top to take the air and maybe smoke a cigarette. However, with the wind blowing strongly into their faces they beat a hasty retreat back inside, but not before Isaiah raised his hand in greeting to the bridge. Before Sakharov could respond in kind, the group had disappeared from view once more.

Sakharov had not spent much time with the diplomats other than to welcome them on board with his first mate and political officer, Alexander Federov. They were of no real concern to him, merely two more passengers to transfer. His focus was fully on the running of the ship and ensuring her safe passage to Archangelsk. He was aware that each of these men had with him a diplomatic pouch that was to be delivered to Moscow. He had no idea what these contained and he preferred it that way. He had already decided to keep contact with the men to a minimum.

Already those vessels in the bay were on high alert. At the mouth of the fjord lay other elements of the escort. The anti-aircraft ships *Pozarica*, *Palomares* and *Alynbank*, together with a number of formidable-looking destroyers, kept watch for enemy aircraft, their gunners at the ready, eyes fixed steadily on the sky whilst they shivered in the freezing weather. These anti-aircraft ships had started life as merchantmen but had been converted, with added gun turrets, director towers and Royal Navy-type bridge superstructures, giving them little resemblance to their original appearance. No longer would they transport fruit, coffee and other such luxuries around the globe; for now, at least, they would carry ammunition, gunners and a determination to keep those around them safe from Luftwaffe attack.

One of these anti-aircraft ships was to travel with the convoy. HMS *Alynbank*, together with another converted merchant ship, HMS *Ulster Queen*, and the Fighting Destroyer Escort, would provide the anti-aircraft cover required to fend off the Junkers Ju-88s and Heinkel He-111s that flew out of the Norwegian airbases at Banak and Bardufoss. There was an expectation that the Germans would launch regular attacks once range and weather conditions permitted. It was a double-edged sword. Bad weather meant fewer air attacks, but at the same time enduring temperatures as low as -30°C and heavy seas full of ice floes; whereas milder weather meant more air attacks and with it the chance of being sunk by a torpedo bomber. It was a no-win situation. There was always going to be a danger of one kind or another.

As the convoy neared Iceland, aircraft of Coastal Command again conducted anti-submarine sweeps in its track. Four Hudsons and three Catalinas carried out lengthy flights, with a further Hudson flying an ice reconnaissance sortie ahead of them. The Admiralty were taking absolutely no chances of the convoy being hit at such an early stage.

* * *

With more anti-submarine sweeps continuing from Coastal Command, the following day the convoy arrived safely in Iceland. Upon arrival it immediately steamed around the west of the island to Seydisfjördur in the north, still in two columns, to negotiate the Denmark Strait. Those ships at anchor at Faxa Bay joined them as they rounded the north of the island and, now that all the merchant ships were present, began to assemble into the ten columns that would sail onward to Russia. The crews of the merchantmen were then met with a most welcome sight. Drawing up alongside them was the Fighter Destroyer Escort. This group contained sixteen destroyers under the command of the flagship, the cruiser HMS *Scylla*. It was a formidable destroyer force, each ship containing very heavy firepower.

And so the ships formed up into normal convoy order, with the *Scylla* taking her place at the front of the merchant ships, and Rear-Admiral Boddam-Whetham, the Commodore of the Convoy in SS *Temple Arch*, leading the sixth column. The columns would be separated by approximately 1,000 yards of open sea, with the ships in each column spaced around 500 yards apart.

Significantly, for the first time on an Arctic convoy, an aircraft carrier, the converted cargo ship HMS *Avenger*, would travel with them as far as the Kola Inlet, to provide immediate air support should they come under Luftwaffe attack.

Constructed at the Sun Shipbuilding Company in Pennsylvania in 1939, HMS *Avenger* started life as *Rio Hudson*, one of four C3 type passenger cargo ships of the 'Rio' class. Weighing 9,100 tonnes, with a 17,500-tonne loaded displacement, she was originally intended to operate the South American routes but was requisitioned by the United States Navy for conversion to an auxiliary aircraft carrier in July 1941. Able to accommodate nearly 200 passengers and with 440,000 cubic feet of cargo space, she was ideal for this switch. A lightweight wooden flight deck was constructed on a truss-work superstructure, which covered 70 per cent of the ship's length, and a small hangar was fashioned beneath the stern of the flight deck. A lift would then bring up the aircraft for launching. In March 1942 she was commissioned into the Royal Navy as HMS *Avenger* and given the pennant number D14, under Commander A.P. Colthurst.

The ship had a complement of three Fairey Swordfish II aircraft (affectionately nicknamed 'Stringbags' due to their ability to carry all manner of equipment) with five crews detached from 825 Squadron, based at RNAS Hatston. These biplanes, which could carry a single torpedo on their undercarriage as well as a small number of depth charges, were to conduct anti-submarine sorties en route. Along with them were six Sea Hurricanes from 802 Squadron, with a further six from 822 Squadron broken down and stored in the hangar below decks. These were to be used against any air attack the Germans might throw at the convoy. Due to the ship being built to accommodate the American Grumman Wildcat, a plane which was then in short supply in Britain, the Sea Hurricanes were not technically able to be launched by the ship's catapult system; the pilots would have to use their skill to take off unaided, using the length of the flight deck to gather enough speed to get airborne. Also, the arrestor hook on the Hurricane was halfway up the fuselage, so the pilots would have to be highly skilled to make a successful landing, especially in rough seas.

Nicknamed a 'Woolworths' carrier as it was considered 'cheap', the sight of the rather strange-looking *Avenger* in the water of Seydisfjordur gave some comfort to the men looking on from the other ships.

One such sailor was 18-year-old Charlie Erswell, a seaman gunner on the brand new 'M' Class destroyer HMS *Milne*.

PQ18 was to be young Charlie's very first sea voyage. Born in Scotland in December 1923 and brought up in Berwick-upon-Tweed and Hornchurch, Essex, he had wanted to go to sea from a very young age and had finally managed to achieve his ambition when he volunteered for the Royal Navy on his eighteenth birthday in December 1941. However, Charlie had already seen a fair share of war. Whilst working as a telegram boy during the Blitz he had come close to being killed on a couple of occasions. The first was when a Heinkel He-111 was shot down over Hornchurch when he was on a night out with a friend, the stricken German aircraft crashing so close by that the heat from the explosion forced him to take shelter behind a garden wall; and then later, when he was working at the GPO office in London and the building above his air-raid shelter was flattened by a bomb.

Now, as he looked out across the water at the ships assembling for the threatening journey ahead, his emotions were somewhat mixed. Although keen to get out there and do his bit, like many others around him he felt anxious and nervous; not so much about the dangers they might face, but hoping that they would not be found wanting when the moment came.

As Charlie cast his eyes over the water he could see, in the fading light, many columns of ships stretching out to the far horizon, and he knew there were maybe more still, beyond his vision. A fleet of ships so gargantuan he had trouble registering it. He had never seen so many and for a moment he was struck with the wonder of it all. Here were ships of all different shapes and sizes, flying the flags of many countries and spaced out in regimented lines ready for the journey ahead. The sheer size of the convoy was awe-inspiring, and he realized that what he was about to take part in was something of monumental importance, of that there was no doubt.

HMS *Milne* was a flotilla leader and therefore the lead ship in Force B (a small group of destroyers) sailing ahead and to starboard of the main body of merchantmen. Should any German aircraft attack the convoy, then it was the *Milne* and the destroyers around her that would be the first to engage them. As a turret trainer in B turret (the gun turret immediately in front of the bridge), it would be up to Charlie to turn the huge twin 4.7-inch guns toward the approaching aircraft. It was an enormous responsibility for such a young man, and he just hoped that he would be able to carry out his duties efficiently.

As Tuesday, 8 September drew to a close, the weather, although still extremely cold, abated somewhat and a slight fog began to descend upon the ships as they formed up. The threat of squalls that could appear without warning across the fjords had lessened, and it was in these almost peaceful conditions that the thirty-nine merchant ships were finally ready to sail.

Strung out around the convoy were the sixteen destroyers of the Fighting Destroyer Escort, all containing significant anti-aircraft and anti-submarine weaponry. On board each of them, Asdic and radar operators were to look out for and provide early warning of enemy aircraft or U-boats as they approached to attack the convoy. A line of seven such destroyers would sail in front of the merchantmen to provide protection. The destroyers HMS *Impulsive* and HMS *Marne* positioned themselves just behind this line to the port and starboard respectively of the *Scylla*. Within this protective destroyer circle sailed a number of corvettes and minesweepers, with more to the rear, including three armed trawlers, each of them towing a Motor Minesweeper to be delivered to the Russians as part of the Lend-Lease Agreement of 1941. This was an Act of Congress signed in March that year by President Franklin D. Roosevelt which allowed the United States to offer material support to any country seen as 'vital to the defence of the United States', whilst at the same time remaining officially neutral. Of course, this had become irrelevant when America joined the war after the bombing of Pearl Harbor in December the same year.

Within the body of the merchantmen more ships of the Royal Navy took up position, including the anti-aircraft ships HMS *Ulster Queen* and HMS *Alynbank* and, to the rear, the two submarines *P614* and *P615*. The aircraft carrier HMS *Avenger* and the designated rescue ship HMS *Copeland* were the last ships of the first two columns. Finally, four oilers including the MV *Atheltemplar* and RFA *Gray Ranger*, took up position towards the rear. These were to provide fuel for the ships as and when required.

With the convoy set up in this way, it was thought the most offensively equipped ships might be hidden from any spotter plane and mistaken, at least for a while, for merchantmen. If the convoy was attacked by U-boats, the destroyers would form a defensive screen, every approach covered by their

Asdic; and should the convoy come under air attack, then the *Scylla* and the anti-aircraft ships would move from their positions to form a defensive line and, along with the guns of the destroyers, hurl a huge barrage skyward to deter any effective bombing runs. At the same time, if required, HMS *Avenger* would move from the port column to give manoeuvring space for her Sea Hurricanes to take off and engage with enemy aircraft. The *Avenger*'s three Swordfish aircraft would carry out regular anti-submarine hunts around the convoy, and should suspicious activity be detected on the Asdic, they would fly out to investigate and engage any U-boats with their torpedoes.

If the convoy came under air attack, the destroyers were to 'close up'; in other words, some would position themselves closer to the lines of merchant ships. Two from the forward screen would pull back and position themselves tight against the front of the convoy, with the *Marne* and *Impulsive* moving to the sides to form a line with the front rank. Four more destroyers would do likewise at the rear. Closing up in this way would effectively place a destroyer at all four corners of the convoy and give added, closer protection to prevent the enemy getting a clear run against the merchant ships, should the outer screen of warships be penetrated.

The two submarines travelled as a precaution in case the enemy decided to utilize their surface ships. Should the convoy come under air attack, they were to submerge to avoid being detected, and if the German heavy ships *Tirpitz*, *Scharnhorst*, *Gneisenau* or *Hipper* were to move to attack the convoy, then it was hoped the submarines might be able to engage and damage them without themselves being detected.

And so, under a fiery sunset, and with the array of the aurora borealis dancing majestically across the distant horizon, PQ18 was finally ready to sail. Every preparation had been carried out to make it a success.

Had the lessons of the failed PQ17 been learned, and was the Royal Navy better prepared? The following few days would provide answers to these questions. As the battle for Stalingrad raged, the outcome of which would determine the whole European war, nearly 100 ships were now at sea to deliver vital supplies to boost the Soviet war effort.

It was imperative that they make it through.

Chapter 3

9–10 September

The *Scylla*'s voyage had not begun well. As the thick steel cables revolved slowly on the foredeck, dragging the heavy chains on board to raise the anchor, they suddenly faltered, shuddered to a halt and then went taut. As Rear-Admiral Burnett and Captain MacIntyre watched from the bridge, it was immediately apparent that the anchor was stuck fast. With a shout of 'Avast heaving!' resounding across the deck, the First Lieutenant and ship's blacksmith were called to sort out the situation. The order was quickly given to cut the cable, which was duly done by the blacksmith, and to attach a buoy, in order to slip the anchor, abandoning it for collection at a later date. One of those tasked to collect the anchor buoy from where it was stowed was Robert Hughes, officer in charge of the blue director. As the freed cable slithered across the deck and down through the hawse-pipe, the buoy was pitched over the side and the ship was now free, gliding elegantly across the water to port.

For some on the *Scylla*, Hughes included, it felt like a bad omen. The incident with the anchor had not been a good sign, and the ship now heading towards a blood-red sky only added to the strange feeling of unease that had suddenly descended upon the crew. This wasn't the best of starts, Hughes thought. He was aware that the battleships HMS *Edinburgh* and HMS *Trinidad* had both been sunk on previous convoys, and he knew that sailing on such a big ship as the *Scylla* did not automatically guarantee a safe run.

* * *

Unable to raise more than 8 knots, the convoy set a north-easterly course towards Bear Island. As it sailed on, with the escort destroyers making sweeps between the columns of merchant ships, Asdic operators in the Electronic Warfare Operations (EWO) rooms on the destroyers kept watchful eyes on their screens, their ears tuned in and listening out for the unmistakable 'ping' of an enemy submarine lurking beneath the surface.

Named after the 'Anti-Submarine Detection Investigation Committee', the Asdic equipment was housed in a dome-like structure on the ship's hull which transmitted high frequency beams in the form of audible 'pings'. If these hit something solid, for example a submarine, then they would be 'bounced back' and picked up in the EWO room. The time that passed between the sound being transmitted and the echo being received determined how far away the submarine was, with the pitch of the echo revealing whether it was approaching or moving away. The job of those who operated the system was vitally important to the safety of the convoy. Early warning of a possible U-boat attack allowed convoy commanders to put into place their defensive strategies or, as was often the case, to send out destroyers and aircraft to hunt and engage with the boats before they had a chance to strike.

However, Asdic was not foolproof. The system was often affected by sea conditions, and it was only really effective at speeds below 18 knots, due to the noise made by the ships' propellers. Eddies, thermoclines (the transition layer between the warmer mixed water at the surface and the cooler, deep water below) and currents all caused problems and could render the system totally ineffectual at times; and once the water was disturbed by an unsuccessful depth charge run it was very difficult for the signal to be picked up again, allowing an experienced U-boat commander to use this time to effect an escape from the area the destroyers might be targeting.

The system did not only pick up submarines. Anything large in the water that was able to 'bounce back' the audible ping could not be disregarded, and so false readings were a constant problem for those working in the EWO rooms. Large shoals of fish, whales and pods of porpoises were often mistaken for U-boats, and many a marine creature became an innocent casualty of war when a depth charge exploded near to it. Sailors would often rush to Action Stations, adrenalin pumping through their veins, ready to man the depth-charge launchers, only to be stood down by the captain once it was determined that what had been detected was no more dangerous than a school of tuna. However, these false alarms were not necessarily a bad thing, as they kept ships' crews at a heightened state of vigilance and honed their skills for when the alarm was genuine.

* * *

The Germans knew PQ18 was on its way. Although the British had cracked the German Enigma code at the secret facility at Bletchley Park, Buckinghamshire, nearly two years previously, the *Beobachtungsdienst* (German Naval Intelligence, also known as *B-Dienst*), based at Bendlerblock, Berlin, had also been intercepting and decoding Royal Navy signals for quite some time. Breaking the Royal Navy's Combined Cypher Number 3 in October of 1941 allowed Rear-Admiral Karl Dönitz, the *Befehlshaber der Unterseeboote* (BdU, Commander of U-boat Operations) to predict, to within a 500 by 200 mile area, just where any British ships were at any one time. He was then able to dispatch his wolf-packs to patrol those areas where he knew, with some confidence, the convoys were.

Unlike the Atlantic convoys, those to Russia fell within range of Luftwaffe bases for the majority of their journey, and so spotter planes could also be sent to the area to confirm their location. On sighting Allied ships, German planes would radio back their exact positions, allowing Dönitz to send the wolf-packs their locations. However, the U-boats needed to surface, or at least be at periscope depth, to receive the transmissions, which were sent periodically from Berlin and relayed via the transmitter sites at Lorient and Sainte-Assise. The radio rooms on the German submarines were manned at all times, and each signal was prefixed with a number to ensure that no messages were missed. The radio operators would decode every message, even if it wasn't for their own U-boat, so the commander had an overall picture of what was taking place within the pack. Through this combination of Luftwaffe patrols, U-boat reports and Royal Navy signals intercepts, the Germans were able to follow the convoys for pretty much the whole route.

Of course, these messages were themselves intercepted by the British and decoded at Bletchley Park, giving the Admiralty notice of just how much the Germans knew and the fact that the wolf-packs were out there, lurking, waiting for an opportunity to strike. Therefore the anti-submarine patrols by Coastal Command aircraft based in Russia, and the Swordfish and destroyers on the convoy itself, were essential for the convoy's protection.

After the disaster of PQ17, the Germans had used the lull in Allied operations to prepare for what they knew would be a major convoy to follow. It was clear that, despite the failure of PQ17, the British would not simply call a halt to the Arctic convoys. If nothing else, they had agreed quotas of materiel with the Soviets and they were honour-bound to fulfil them. The loss of so much cargo on PQ17 would mean they had to deliver a much larger consignment the next time, and they would also need to ensure that the next convoy was much better protected.

And so the Luftwaffe squadrons operating from the northern Norwegian airbases were reinforced, and more U-boat wolf-packs operating out of Kriegsmarine bases on the Norwegian coast, such as Bergen, Narvik and Trondheim, were ordered to patrol the route they expected the new convoy to take. With so many Arctic convoys having already sailed, and given the information received from B-Dienst, the Germans could estimate roughly where the British were going to be. They just needed to know when they were going to be there.

* * *

The convoy was not long out of Iceland before something was sighted in the sky to the north. Although Coastal Command had been flying Catalina and Hudson sorties regularly in preparation for the journey, it was evident that the aircraft now circling to the port side was not one of those. This was clearly a four-engine Focke-Wulf FW200 Condor of the Luftwaffe, unmistakable even through the fine mist-like rain that was now falling from a dull grey sky. To many who had sailed on the Atlantic convoys, this aircraft was easily recognizable, since it had sunk many merchant ships on that run. However, the Condor had now been switched to operate purely as a reconnaissance aircraft; there was no doubt it had sighted the convoy and would immediately be reporting its position and direction of travel. It would not be long before that information was passed on through the intelligence network to the patrolling wolf-packs.

Immediately, the guns of the destroyers on the port side opened up. Turret-trainers and gun-layers turned and pointed their barrels at the plane, under instructions from those working in the ships' directors. Together with the 4.7-inch shells from the heavy cannon, Oerlikon and Bofors gunners added to the cacophony, creating a formidable barrage. Undeterred by this gunfire, and using the clouds for cover, the pilot banked his aircraft to come in for a closer look, his co-pilot and crew busily counting the ships below.

On board the aircraft carrier HMS *Avenger* a Sea Hurricane pilot ran to his aircraft and climbed into the cockpit. After hooking up his comms and oxygen lines, he gunned the engine and within a couple of minutes was racing down the runway and into the air on a mission to intercept.

Seeing the Hurricane take off from the carrier, and having gained the information he needed, the pilot of the Condor decided it was time to leave and turned away from the ships. Once more using the cover of the clouds, he was soon gone from view. With the German aircraft now posing no threat, having left the scene at some speed, the Hurricane returned to the *Avenger*, landing safely back on board.

If nothing else, this first brush with the enemy had been a good drill for those on the destroyers and anti-aircraft ships, especially those for whom PQ18 was their first voyage. Although the plane had not been shot down, it had at least been shown the firepower the defensive screen could produce and how efficiently and quickly the gunners were able to react. As well as heading away with vital intelligence, the crew of the Condor would also now be aware that destroying PQ18 would not be as easy a task as for its predecessor.

Later that morning, a number of ships broke away from the convoy and headed at full speed towards the island of Spitzbergen in the far north. This was Force P, consisting of the destroyers HMS *Windsor*, HMS *Cowdray* and

HMS *Oakley* with tankers of the Royal Fleet Auxiliary (RFA *Blue Ranger* and RFA *Oligarch*). Force P was under orders to establish a refuelling base at Lowe Sound, where escort ships could detach themselves to refuel en route. The remaining ships would be serviced by the four oilers travelling at the rear of the convoy.

* * *

Further north and out of sight of the convoy, 28-year-old Kapitänleutnant Heino Bohmann, skipper of U-boat *U-88*, stood with his officers on the conning tower of the 67m-long submarine. As she sped along at a steady rate of 15 knots, the rough waves of the Norwegian Sea bounced off her steel-grey hull, creating a constant spray of seawater which mixed with the fine rain and fell upon the four shivering submariners. Bohmann had his binoculars firmly clamped to his eyes, scanning the horizon for any activity, but could see nothing other than the rise and fall of the dark waves and the rain that was creating a foggy haze, making it somewhat difficult to focus. For the umpteenth time he wiped the water from the lenses and put them to his eyes again, sweeping in an arc from port to starboard. Happy that there was nothing to concern him unduly, he made the decision to remain on the surface, where the boat could travel nearly three times as quickly as submerged. It also meant they could top up the batteries and receive any signals traffic from the Kriegsmarine.

He had received word earlier that the British were on the move and headed in their direction. The next few days could prove to be very interesting, he thought; there might be a chance for more glory. Forming part of the 11th Flotilla, operating out of Bergen on the Norwegian coast as part of the *Trägertod* wolf-pack, *U-88* had been at sea for nearly seventeen days, and Bohmann's 45-man crew were beginning to get restless. This was now the second longest patrol he had carried out, the previous one having taken twenty-five days. With information coming through that the latest British convoy had now set sail, he envisaged it would be some time yet before any of his men would see land again.

Bohmann had been in the Kriegsmarine for over eight years, taking command of *U-88* in October 1941. He had recently won the Iron Cross First Class for actions undertaken on 5 July 1942, when his boat had sunk two merchant ships from the dispersed convoy PQ17.

Bohmann was aware that he had won his medal quite easily. The two merchant ships he had sent to the bottom of the Arctic Ocean on that day had been unprotected and travelling very slowly. They had been relatively easy pickings. Sitting on the saddle in the tiny 'Commander's Control Room' at the attack periscope within the conning tower, he had been able to focus completely on the task at hand. This small room was only big enough for himself and one other person, and this separation from the rest of the crew, who were only a few feet away in the central control room, allowed him to operate without distraction. *U-88* had chased the first ship for close to three hours before Bohmann managed to slam a torpedo into her side. However, it had failed to explode. Undeterred, Bohmann fired a second torpedo, again hitting the target, this time with a much more successful outcome. It had not taken long for the ship to go down. The second merchantman he sent to the bottom had been much easier, taking just a single shot to sink.

He knew that the majority of U-boat commanders had yet to score any kills, most patrols returning to their bases without firing a shot, and so he had been very fortunate to have destroyed two ships. Well out of range of any British airbases, and with no fear of an enemy destroyer finding them on Asdic and dropping depth charges on top of them, it could not have been simpler.

However, he wasn't so naive as to believe success against this new convoy would be as easy. The British had clearly learned their lesson, and if he was to score any more kills in the coming days, he knew his crew had to be alert, focused and determined, and it was up to him to ensure that they were.

After another hour outside, the cold was beginning to bite, becoming almost unbearable. He looked at his colleagues and could see that they too were feeling it, their shoulders hunched and their scarves pulled up across their bearded faces. He gave the order to go back below deck; there was no point freezing to death out here. As was U-boat commander practice, he waited until everyone had gone down the hatch before he followed them, the last to leave the conning tower. He took one last breath of fresh air and then shut the hatch behind him, turning the closing wheel tightly to ensure a watertight seal.

Once safely inside, he gave the order to dive and continue on course at periscope depth.

* * *

Travelling through ice floes, heavy snow squalls and patchy fog, with the temperature a bracing 15°C below zero, PQ18 pressed on. Ice was now starting to form on decks and superstructures as the sleet and snow poured down, freezing almost instantly on impact and covering everything in a fine blanket of whiteness which reflected blindingly whenever the sun deigned to break through the dark grey clouds. Sailors had already taken to wearing just about every item of clothing they possessed in an attempt to stay warm. The order not to shave, so as to conserve the ships' fresh water, was now accepted almost happily by most, their beards and stubble giving an added layer of protection from the cold. The chance of a hot shower would have been very welcome, but personal hygiene, for the lower ranks at least, was on hold for the foreseeable future.

For those having to work outside, the extreme cold was becoming almost intolerable. In some cases any moisture on outer clothing froze solid; lammy coats (see Glossary), windcheaters and jerkins had to be bashed with brooms and other such items to restore their pliability once back inside mess decks; gloved and mittened hands were thawed out with hot cups of tea and kye; and frozen eyelashes would break off, causing severe irritation and reddening of the eyes.

With daylight now lasting almost twenty hours, it was understandable that many on the ships did not notice when one day turned into the next. Thursday, 10 September dawned to freezing temperatures and heavy snow squalls which made conditions outside and on open bridges unbearable. As the ships sailed on, their bows rhythmically dipped deep into the waves, throwing seawater back over the frozen decks. The bows would then rise as the ships pressed forward, the water draining back through the scuppers into the unforgiving ocean.

On board HMS *Avenger*, a Swordfish was being prepped for flight. To attempt a sortie in this weather was considered madness by some, but to the well-trained and experienced pilots of 825 Squadron it was something they took in their stride. Wrapping up in as much warm clothing as was possible yet still be able to operate the aircraft effectively, the pilots, navigators and gunners of the much-loved biplane would have to endure a much rougher voyage than most. The open cockpit left the three-man crew exposed to the elements, and with the wind-chill factor adding to the already freezing temperatures, their missions became doubly difficult. Not only did they have to contend with the weather, they also had to manage taking off and landing on a short runway, often in a heavy sea in which the carrier was pitching and rolling almost chaotically. Once airborne, spotting U-boats, or their periscopes, would also be a challenge in such tumultuous seas. The respect all the sailors had for these men was, therefore, justifiably immense.

It was around midday when the 'Stringbag' took off from the makeshift deck, the pilot expertly lifting it into the skies, on the hunt for U-boats that, by now, everyone was aware were out there. How much they would be able to see was debatable as the fine rain had now turned to snow and was coming down heavily. Coupled with the Asdic operators on the destroyers and anti-submarine ships, the Swordfish formed part of the defence against this 'scourge from the deep'. Should a U-boat be spotted on the surface, they could either attack it with their single torpedo or, should the submarine dive, call in its co-ordinates to the destroyers. The U-boat could then be picked up on the Asdic and a depth-charge attack take place on its position. Without requiring a direct hit, a barrel charge, if set to explode at the correct depth, could cause a shock wave violent enough to crack a submarine's hull, either forcing her to the surface where she could be engaged by, or surrender to, the destroyers; or it might be enough to send her to the bottom of the ocean forever. The likelihood of anyone surviving in a damaged and sinking U-boat was virtually zero.

For an hour the Swordfish circled the convoy, all the while on the lookout for enemy activity. After sighting no U-boats or surface ships, it made a perfect landing back on the *Avenger*, to the cheers and admiration of all who witnessed it. The fact that the aircraft could only manage a maximum speed of around 90mph was a help when it came to taking off from and landing on such a short runway.

* * *

But it was not only the aircraft of the convoy itself which were on the alert for the presence of enemy surface ships; much had been put in place prior to the embarkation of PQ18 to warn it of any movement from the Kriegsmarine's heavy ships, most notably the *Tirpitz*.

The responsibility to provide air protection to both the convoys and the distant covering naval forces lay with Coastal Command. Due to the threat of Kriegsmarine ships based in Altenfjord, it was now necessary to station aircraft in Russia itself under the codename 'Operation Orator'. Forty-seven-year-old Group Captain Frank Hopps was selected to head British forces in Russia and tasked with the job of providing this protection. The forces placed at Hopps' disposal included Catalina flying boats of 210 Squadron, positioned to give warning to the British submarines patrolling seaward of them and to prevent enemy ships from leaving the fjords undetected. If the heavy German cruisers left harbour, the Catalinas were to shadow them. Also at Hopps' disposal were two Hampden torpedo-bomber squadrons (144 and 455 Squadron) based at Afrikanda, south of Murmansk, who were to be at readiness to attack enemy surface vessels in the event of their putting to sea to attack the convoy.

The primary task of the Catalinas was to maintain anti-surface ship patrols and to provide escort to PQ18, up to the point where the convoy passed the returning QP14 near the Kola Inlet, with the focus then switching to the ships returning to Britain, some of which had endured the horrors of the ill-fated PQ17. They were also to engage with any U-boats they might come across.

To support these torpedo-carrying Catalinas, a ground party with torpedoes, a compressor and other ground equipment was sent in the ship USNS *Tuscaloosa*, which left Glasgow on 12 August 1942 for Vaenga, arriving eleven days later in readiness for PQ18's embarkation. However, it was not possible to take enough maintenance personnel for the Flying Boat squadrons on the *Tuscaloosa*, as the aircraft were still required to operate from Sullom Voe in Orkney at the same time as they were preparing for operations in northern Russia. Three Catalina Flying Boats of 422 Squadron were therefore employed to transport essential personnel and stores later that month.

It had been the intention to base the flying boats at Lake Lakhta on the White Sea, but due to the difficulties of communication, Hopps decided to make Grasnaya, near Murmansk, the main operational flying boat base as far as the entrance to the White Sea; it was much nearer to the patrol area and the convoy route. The only argument against using Grasnaya was that it was close to the enemy front line and therefore susceptible to possible air attack. This was reluctantly accepted by Hopps as a hazard of war, and so Lake Lakhta was relegated to a repairing and rest station.

Thirteen Catalinas of 210 Squadron arrived in Russia in early September, and eleven Hampdens of 144 Squadron and thirteen of 455 Squadron landed safely on 5 September. However, one aircraft of 144 Squadron crash-landed at the Kola Inlet and another, belonging to 455 Squadron, crashed near Kandalaksha on the same day. Four aircraft of 144 Squadron and two of 455 Squadron were also lost in transit, two coming down in Sweden, with only four survivors from both crews, and three crashing in Norway, with three men confirmed as killed. The fate of the other plane was unknown.

Additional air cover was to be provided from bases in Iceland and Britain when within range.

To add to this air cover, and to give early warning to the Admiralty that the German Norwegian fleet might be on the move, a Photo Reconnaissance Unit (1PRU) of four Spitfires was sent to Vaenga to carry out daily sorties and keep an eye on the ships operating out of Altenfjord. Three were dispatched on 1 September, with another to follow on 16 September. Any information garnered was to be relayed to the Admiralty, who would then pass it on to Rear-Admiral Burnett on the *Scylla*.

* * *

It wasn't long before another spotter plane was sighted in the skies ahead. Always ready for action, four of the *Avenger*'s Sea Hurricanes were immediately scrambled to intercept it. As on the previous day, the German pilot, seeing such a show of strength from the British, turned away and headed for home, his job done, pursued for a short while by the Hurricanes.

It was now becoming quite evident that the Germans knew exactly where the convoy was, and their U-boat wolf-packs were already stalking the ships, waiting to strike when the time was right. Around the convoy, the destroyers and anti-submarine ships threw out depth charges, pounding the sea wherever an Asdic showed up a potential enemy submarine.

The noise of the underwater explosions reverberated throughout the convoy. Those cooped up in boiler rooms and below deck, unaware of what was taking place above them, looked at each other nervously as they went about their duties. Was the convoy under attack? Had any of the ships been hit? Did a U-boat at that very moment have their ship in her sights? Was a torpedo on its way to slam into their side and send them to a deep, watery grave? Some became so nervous they would ring through to the bridge to check what was going on, asking if there was any reason for them to be worried. After reassurance from their officers, they then continued with their work. However, as each new explosion echoed around their confined spaces, it wasn't long before that anxiety returned.

With temperatures plummeting even further, orders were given to check and re-check guns, and de-icing parties were sent out to ensure the lifeboats and davits were clear in case a ship had to be abandoned. Sick bays began to fill with sailors with skin burns; these were caused when men, finding it easier to work without gloves, discovered that their hands, on coming into contact with freezing metal handrails, became fixed as though stuck with glue. Of course, once they pulled them away, a layer of skin was left on the ship as a reminder of their negligence. Although cumbersome and sometimes difficult to work in, the mittens supplied by the Navy became an essential piece of kit.

Ahead of them, and out of view, a Catalina and two Liberators from Coastal Command carried out an anti-submarine sweep. However, they returned to base a few hours later having located nothing.

Chapter 4

11–12 September

Aboard HMS *Milne* young Charlie Erswell was feeling confident. The appearance of the two spotter planes over the last couple of days, and the escort's swift reaction in sending them packing, gave him a sense that the Royal Navy was in total control of the situation. Since leaving Iceland, the crew had constantly been put through their drills, whether at Action Stations or not, and although they had yet to face an attack they knew that it was just a matter of time before the Germans showed themselves in force. With each passing hour, the further they sailed away from the protection of the planes of Coastal Command and the closer they got to the Norwegian Luftwaffe airbases, the greater the threat of air attack became. And with daylight lasting longer the further north they travelled, the enemy had plenty of opportunity to launch such an assault.

The cold Charlie was feeling inside B turret was as nothing compared to those having to man the Bofors and Oerlikons. At least inside the turret there was a degree of protection from the elements, even if it did feel as though he was working inside a freezer. Those poor souls who had to operate their weapons whilst exposed to the harsh Arctic weather had it much worse, and he did not envy them one bit.

Beside him was his best friend, Charlie 'Robbo' Robinson, B turret's gun layer. As Charlie turned the turret, Robbo's job was to raise and lower the 4.7-inch guns, pointing them as instructed by the Petty Officer who stood behind him, himself following the orders from the ship's director, the small fire control room situated above the bridge that had overall control of the guns. Two more shipmates made up the remainder of the turret crew, their job being to load the guns with shells that were sent up on the lifts from the magazine below.

The Petty Officer had seemed unconcerned when the spotter planes had appeared. He had sailed the Kola Run (as sailors called the Arctic route to Murmansk) before and told them this was nothing new and only to be expected. It was quite normal for enemy aircraft to be seen in the sky at this stage of the journey, and they offered no immediate threat. However, his words did not prevent a nervous apprehension spreading among those whose first voyage, and consequently their first sight of the enemy, this was. The planes' appearance made it feel altogether very real. At all times, the crew had to be vigilant.

Sailing to port of the *Milne* was the escort flagship HMS *Scylla*. Robert Hughes, on duty in the blue director, was equally alert. Those in the directors had a comms link to both the bridge and the EWO room, where they would be pre-warned of any enemy air activity picked up on the ship's radar screens. Trained to a very high standard, Hughes was also confident of doing a good job when the time came. And the firepower of the *Scylla* was something to behold…

HMS *Scylla*, a 'Dido Class' light cruiser, was the most heavily armed ship of the convoy. Even the bespoke anti-aircraft ships, HMS *Ulster Queen* and HMS *Alynbank*, although formidable in their own right, did not possess weaponry on the same scale. Equipped with three 40mm pom-pom anti-aircraft guns, a QF 4-inch naval gun, two Vickers quadruple 0.5-inch machine guns and two triple 21-inch torpedo tubes situated amidships, she was an impressive sight.

But it was the eight 4.5-inch heavy cannon, housed in pairs in the four turrets that were her most powerful weapons. Hughes, a Sub-Lieutenant in the 'blue' director, controlled two of these turrets, X and Y, situated at the stern of the ship; his friend Sub-Lieutenant Rowland had charge of A and B guns on the foredeck.

Each director had a team of five and could control either all eight guns together, or the four nearest to it. At Action Stations each director would be manned by a Control Officer and crew, but during quieter periods, such as Cruising Stations, only the 'red' director would be manned, with Hughes and Rowland working opposite watches. As the threat of attack diminished, the directors would not be manned at all, the officers taking up duties on the bridge instead.

The allocation of the guns to the directors was the job of the Gunnery Officer (on the *Scylla* this was Lieutenant 'Guns' Wainwright) or the Air Defence Officers who were normally situated at the rear of the bridge. By turning a switch, the Gunnery Officer could give control of the guns to either of the Control Officers in the directors, and another turn gave each director its own four guns. This therefore demanded close co-operation between these officers and those in the directors. Should the situation demand it, a Control Officer could request that all guns be given to him if he believed there was an imminent danger to the ship.

The Air Defence Officer would show a target to each director by means of the target-bearing indicators. These were two hugely powerful binoculars on a power-operated mounting each side of the air defence position. Pressure on a switch adjacent to them would ring a bell in the director, and a pointer would then swing on a dial. When this pointer was centred, the target would be revealed in the sights.

By use of geometry (including Pythagoras theorem), the director team were able to judge the direction, elevation, range, speed and course of an attacking aircraft and get the turret teams to adjust their positions accordingly. By estimating where the attacking aircraft would be in the time it took for the turret teams to train, lay and load the guns, and the duration of travel for the shell to reach the target, the director could effectively put up a defensive barrage. Once all the lights were lit in the director tower, showing that the guns were loaded and ready to fire, the Control Officer would pull the trigger, releasing eight shells into the sky. This would have to be done many times during an aerial attack, and the pointers would have to be constantly readjusted. (NB In the destroyers, the three turrets were controlled by just the one director tower.)

* * *

The convoy had now passed Jan Mayen Island and was steaming steadily at around 8 knots on a north-easterly course. With no enemy activity being detected, Rear-Admiral Burnett on the *Scylla* gave the order for Force B to detach from the convoy and rendezvous with Force P at Spitzbergen to refuel. Force P, which had set off two days previously, were now anchored in Lowe Sound and were expecting them.

Force B, consisting of HMS *Scylla* and the 'M' Class destroyers HMS *Milne*, HMS *Meteor*, HMS *Marne* and HMS *Martin*, proceeded north at full speed, leaving the protection of the convoy to Force A. The plan was that, once refuelled, they would return at full speed to rejoin the convoy east of Bear Island.

Unencumbered by the merchant ships, Force B was able to travel at around 30 knots and make good time in reaching Spitzbergen. The coastline was a welcome sight to Charlie Erswell and the crew of the *Milne*. As the ships entered the Sound, they gazed in wonder at the ice-covered terrain and the dark mass of a glacier at the far end of the inlet; parts of it had broken off, falling into the water to form small icebergs, the sun's rays bouncing off their uneven surfaces and giving them a jewel-like appearance. Other than a small settlement, there looked to be no signs of life on land, but for a fleeting second Charlie thought he saw movement high up on a snowy ridge. He scanned the horizon seeking the thing that had caught his eye, now lost from view. Not sure what it could have been, he mentioned it to his Petty Officer, who suggested it might well have been a polar bear; it was not uncommon for them to venture this far south.

The two oil tankers lined the Sound, and as each ship docked to their sides, there was bustling activity on the decks of the destroyers as fuel lines were thrown across and connected. As the destroyers passed each other, their crews waved in greeting. There may have been a rivalry between the ships' companies whilst in port, but out in the frozen wastes of the Arctic Ocean there was a mutual respect, especially for those on SS *Blue Ranger* and SS *Oligarch*, who were providing the heated fuel for them to continue on their way.

* * *

By now the convoy was approximately 230 miles south-west of Spitzbergen, with Bear Island 270 miles to the east. The course would send it around the north of the island in an easterly direction, keeping as far away from the Luftwaffe airbases as possible, before then heading south towards the Kola Inlet, where the Fighting Destroyer Escort would then pick up the returning QP14, leaving the convoy to make the final run to Archangelsk with the rest of the escorts, supported by ships from the Soviet Union who would meet them there.

Although keeping as far away from the German airbases as it could, PQ18 would still inevitably come within their range. Reducing the threat of air attack was something the Navy could control to some degree. However, the threat from the deep – that they could do very little about.

* * *

Heino Bohmann stood on *U-88*'s conning tower and looked towards the south. If the information he had received from B-Dienst was correct, then PQ18 could not be too far away. He knew that being on the surface was something of a compromise. From here he could travel at a rate almost twice that of the approaching convoy, whereas below the water he would be reduced to almost half the enemy's speed. The trick was to get into a position where, once submerged, he was able to get off a shot before the ships passed, at the same time avoiding detection. The most effective time to engage was at dusk, when a surface attack could be carried out. That way, it would be harder for eagle-eyed spotters to see the conning tower or the track of an approaching torpedo. However, there was always the enemy's Asdic to worry about, so he would demand absolute silence from all the crew when the time came.

For a brief moment he thought he saw something in the air to the south. Quickly he put his binoculars to his eyes and scanned the sky. What he at first thought was a bird was clearly not. It was the unmistakable silhouette of a biplane, one of those ancient-looking Swordfish aircraft used by the Royal Navy, worryingly to great effect. And more troubling still, it was headed in their direction.

'Alarm!' he yelled. 'Below decks now, everyone. Clear the tower!'

He followed the other officers through the hatch and back into the submarine, screaming all the while the order to dive, not believing his bad luck. He had only been at the surface a matter of a few minutes. The convoy must have been closer than he realized, and it was clear that the Swordfish had seen him. He knew that the aircraft, due to its slow speed, was highly manoeuvrable and carried a torpedo on its fuselage that could quite easily sink his boat. Maybe, he thought, they could have stayed on the surface and used the 88mm deck gun to shoot the aircraft down; but he knew the chances of that were slim, and it wasn't as though the plane was alone. The convoy, containing a large number of Royal Navy ships, must be very close by, and the Swordfish pilot would have already passed on their position to the destroyers. It was only a matter of time before they would be heading in his direction at full speed.

To enable a quick dive it was necessary to increase speed, with the diesel engines shut down and power switched to the electric motors. The hatch and vents were quickly closed, the tanks flooded and the hydroplanes set to dive. Bohmann felt a sense of pride at how quickly his crew moved so to achieve this. However, the danger was by no means over.

The only thing to do now was to dive as deep as possible and wait it out.

* * *

Bohmann was quite correct.

The crew of the Swordfish, carrying out a routine patrol around the perimeter of the convoy, had sighted the *U-88* and gone to investigate. They witnessed the unmistakable shape of a conning tower disappearing beneath the waves but were too far away to engage. They immediately radioed back to the destroyers what they had seen and dropped a marker buoy on the surface where the submarine was last sighted.

HMS *Faulknor*, the 'F' Class flotilla leader positioned on the far port side of the front row of destroyers and the closest ship to the site, had picked up a faint contact on their Asdic and was at that very moment heading to the area to investigate.

In only a few minutes the destroyer was in position and had picked up a much stronger contact. Her captain, Alan Scott-Moncrieff, gave the order to prepare a depth-charge run. Quickly and expertly, the crew ran to their tasks, setting the timers on the charges and loading them on to the throwers positioned at the sides and stern of the ship. They then waited patiently for the order to launch them.

* * *

Thirty metres below the waves, Bohmann held his breath. He had ordered the boat to proceed at only 2 knots on a silent running, her stern pointed slightly upwards to make it more difficult for the destroyer's Asdic operator to locate them. Once this was done, those crewmen who were not required in the central control room were sent to their bunks, and everyone was instructed to maintain absolute silence.

After only a few moments, they could clearly hear the sound of a destroyer's propellers and the distinctive 'ping' as its Asdic scanned the area seeking them out.

Despite the cold in the U-boat, he could feel sweat running down the back of his neck and he nervously rubbed his clammy hands against his trouser leg. He looked around the room and could see the desperation in all his men's bearded faces. Everyone stood as still as a statue, hardly daring to breathe. They too were perspiring, and he could see one or two with tears starting to form in their eyes. Lying on their bunks in the accommodation area, non-essential crew looked longingly at photographs of their wives, children and sweethearts, some praying silently.

Bohmann was now starting to regret not staying on the surface when they had been spotted. Maybe they would have stood more of a chance in the open sea. But he knew there was no possibility of outrunning a Royal Navy destroyer; they would have either been blown out of the water or, more likely, rammed. Diving had been his only option.

He had already made up his mind that if they were hit and it looked like there was no way out, he would attempt to surface and throw *U-88* on the mercy of the British. Hopefully they would accept his surrender. At least then his crew might be saved.

He looked across to the hydrophone operator, who was listening intently at his equipment. Catching his captain's eye, the operator raised his eyebrows, the expression on his face indicating that the ship above was very close, almost directly on top of them. Bohmann frowned. He knew the destroyer did not need a direct hit to sink them. The concussion shock wave that a depth charge produced would be enough to breach the hull if it was close enough, and a hull breach at this depth would make it impossible to survive. He just prayed they were deep enough.

Like all the others around him, he held his breath.

* * *

In the Electronic Warfare Operations room on the *Faulknor*, the Asdic operator listened intently for any noise that would give away the U-boat's exact position. On his screen he could see a large object almost directly beneath them. He called over the supervising officer to show him. On observing this, the officer grabbed the telephone and called the bridge.

Once informed, Captain Scott-Moncrieff gave the order to launch the depth charges.

Seconds later, the charges were fired from their launchers, hitting the surface and quickly sinking beneath the waves, while the *Faulknor* sped ahead to avoid being caught by the explosions that were soon to follow.

* * *

Bohmann was thrown violently to the side, the hydrophone operator fell from his seat and the whole boat immediately listed to port. At the same time he was aware of a thud, followed immediately by a scream as someone in the accommodation area was thrown from his bunk to the floor.

One or two others cried out in pain and despair, and he immediately told them to be quiet.

That first explosion had been very close, and only a couple of seconds later, another boom reverberated around the boat. He could feel the pressure heighten as the concussive effect of the depth charge caused *U-88* to lurch from side to side. He was then thrown to the floor himself, hitting his head on the cold, hard steel. He realized he was losing control of the situation and needed to surface as soon as possible, but as he got back to his feet, he saw that all was now lost. Seawater was pouring into the boat from all sides.

Just as he had feared, the hull had been breached.

Desperately, he ordered the tanks to be vented. He needed to get to the surface quickly if there was to be any chance of survival at all.

And then more and more explosions resounded through the water. Rivets pinged from their housings and equipment smashed all around him. Then the lights went out, and they were plunged into total darkness. The cries of his crew filled his ears, as yet more underwater explosions caused him to be thrown mercilessly to the side, striking his head once more. As he fell into unconsciousness, he knew this was the end.

* * *

On the surface, sea water was continuing to fly high into the air as the depth charges exploded. The whole sea seemed to reverberate and shimmer around the *Faulknor* as each charge detonated. As the destroyer turned to carry out another run, it quickly became clear that this was not going to be necessary. On the surface there appeared a large oil slick which grew with each passing second. A sample was hurriedly taken which proved immediately to be diesel, and with the Asdic operator reporting to his officer that his equipment was now showing clear, Scott-Moncrieff was left in no doubt that the U-boat had been destroyed. He ordered a search of the area, but after fifteen minutes nothing further was found other than a large black patch within the ice floes that marked the fresh graves of forty-six German submariners.

But this was not a time for celebration. The loss of so many lives beneath the sea was not something to savour. It was something that just had to be done.

With the immediate threat now nullified, Scott-Moncrieff ordered the *Faulknor*, her job done, to return to her position in the convoy .

* * *

That afternoon at Vaenga, 1,250 miles south-east of the convoy's position, Flying Officer Donald Furniss of 1PRU (1 Photograph Reconnaissance Unit), sent to Russia earlier that month, climbed into the cockpit of his Spitfire. He found it rather odd to see that, in place of the RAF roundel that usually adorned the side of his aircraft, a red star of the Soviet Union had been painted next to the aircraft number, BP891. He understood that once the short detachment to Russia was over, the aircraft they had brought with them would be left behind for the Russian Air Force.

This was to be the unit's second flight of the day, the first having been undertaken that morning by his colleague, Flight Lieutenant Edward (Tim) Fairhurst. This would be a round trip of almost 1,500 miles to carry out a reconnaissance of Altenfjord, where the German cruisers,*Admiral Hipper*, *Admiral Scheer* and *Köln*, along with a further eight warships, were known to be anchored. It was vitally important that the Admiralty know where these ships were at all times. Should they leave Altenfjord to engage with PQ18, then their threat would need to be met. Word would be sent to the Cruiser Cover Force headed by Vice-Admiral Stuart Bonham-Carter and the Distant Covering

Force under the command of Vice-Admiral Bruce Fraser to intercept and engage with the German fleet. Also, the two squadrons of Hampdens based at Afrikanda, under Group Captain Hopps would be scrambled.

Furniss's reconnaissance mission was therefore essential to the safety of the men sailing on PQ18.

Taking off at 1540 hrs and climbing to a height of between 15,000 and 19,000ft, his sortie would take him on a round trip along the Norwegian coast covering Altenfjord, Langfjord, Sorfjord, Ornoya and Torsvaag.

Carrying out reconnaissance missions at this time of day, when the sun was still high in the sky, was filled with complications. Maintaining high altitude and using the clouds for cover were extremely important. The last thing Furniss wanted was to bump into a Luftwaffe fighter patrol, but he knew the chances of that happening were quite slim; or to be hit by anti-aircraft fire, should he be spotted on the enemy's radar. But even if he did run into trouble, he would only be staying in an area long enough to take photographs, and the speed produced by the Spitfire's Merlin 46 engine would soon have him away and out of any danger from ground fire.

The main area he had to consider was Altenfjord, where the German heavy cruisers were last known to have docked. He knew the importance of his mission. Senior officers and planners would be waiting for the information he would gather, so it was imperative he got some good shots of the harbour and visual confirmation that the ships were still there. Later, as he approached the fjord, he climbed to 19,000ft. This area would be the most heavily protected due to the presence of the Kriegsmarine ships.

Banking slightly to get a better view, he looked through a gap in the clouds and saw exactly what he wanted to see. Below him, some anchored in open water and others docked at the quayside, lay a number of German battleships, none of which showed any signs of movement. Levelling out once more, he circled round and started to press the button on his control column which triggered the F24 reconnaissance camera fixed to his undercarriage.

Having the information he needed, he immediately set a course back to Vaenga, landing safely back on the runway at 1900 hrs. He climbed out of the cockpit and handed the aircraft over to Sergeant Greenwood, who headed the five-man ground crew. After they had retrieved the film from the camera and handed it to him, he walked to the headquarters building to give his debrief on what had been a routine and successful mission.

His job done and his report passed over to his Commanding Officer, Squadron Leader Lawrence Wager, Furniss went to find some supper. As he stepped out into the cold Russian evening he shivered for a moment and took out a packet of cigarettes and a box of matches from his jacket pocket.

Throwing the used match to the ground, he shuddered again and looked north to the cloudy, grey sky. He did not envy those poor buggers on the ships right now. Furniss knew that although the missions he and his colleagues were flying were extremely hazardous, and the conditions in which they were living in Russia were not exactly up to the RAF's usual standard, at least he could come back after each sortie, get warm and find a decent supply of hot food to fill his belly, even if it wasn't the best he had ever eaten.

But he knew that the men out there on those ships, currently enduring the dangers of the Arctic weather, the constant threat of U-boats and expected attack by the torpedo-bombers of the Luftwaffe, were having it much, much tougher than he was.

If he could play a small part in providing early warning of a surface ship attack, then he was more than happy to do so, whatever the consequences.

Throwing his half-finished cigarette to the ground, he set off in search of that hot meal.

* * *

At 0600 hrs on Saturday, 12 September, the Cruiser Covering Force (CCF), commanded by Vice-Admiral Stuart Bonham-Carter, left Hvalfjörd in Iceland. Codenamed Operation EVY, the eight ships set a course north-north-west at a cruising speed of 17 knots. The patrol route would take them to a point 270 miles north of Jan Mayen Island, before they were then to proceed to Spitzbergen to refuel two days later.

Should the Admiralty be made aware that Kriegsmarine surface ships had left port, then the CCF was to move to intercept and engage. However, as Bonham-Carter had mentioned in his orders distributed on 4 September, it was not his intention to engage any enemy force that included the *Tirpitz*.

Three of the ships proceeding north were to leave Operation EVY once refuelled at Spitzbergen. HMS *Cumberland*, HMS *Eclipse* and HMS *Sheffield* would then detach to carry out Operation Gearbox II, and once that was completed, rejoin the forces of Operation EVY to continue the patrols. Gearbox II was a mission to supply and reinforce Allied forces at Spitzbergen, the ships carrying a contingent of Norwegian troops and supplies with them from Iceland.

With the Cruiser Covering Force out on the open sea, all the participants in PQ18 were now in play.

* * *

Topped up with fuel and eager to get back to the convoy, the ships of Force B, led by the flagship HMS *Scylla* and the flotilla leader HMS *Milne*, steamed south at full speed to rendezvous with them. The weather had shown no signs of improvement, but as they left Lowe Sound the low cloud turned into a heavy fog which cleared only after a couple of hours.

It wasn't long before Action Stations reverberated through the ships.

On board HMS *Milne*, Charlie Erswell and his friend 'Robbo' Robinson ran quickly to their positions in B turret. The unmistakable drone of an aircraft engine could be heard above the noise, and when the men looked to the sky, they could see a lone Heinkel He-111 between the clouds off the starboard bow.

'Probably another observation aircraft out looking for us,' said the Petty Officer standing behind them.

Immediately, the pom-poms and Oerlikons opened up at the approaching aircraft. For a brief moment it looked as though the Heinkel pilot was preparing to attack, but seeing the firepower he would need to face and thinking better of it, he turned his plane around and headed away to safety.

For Charlie, Robbo and the rest of the crew, there was a feeling of exhilaration, which was also felt throughout the ship. This was the first time the *Milne*'s guns had been fired in anger, and although they had not shot the He-111 from the sky, they had done enough to scare it off and protect the ships.

In late afternoon a sailor on duty in the *Scylla*'s crow's nest spotted something in the distance to the south. Admiral Burnett and Captain MacIntyre were immediately called to the bridge. In the blue director Robert Hughes ordered the powerful telescopes to traverse the horizon and, once focused, saw the tops of masts and a slight haze of smoke filling the Arctic air. It was the ships of PQ18.

With the sun beginning to drop in the sky, the ships of Force B settled back into position at the front of the formidable convoy. By now, PQ18 was almost 320 miles directly west of Bear Island and continuing on a north-easterly heading. So far, things were going quite well. As yet, all the ships that had set out from Iceland a few days ago were still proceeding safely on the surface. A U-boat had been sent to the bottom of the sea and enemy aircraft had been sent packing. Confidence was growing that the convoy could make it to Archangelsk safely.

However, a few hundred miles away at the Luftwaffe airbases at Banak and Bardufoss, German planes were being armed and fuelled and their pilots briefed, ready for an audacious operation that was planned for the following day.

Rear-Admiral Burnett, Commodore Boddam-Whetham and the officers of PQ18 had little idea as yet that Sunday, 13 September 1942 would be a momentous day in the history of the Arctic convoys.

Chapter 5

13 September – Early Morning

Aboard the SS *Stalingrad*, Captain Sakharov was beginning to feel a little uneasy. Thus far the convoy had gone unmolested, and the sinking of the U-boat by HMS *Faulknor* had given all of them a morale boost, but this was coupled with the knowledge that the wolf-packs were on the prowl. It was evident that the enhanced escort for this convoy was already proving to be necessary. However, although this gave Sakharov some comfort and confidence, it was tempered by the knowledge that the waters the convoy was now entering would provide more of a challenge to them all, not only due to the freezing temperatures and hazardous weather, but also because this was where enemy air attack was most likely to occur.

Dawn had broken to a calmer sea than on the previous day. A couple of Junkers Ju-88s had made an appearance shortly after daybreak but had been seen off by the anti-aircraft guns of the destroyers and had not lingered for long, avoiding the flak and the fog which had fallen an hour or so later.

Having been brought his breakfast at change of watch at 0800 hours by First Lieutenant Yermilov, who was relieving the navigator, Valentin Dartau, Sakharov checked the instruments on the panels. Before leaving the wheelhouse, Dartau had given the captain an update on the ship's exact position. The air temperature outside was a moderate -2°C, with the sea water at 4.5°C. He gazed out of the window, wondering what the new day would bring. Occasionally the fog drifted away, allowing the sun to make a brief appearance, its glare bouncing back off the waves, dazzling against the bright white of the ice floes and causing Sakharov to blink and shield his eyes momentarily.

Like everybody else, he had seen the spotter planes circling and understood that the Germans knew exactly where they were and it was only a matter of time before the enemy showed themselves in force. He looked to his right at the escort ships, painted white and pale green, the colours the Navy had adopted for the Arctic convoys; the white on their hulls merged slightly with the floes they pushed aside as they drove forward. He could see men on their decks manning the guns and carrying out other duties, and he felt for them. Although quite tolerable now, the temperature was likely to drop to at least -15°C as the day wore on, and the wind chill would make it feel even colder.

He watched as the working parties, wrapped up in duffel coats, jerkins and lammy coats, chipped away at the ice on guns and machinery. Below him on the foredeck, he had his own men doing the same thing.

He frowned to himself. No sooner were the ice and snow cleared than they formed again, coating everything in a white film, making the ships appear ghostlike as they fought their way through the swell. The sea spray froze as soon as it hit anything solid: superstructures, cargoes strapped to the decks, anchor chains and anything else out in the open. It was a constant battle and would never really be won until they returned to milder climes. But that was a long time away just yet.

As usual in this part of the world at this time of year, the sun had shown its face very early, after only two or three hours of darkness had separated one period of daylight from the next. It all seemed to merge into one never-ending day. The irony of it all was that had this convoy sailed only a few weeks later, the exact opposite would have occurred, the winter sun making only a brief appearance during the daytime. It was only by looking at his wristwatch or the large clock that adorned the wall at the back of the wheelhouse that Sakharov actually knew what time it was.

Below decks life was becoming monotonous. During their brief rest periods the crew would either catch up with sleep or play cards to pass away the hours. Those passengers carrying injuries lay idly in their bunks, looked after by the medical orderlies who had joined them on the journey. The civilian passengers were doing their best to keep themselves and the youngsters with them occupied. Sakharov wasn't too happy at having to carry them but, he supposed, someone had to do it, and since this was a Russian ship, it was down to him to take responsibility for repatriating his fellow countrymen and women: the mothers with small children playing silly games to stop them becoming bored; the diplomatic staff keeping themselves to themselves, enduring the journey out of necessity and just hoping the whole thing would be over soon. In general, the diplomats had remained apart, their diplomatic pouches secured safely in their cabins, leaving Sakharov to concentrate fully on sailing the ship to Archangelsk safely.

And so the *Stalingrad* forged on; but for Captain Sakharov and everyone else on board, things were about to become a little more exciting. They just did not know it yet.

* * *

His eyes fixed to the navigation periscope, Korvettenkapitän Reinhard von Hymmen, skipper of *U-408* of the *Trägertod* wolf-pack, twisted its handles to increase magnification and then flicked the mechanism to reduce the reflective surface within the periscope head, which was at that moment just above the surface. The last thing he needed was for the sun to be reflected off it and the periscope be spotted by an eagle-eyed sailor on one of the ships he could now see cutting across his vision. He knew that if they saw it they would immediately dispatch a destroyer to engage with him. He had learned that another U-boat, the *U-88*, had been sunk with all hands the previous day, and he knew he had to be extremely careful lest he and his crew suffer the same fate.

Having left Skomenfjord in northern Norway on the morning of 10 September, six days after his twenty-eighth birthday, von Hymmen had been able to quickly take up a position with the wolf-pack. This was only his second U-boat patrol and he was eager for success. He had managed to get ahead of the convoy and had submerged when, from the information he had received by signal from B-Dienst, he understood the ships to be approaching.

It wasn't long before he sighted them, a vast armada heading in a north-easterly direction. This was a bigger convoy than anything he had seen before. What appeared before him were dozens of merchant ships, all lying low in the water, their holds no doubt filled to the brim, slowly lumbering across his vision. Around them, the unmistakable forms of British destroyers, keeping watch like shepherds with their flock, patiently overseeing the sheep and keeping the wolves at bay. But von Hymmen was determined to be one wolf who would have his day.

As he observed this multitude of targets passing by, he understood that if he managed this right, there was a very good chance that *U-408* could sink some shipping this morning, sending to the bottom of the sea supplies bound for the Red Army. Added to this was the fact that, with the loss of the *U-88* so fresh in the minds of his men, the sinking of some Allied ships would do wonders for their morale, and for the spirits of crews on the other U-boats of the patrol.

Although it was very tempting to strike a destroyer of the Royal Navy, von Hymmen knew the real targets were those lumbering merchant ships with their cargoes of tanks, aircraft, fuel and ammunition, all destined to be pitched against his countrymen on the Eastern Front, and so he focused his mind on them, reluctantly ignoring the destroyers.

Ideally, he would have liked to engage the enemy on the surface, but this was impossible. The sea was quite calm, although slight mist and a grey sky made it less likely that his periscope would be seen. But he could not pass up this opportunity of striking at the convoy. Although there was always a risk of being picked up on the enemy's Asdic, the chance might not come around again soon, and so he decided to attack.

Pulling the navigation periscope down into the well, he gave the order to prepare the bow torpedo tubes and moved to the attack periscope in the somewhat cramped commander's control room within the conning tower. With room only for himself and one more crew member to operate the torpedo calculator, he settled himself on the saddle and drew up the periscope. He knew the torpedo tubes would already be armed as this would be the first attack of the patrol, the missiles having been fitted in the tubes before leaving Skomenfjord.

As he called out the distances, the torpedo calculator adjusted his settings, which were automatically relayed to the petty officer and torpedo mechanic in the bow torpedo room. Von Hymmen had already decided to fire a salvo of three torpedoes at the starboard column. This would give him a better chance of scoring a hit. Once the settings were completed, those in the torpedo room awaited the order from the captain.

After a brief pause to reflect, knowing that the torpedo tracks might give their position away if spotted, von Hymmen said calmly, '*Los*', the order to fire. The order was relayed throughout the boat, and when it reached the torpedo room a couple of seconds later, the mechanic pulled the levers and the torpedoes were released. Immediately, von Hymmen clicked his stopwatch. At the same time, his crew expertly adjusted the ballast to account for the loss of weight and increased buoyancy resulting from the torpedoes leaving the boat. The last thing von Hymmen wanted was an uncontrolled ascent to the surface, giving away their position and provoking a counter-attack by the destroyers.

He glanced over to the seaman at the hydrophone, who looked back at him expressionlessly. All they could do now was wait patiently and see if the attack was successful.

* * *

Maintaining a speed of just over 9 knots, the *Stalingrad* continued on her course.

In the wheelhouse, Sakharov and Yermilov had now been joined by a small party of sailors who were taking turns at the wheel. The job itself was not too difficult – they merely had to maintain a straight course – but their involvement on the bridge gave them a sense of inclusion; that they were valued by the senior officers on board.

Sakharov looked up. Valentin Dartau, who had been relieved earlier, appeared on the bridge having eaten his breakfast, and although he had taken the previous watch, he was still looking wide awake.

Sakharov spoke to him.

'Valentin, seeing we both can't sleep and you're here, check the sonar and let's see how much water we have under the keel.'

Dartau switched on the sonar, and once the device was warmed, the stylus drew a line on the tape revealing a depth under the ship of just over 1,700 metres.

What happened next was without warning. A massive explosion on the starboard side threw all on the bridge to the floor, shattering the windows and spraying glass over them all. For a second the ship seemed to stall, as though in a momentary void, before jerking and shaking violently. For the moment Sakharov was dazed, not fully understanding what had happened. Slowly he got to his feet and in an instant understood that his worst fears had been realized.

The *Stalingrad* had clearly been hit by a torpedo and, from what he could see, was already sinking fast.

He shook his head to clear the ringing in his ears and moved to the shattered windows of the wheelhouse. The torpedo had hit amidships, exploding in the boiler room, no doubt killing everyone inside instantly. If there was one saving grace, it was that the ammunition in the holds had not been hit; otherwise everyone on board would have been instantly vaporized. He could see a huge hole in the ship's starboard side, and seawater was pouring in fast. Fires were starting to burn all around, and the superstructure they were occupying swayed dangerously back and forth.

Above the noise of the explosion, which was still reverberating around the ship, he could hear the screams and cries of the injured and others scared out of their wits. The superstructure groaned as the metal twisted and broke away from the deck. To his horror, Sakharov saw that all but one of the lifeboats on the starboard side had been destroyed, smashed to pieces, the fragments floating out to sea as the ship listed even further. From what he could see, she was going down fast, and they didn't have much time before she went under. They had only a few minutes at best to save themselves.

He turned to his colleagues, who were by now getting to their feet.

'Go! Run! I order you to escape however you can!'

He grabbed the microphone and broadcast a similar message throughout the ship, hoping that the sound system was still operative and it would be heard by those able to save themselves. Quickly he donned a life jacket and left the wheelhouse.

By now the air was filled with smoke and dust, and it was becoming very difficult to see. To the sounds of people coughing and vomiting as they choked on the acrid smoke, Sakharov shouted to those able to hear that they should make for the port side lifeboats, to abandon ship, for all was lost.

* * *

Von Hymmen was elated. He had moved back into the central control room and been given the thumbs up from the submariner at the hydrophone. He clicked the stopwatch. Five minutes and twenty-seven seconds. A confirmed hit. He grinned at everyone near him and saw that they were as pleased as he was.

He was about to give the order to dive deeper and to carry out evasive manoeuvres when the hydrophone operator held up his hand again. He raised two fingers, indicating a second hit.

'A different ship,' stated the operator. 'Two hits on two separate ships.'

Von Hymmen grabbed the navigation periscope and raised it. He had to see for himself what was happening on the surface.

* * *

The hydrophone operator on *U-408* was quite correct.

On seeing and feeling the blast of the explosion on the SS *Stalingrad*, the captain of the United States Liberty ship SS *Oliver Ellsworth*, sailing two ships behind in the starboard column, immediately realized what was happening. He also knew that U-boats tended to fire more than one torpedo in a spread, hoping that at least one would score a hit.

In order to avoid hitting the stricken *Stalingrad*, he immediately ordered his ship to turn hard to port. Unfortunately for him, and his ship, this put the *Oliver Ellsworth* in the path of the third torpedo.

A huge explosion rocked the ship as the missile rammed into her side, between holds numbers four and five. As fires broke out and quickly spread, the captain ordered the engines to be stopped and gave the order to abandon ship, fearing the munitions he was carrying in the holds would explode and kill all on board. He could see immediately that the ship was doomed, although she wasn't going to go down as quickly as the *Stalingrad*, which he could now see listing badly to starboard.

* * *

Upon seeing the damage his torpedoes had caused, von Hymmen lowered the periscope and gave the order for *U-408* to dive deeper and carry out evasive manoeuvres. It would not be long before the escort ships, the destroyers and anti-submarine trawlers, would come looking for him. His work done for now, he needed to get the boat away to safety.

Despite his success, he did not smile. This was a dirty business, there was no doubt about it. He consoled himself with the thought that, although he had caused great damage this day and no doubt the deaths of a number of fellow mariners, this, after all, was war. This is what happened in war. There was simply no getting away from it.

* * *

On board *Stalingrad*, the situation was deteriorating. The ship was listing badly to starboard and shaking violently as fires raged and the metal superstructure twisted and grated, causing the ship to groan wildly, almost like an animal in its death throes. Sakharov had ordered everyone to evacuate the wheelhouse; it was simply not safe to stay there any longer. First Lieutenant Yermilov was now mustering as many passengers and crew as he could to the surviving lifeboats on the port side, bawling instructions at them through a megaphone. Sakharov noticed a heavily pregnant woman, clearly in huge distress, being assisted by two sailors and hoped to God she would be all right. The second mate, Strelkov, was also on deck frantically trying to release the boats into the water and impose some sort of order on the evacuation.

Burning oil was now covering the sea to the starboard side, and Sakharov was horrified to see a few of his men in the water, battling against both the heat of the fire and the icy cold of the water into which they had jumped. It was a hard choice: possible death by fire and smoke on board ship, or take your chances in the freezing waters of the Arctic. Through breaks in the smoke, as the wind blew it away slightly, he could see a destroyer on the port side, together with HMS *Copeland*, the convoy's designated rescue ship, heading in their direction, and for a moment his spirits lifted. If they could just get as many people into the boats as possible, then they might be able to save most of the passengers and crew. He could only hope.

Meanwhile, on leaving the wheelhouse, the ship's navigator, Valentin Dartau, had to go to his cabin once the captain had given the order to abandon ship. He needed to collect his life-jacket and cursed himself for not having kept it with him. If he got out of this alive, this would be a lesson very well learned.

Holding his breath, he entered the smoke-filled walkway and headed towards his cabin. He could hear people coughing and shouting, and when he was a couple of yards from his berth he saw the smoke starting to become thicker. There was then the sound of another explosion, causing the ship to lurch once more and making him stumble against the side wall. Holding his breath, he stepped into his cabin. Taking the lifejacket from where he had left it on his cot, he threw it over his head and stepped back out into the walkway, turning to the left, away from where the smoke was thickest. Half running and half stumbling, he fastened the straps as he went, eventually making it back out onto the deck, where he almost tripped over the bodies of two clearly dead sailors. Numerous smaller explosions were now occurring throughout the ship as the flames reached more combustible material, throwing white-hot metal into the air as the superstructure started to disintegrate. Turning to his left, he watched helplessly as two more sailors and a female passenger jumped into the sea.

Dartau could now see his only means of escape was to make it to the lifeboats, into which sailors and passengers were starting to clamber. He rushed into the complex of cabins where the infirmary was housed and, together with seven or eight of the wounded sailors, managed to make it to the starboard side, where one serviceable lifeboat still remained. Quickly they released it from its davits and, once it hit the water, scrambled aboard. For a brief second he heaved a sigh of relief.

By now Captain Sakharov knew his ship did not have long left before she would be completely submerged, taking down with her anyone unlucky enough still to be on board. The last of the available lifeboats had been dropped into the water, their coxswains frantically shouting at those manning the oars to work harder, to pull them away from the ship lest it take them down with her.

Sakharov once more looked around to assess the situation. Above the din of the dying ship and the roaring of the flames, the screams of those in the freezing water crying desperately for help pierced his ears. He saw the ship rising in the water and knew this was the prelude to her sinking, as the water flooded the stern, lifting her bow into the air. There was nothing he could do now for anyone. It was time for him to leave.

* * *

Those on the other ships had felt the explosions on the *Stalingrad* and *Oliver Ellsworth* almost as soon as they occurred. The sounds carried to all the vessels, and the wash that was created hit each of them in turn. Immediately, Burnett on board the *Scylla* ordered the nearest destroyers on the starboard side to hunt for the U-boat that had carried out the attack, whilst the rescue ship HMS *Copeland* and the anti-submarine trawler HMS *St Kenan* were dispatched to pick up any survivors.

Hot burning oil now surrounded the *Stalingrad*, and fires aboard the *Oliver Ellsworth* were burning furiously. With both ships carrying high explosives, nothing could be done other than to abandon them. Neither could be saved. The *Stalingrad* looked to be in more distress, her bow slowly rising into the air as a myriad of small explosions now flickered down the length of the ship.

Everyone watching knew that all was lost. The only thing was to hope that as many sailors as were able had managed to escape these infernos.

The convoy was not to stop at any cost. Those ships travelling behind the two stricken vessels could only sail by, leaving the designated rescue ships to pick up the survivors. If U-boats were out there, as they most clearly were, then to stop and give assistance was only tempting the same fate as had befallen those currently dying in front of them. As sailors clung on desperately to floating debris and waved frantically from lifeboats for assistance, those not involved in the rescue effort could only sail past, unable to help in any way.

* * *

Sakharov took a breath and jumped. The fact he was wearing the thickest and warmest clothing available did not detract from the shock of the cold as he hit the water and went under. It was enough to take his breath away. With the average human temperature being 37°C, and the water, as he knew, being only just over 4°C, he was in real danger of his body shutting down very quickly and freezing to death. Letting his muscles relax as best he could, he kicked out and a second or two later reached the surface, where the life-jacket he was wearing then did its job in keeping him afloat.

For a second he did not move and let the heat from the burning oil wash over him. He could see it was spreading fast and so, gathering his faculties together, he started to swim away from it and the ship, in the direction of some floating debris. If he could only clamber onto this he might have a chance of saving himself.

He was aware of the rescue ship and another coming his way and knew he needed to get as close to them as he could if he was to survive. He turned his head around and saw, to his horror, that the ship was now half submerged, her bow almost perpendicular. It would be only a matter of seconds before she went under completely. He started to swim for his life.

Then he felt the sea pull at him and he was forced backwards and under the water as the sinking ship dragged the surface water down with her. There was no way he could resist it. Again, he struggled wildly for the surface, but the sea was pulling him down, as though an invisible ocean god was trying to claim him, not letting him go. Kicking for all he was worth and fighting desperately for his life, he made a last-ditch bid for survival, working as hard as he could against the current. And then, almost miraculously, he was at the surface again and could breathe in the freezing air. Spotting some floating wood a few yards away, he made for it it and managed to haul the top half of his body out of the water. He closed his eyes, exhausted.

When he opened them a minute or so later, he saw that his ship, the SS *Stalingrad*, had gone. She had disappeared from the face of the earth as though she had never existed, taking with her all the precious cargo so desperately needed by his brothers and sisters fighting for the motherland in the Soviet Union. Tanks, explosives, ammunition, foods, medicines – all gone to the bottom of the sea forever. And how many souls had gone with her, he wondered? How many people had perished this morning, victims of the underwater terror that plagued every seafarer in this war? He pondered if there had been anything he could have done to prevent it, but immediately knew there was not. He assumed that the covering force had not picked up anything on their Asdic, as he knew that otherwise they would have called Action Stations and gone on the hunt with a depth-charge run. There was nobody to blame for this disaster other than the U-boat commander who had fired the torpedoes.

He could see another ship burning and the sea around her filled with lifeboats. For a U-boat commander to have scored two kills from one spread of torpedoes meant he was either a brilliant tactician or very lucky. Sakharov sighed; it was probably a mix of the two, he thought. Skill and luck. He himself had just been unlucky. Very unlucky indeed.

* * *

On board one of the lifeboats, things were going from bad to worse. Having managed to assist the heavily pregnant woman on board, the distress and shock she had endured had caused her to go into premature labour. Whilst they waited to be picked up by the rescue ship, the baby started to show itself.

In freezing temperatures, in a lifeboat in the middle of the Arctic Ocean, the woman gave birth to her child, but not surprisingly, the infant was stillborn. Wrapping its lifeless form in a blanket taken from the lifeboat supplies, a sailor placed it delicately on the chest of the weeping mother, then sat back and waited for them to be picked up.

* * *

For nearly forty minutes Captain Sakharov remained in the water awaiting rescue. He was aware of the *Copeland* and *St Kenan* working hard to pick up survivors, but when the *Copeland* finally reached him, he was frozen to the core. Hauled aboard, he was immediately assisted below deck, where his wet and frozen clothes were taken off and attempts made to get some warmth back into him.

The fact that he had survived so long in the water was nothing short of a miracle. He was to learn that out of a total complement of eighty-seven passengers and crew on the SS *Stalingrad*, twenty-one had lost their lives, including the first mate and political officer, Alexander Federov, the second mate, Strelkov and the two diplomats, Shmakov and Khromov, their diplomatic pouches, whatever they contained, going to the bottom of the sea with them. Khromov had been witnessed by Plavinsky, the chief engineer, trying desperately to rescue one of the pouches, and had drowned in the attempt.

In total it had taken only three minutes and forty-eight seconds for the ship to go under after being hit. It was astonishing that so many had been saved.

As Sakharov sipped a hot cup of tea, outside, a few hundred yards away, the SS *Oliver Ellsworth* lay dead in the water. Once it was established that all the survivors had been picked up, HMS *St Kenan*, commanded by Lieutenant Robert Simpson, fired a volley of shells into her side, causing the ship to burn furiously. Shortly afterwards, the rescue ships having sped away to catch up with the rest of the convoy, she eventually succumbed and sank beneath the waves. A single armed guard was the only casualty, having drowned when abandoning ship. The other sixty-nine crew had managed to escape to safety.

The sinking of the two ships had an immediate and profound effect on the rest of the convoy. The wolf-packs had raised their heads and struck a vital blow at both the delivery of the cargoes and the morale of those on the ships. For nobody was under the illusion that this was as bad as it would get. They had now entered waters that were filled with U-boats and within range of all that the Luftwaffe had to throw at them.

They knew this was only the start.

And it was barely ten o'clock in the morning.

Chapter 6

13 September – Late Morning

The sinking of the SS *Stalingrad* and SS *Oliver Ellsworth*, with the loss of twenty-two lives, brought the reality and horror of war home to all those in the convoy making their maiden voyages. The shock of seeing how vulnerable such large vessels were as they sank beneath the waves, and hearing the desperate screams of those souls unfortunate enough to find themselves in the water knowing they were about to die, would have a lasting effect on all those who bore witness to it. They now understood that these large ships did not give them the automatic protection they may have expected, and they realized that, but for the grace of God, it could very easily have been them in the water.

There were many onboard who questioned why the convoys were sailing at all. Hadn't Britain fought alone following the fall of France in June 1940? The Soviets, still nominal allies of the Nazis at that time, had offered no assistance. So why were British sailors risking their lives to help them now? Such conversations were taking place in mess decks throughout the convoy and the escort ships.

The reason for the Russian convoys was quite complex, born of political need and practical necessity. In August 1939, the leaders of Nazi Germany and the Soviet Union signed a non-aggression pact (often referred to as the 'Molotov-Ribbentrop Pact' or the 'Hitler-Stalin Pact'). This agreement between the two dictatorships basically stated that they would refrain from going to war with each other and would not meddle in each other's foreign policy. Hitler was thus allowed free rein to invade Poland, France and the rest of Central and Western Europe without fear of Stalin putting up any kind of opposition. In fact, the Soviets themselves saw an opportunity for expansion and, following a secret clause in this agreement with the Nazis, on 17 September 1939 invaded Poland from the east, taking control of all the land from Wilno in the north to Lwów in the south. The Soviets also seized the opportunity to invade Finland in what became known as the 'Winter War', to acquire the regions of Salla and Karelia. This later led to an unlikely alliance between the Nazis and the Finns.

Less than a year later, after the fall of France and the evacuation of its army from the beaches of Dunkirk, Britain and its empire was the only force still opposing the might of the German war machine. Effectively, the British were on their own.

After failing to gain air superiority in the Battle of Britain the Nazis realized that an invasion of southern England was never going to happen; and the Blitz that followed proved equally ineffective in forcing Britain to surrender. Achieving no breakthrough against the British, Hitler instead turned his attentions to the east.

On 22 June 1941 the Germans launched Operation Barbarossa, the invasion of the Soviet Union. Taken completely by surprise, the Red Army was quickly forced to retreat, giving up the land they had gained in Poland and falling back deep into Russian territory. Trusting Hitler to keep his word by honouring the terms of their non-aggression agreement had proved to be a huge misjudgment by Stalin.

With this new Blitzkrieg being extremely effective on the Eastern Front, just as it had been in the Battle for France when the British Expeditionary Force and the French Army had been defeated and the British thrown back to Dunkirk, there was now a very real possibility that the Russians would be forced into a humiliating surrender before they had time to effectively mobilize their forces. Factories that could aid Soviet war production were being overrun, and those not yet under German occupation were hastily deconstructed and moved further east. Realizing his failure to appreciate the duplicity of the Nazis, and fearing defeat, Stalin appealed directly to Winston Churchill to provide material help in order to resist the German advance.

Seeing an opportunity to gain what could potentially be a powerful ally, Churchill agreed to Stalin's request for aid and ordered a convoy of ships to take war supplies to the Soviet Union. With the closest deep-water ports being in the north of the country at Murmansk on the Barents Sea and Archangelsk on the White Sea, a route via Iceland was determined to be the quickest way to deliver much needed resources to the Soviets. On 18 August 1941 the first of the Arctic convoys, codenamed Operation Dervish, set sail from Liverpool. Seven merchantmen with an escort of fourteen Royal Navy ships arrived in Archangelsk thirteen days later, unnoticed by the Germans.

The idea of merchant ships travelling in convoy was hundreds of years old. Back in the age of sail, pirates and privateers were less likely to attack ships that were being escorted by the Royal Navy. During the First World War, the convoy system was used extensively, and merchant ships travelling in this way were more likely to make it to their port of destination unscathed. Ships sailing independently, without protection, were at greater danger of being sunk or captured. Ports were also able to organize themselves better for unloading, since convoys would generally arrive on time.

However, there were drawbacks to the convoy system. All ships were constrained to sail at the speed of the slowest vessel, and this led to supplies reaching destinations later than they might have done. Ships sailing in the outer columns of a convoy were also more susceptible to U-boat and aerial attack purely due to their position, and so it was with much thought and consideration that commodores allocated these positions, based on ships' armaments and the importance of their cargoes. The simple fact, however, was that someone had to occupy those positions, and it was up to the Royal Navy escorts to ensure they were sufficiently protected.

The success of Dervish led to more convoys sailing the Arctic route, becoming bigger each time as quotas were agreed between the two governments. However, as the convoys grew, so too did the attacks on them, and after the Germans' success in virtually wiping out convoy PQ17 their confidence was high that they could put an end to them completely by destroying PQ18.

However, the British had other ideas.

* * *

Despite the tragic sinking of the two ships, PQ18 continued on at a steady 8 knots. Boddam-Whetham on board the SS *Temple Arch* and Rear-Admiral Bob Burnett on the escort flagship HMS *Scylla* remained in constant contact, for they both knew that this was a precarious time for the whole convoy. With information being received from the Admiralty of the general locations of the U-boat wolf-packs, they knew there were many close by, ready to inflict similar damage on the other ships. They needed to remain vigilant and trust that Asdic, the Swordfish patrols and the Catalinas carrying out their reconnaissance missions ahead of them would be enough to keep the German submarines at bay.

However, as morning turned into early afternoon, it became apparent that the air attacks they had been expecting at this point in the journey were finally starting to materialize. Through breaks in the clouds, a small group of Junkers Ju-88 dive-bombers had appeared and began to harass the convoy.

Sub-Lieutenant Robert Hughes, on duty in the blue director on the *Scylla*, was on high alert. With the target-bearing indicators clanging in his ears as a Ju-88 crept into his sights, eight shells at a time were fired in the direction of the aircraft, forcing it to seek sanctuary once more in the clouds. Swinging the director around to find another target, the frustration of the crew at the taunting tactics of the German pilots led to some calling out for them to come down from the clouds to be 'shot at properly'. As yet, the short-range weaponry had not opened fire, the planes not coming within their range. The Germans knew what they were doing, it seemed.

Things were similar for Charlie Erswell in B turret on HMS *Milne*. Together with the team, he worked furiously, turning the training gear handles to line up the pointer; he was beginning to sweat, despite the temperature being well below freezing. Constantly readjusting as the director picked up new targets, he swung the turret from left to right, his friend Robbo Robinson at his side working equally hard, pumping shells into the breech with the other loader; they were then fired the moment the lights turned green in the director, a few feet above and behind them.

The gun turret soon filled with the stench of cordite fumes, sweat and vomit from the metal bucket in the corner that was being used by those still afflicted with seasickness. (Charlie was fortunate enough not to suffer from it.) The noise was deafening as the booms of the twin 4.7-inch guns reverberated around the enclosed space, combining with the clanging of the empty shells as they were ejected from the breeches and the shouted orders of the Petty Officer standing directly behind them. It was all they could do to concentrate on the task in hand, but concentrate they did, never missing a beat. It was the fear of failing, of letting down their colleagues, that spurred them on to do a good job.

Outside the turret Charlie could hear the sound of explosions as the German bombs detonated on the surface of the sea. Luckily, none had yet found its mark, the blasts merely throwing seawater skyward between the ships.

This small contingent of German aircraft were becoming a pest. On board the *Avenger*, Commander Colthurst gave the order to scramble the Sea Hurricanes, and within seconds five pilots hurried to their aircraft across a wet and slippery flight deck. Moments later, after settling into their cockpits, the sweet sound of the Hurricanes' Rolls Royce Merlin engines filled the air as the aircraft prepared to take off. One by one they sped along the runway, their de Havilland propellers buzzing like a swarm of bees as they lifted into a grey, sleet-filled sky and headed towards the irritating Ju-88s still actively seeking gaps in the clouds through which to attack the ships below.

For a few minutes the Hurricanes harassed the Ju-88s, who were still attempting to drop their bombs on the ships below despite this new threat. There was a real danger of the British planes being hit by the flak from the ships, but they went about their task nevertheless. Eventually, the German pilots, realizing they were in very real danger of being shot down, turned away and headed south, back towards the sanctuary of their bases in Norway.

However, their job had been done. Not only was their mission to try and sink merchant ships, it was also to draw out the Sea Hurricanes from the *Avenger*.

For a much greater force was at that very moment heading in the direction of PQ18, led by the experienced torpedo-bomber pilot Werner Klümper of Squadron I/KG26 of the Luftwaffe.

* * *

As the Ju-88s sped away, followed for a short distance by the Sea Hurricanes, the gunners on the destroyers experienced a brief moment of calm. Taking the opportunity to light up cigarettes and grab some refreshment, they were pleased at how they had just performed. To them, the German attack had been completely unsuccessful. They had worked hard and that work had paid off, with not a single ship suffering as much as a scratch to her paintwork. After having witnessed two merchantmen sink beneath the waves only a few hours earlier, this was a welcome victory.

On the *Milne*, the men of B turret were feeling confident. This had been their first real skirmish with the Luftwaffe, and they knew they had done well. Although they had not shot down any aircraft, they had done enough to protect the ships. Along with the rest of the team, Charlie Erswell was feeling optimistic. However, this sanguine mood was cut short by words of harsh reality from his Petty Officer.

'Well done, lads. You did well,' he started. 'But rest assured, they'll be back. And they'll be back in bigger numbers than that lot just now, believe me. Be prepared and keep yourselves warm.'

It was hard to keep warm, for the temperature was by now well below freezing. As the men smoked, mittens off so they could hold their cigarettes, they were careful not to put their bare hands on anything solid. The last thing anyone needed right now was to have his flesh stick to the icy metal, causing an injury that would render him incapable of operating his equipment.

For a while they chatted and moved about, stamping their feet to keep the blood flowing and the cold out.

Across the water, the five Sea Hurricanes that had successfully seen off the German planes made perfect landings back on the flight deck of the *Avenger*. Returning to refuel and re-arm, ready for another attack that would surely come.

Interrupting the sailors' short break, the wailing of the klaxons filled the air once again, calling them to action stations. As they threw their cigarettes away, the distinctive sound of Lieutenant Commander Campbell's voice came over the loudspeakers.

'Be prepared. There are forty-four aircraft approaching from the south. Do your duty, gentleman. And good luck.'

As the men rushed back to the turret, Robbo, Charlie's friend, stopped for a moment and looked to the south. Across the skyline a long row of dark objects filled the sky.

'They're not planes,' he said, half in hope. 'They're birds.'

Charlie followed his gaze, squinting to try and determine exactly what it was that was approaching. From behind him the Petty Officer spoke.

'They're planes,' he said matter-of-factly. 'Junkers and Heinkels. And each of them will be carrying two torpedoes. That's enough firepower to sink the whole convoy. Get to your stations, lads.'

Needing no more convincing, Charlie hastened to the turret and sat at his position, grabbing the winding handles. He was ready. If the Germans wanted a fight, he was going to give them one.

Of course, Lieutenant Commander Campbell and the Petty Officer were quite correct. They indeed were German aircraft that had been picked up on the ships' radar, stretched out in a line across the sky as they dropped to just above sea level to carry out the *Goldene Zange* (Golden Comb) attack against the convoy.

Gunners on all the destroyers settled into their positions ready to face them and awaited orders to open fire.

* * *

Having nearly got lost and come close to abandoning the attack on the run in, Major Werner Klümper, commander of Squadron I/KG26, had now located the convoy and managed to get all his aircraft into position to attack. The convoy looked formidable, there was no doubt about it, and with so many destroyers and anti-aircraft ships now aware of their approach, he was expecting significant opposition. He just hoped that the planes of the aircraft carrier were now back on board and not yet ready to get airborne again, the diversionary attack by the small contingent of planes that had set out earlier having done its job.

Flicking the mic open, he spoke to the other pilots, wishing them good luck. He took a breath and focused.

This was it. He pushed the throttle forward.

It was time to put a stop to these Arctic convoys once and for all.

* * *

Rear-Admiral Burnett, standing with Captain MacIntyre on the bridge of HMS *Scylla*, gazed to the south. On receiving the radar contact of the approaching aircraft he had ordered the ship moved forward, into a predetermined position to repel the coming aerial attack. However, the Sea Hurricanes on the *Avenger* were not yet ready to take back to the skies, having returned only a few minutes earlier following the previous skirmish that he now understood to have been nothing more than a prelude to this larger assault. He could see the destroyers on the starboard side of the escort all turning their turrets to point their heavy guns at the oncoming planes. They were as ready as they could be.

Putting his binoculars to his eyes he scanned the horizon. The radar had picked up forty-four aircraft, but as he looked on it seemed a lot more. They were in a long line, not grouped together. They appeared to be bobbing as they approached, rising and falling like a shoal of porpoises, their undercarriages almost touching the surface of the sea as they came ever closer. Immediately he understood the German plan and, in a way, quite admired the simple genius of it. If they released all their torpedoes at once, all in a long line, it would be very difficult for the ships to avoid them. There was no doubt in his mind that, in the next few minutes, some of the vessels he was there to protect would be hit.

And there was little he could do to stop it.

* * *

Above the bridge, in the director, Robert Hughes could not believe what he was hearing. Through his headset, the Air Defence Officer was telling him there were over twenty-five planes heading in their direction. Immediately, he ordered the turrets to train right, and before he had time to get his head around what he was being told, saw for himself the danger approaching.

Rising above the horizon, in a long line, were many aircraft. They seemed to be bobbing up and down, as though one living organism, snake-like and repulsive, as they grew ever closer. He asked for the range and was told they were still 10 miles out. With the effective range of the *Scylla*'s guns being 7 miles, he could only wait. For a moment all was quiet in the director as they carried on watching and waiting, the only noise being Freeman beside him counting the number of aircraft approaching.

'Twenty-five, twenty-six, twenty-seven . . .'

'Keep on giving me the ranges!' Hughes ordered, his stomach sick with anticipation.

'Oh-two-oh,' came the reply, effective range being 'Oh-one-four', or 14,000 yards.

They fixed their sights on the plane at the extreme right. Those in the turrets waited for instructions, shells already loaded in the QF4.5-inch guns.

'Oh-one-six', came the new range.

Outside, further to starboard, the guns of the destroyers in the outer screen opened up as the planes came within range.

Freeman beside him, still counting: 'I make it forty-two, Robert.'

And then the magic number. 'Range oh-one-four. Have plot and height, sir. Ready, sir.'

Hughes paused for a moment and then he spoke. Calmly and clearly.

'Open fire!'

The *Scylla* rocked to the barrage that was let fly, the noise deafening as the missiles shot skyward, exploding in a murderous spray of flak. Below, in the turrets, more shells were immediately pumped into the breeches and, as the green lights lit up in the fire control system, eight more shells were sent flying into the air.

Hughes could see immediately that the first salvo had been successful. With smoke erupting from it, the right-hand plane veered to starboard, colliding with another He-111 that was rising in that strange way they had observed earlier, both aircraft tumbling into the sea.

'Two of them!' shouted Hughes, momentarily elated at this small triumph, before fixing his focus back on the task in hand. 'Shift target left.'

They continued to fire at the oncoming threat. However, the initial success was not to be repeated, and with the planes so low and the danger of hitting the other ships very real, he gave the order to cease firing. However, the noise of battle still raged as the close-range weaponry of the ships around them continued to spray fire into the air.

* * *

On board the *Milne* Charlie Erswell worked furiously. Despite the biting cold, he was sweating, winding the training gear handles as fast as he could to line up the pointers, swinging the turret this way and that, as his shipmates fed shell after shell into the breeches of the two 4.7-inch guns. He felt no fear. The concentration and focus required to do his job effectively was enough to put aside any nervousness he might have felt. He could not allow thoughts of anything other than what he was doing to enter his head. This was it, this was what he had spent weeks at the training ship HMS *Ganges* and Chatham Barracks training to do, and he was determined to put it into practice. He was determined to do his bit.

* * *

On the commodore ship SS *Temple Arch*, Boddam-Whetham, the convoy commander, had his binoculars glued to his eyes looking at the same scene. Instead of admiration for the tactical plan of the enemy, he felt a certain amount of fear for those ships on the starboard side. They would take the brunt of the attack, there was no doubting it. There was only one thing he could do.

The sound of gunfire filled his ears as the destroyers fired their anti-aircraft shells at the oncoming aircraft; they exploded in the air, spraying shrapnel in all directions. The sky was filled with these dangerous bursts, but still the German planes came on, seemingly uncaring of the maelstrom they were flying into.

They were now close enough for him to see the huge torpedoes on their undercarriages, and he watched with horror as these began to drop when the planes overshot the destroyer screen. The long missiles hit the water and approached his ships in a deadly line.

Without hesitation he shouted his orders. The ships were to turn forty-five degrees to port. This way, they would significantly reduce the target area, and hopefully the torpedoes would sail harmlessly by. Prior to sailing, he had given instructions about how to respond to a massed torpedo attack, and those commanding the ships at the head of each column should therefore be aware of what to do.

As the horn sounded, screeching out across the waves, the signal pennant was hastily raised. Seeing the signal, the ships around the *Temple Arch* began to turn, acknowledging the order. However, as the torpedoes came ever closer, Boddam-Whetham saw to his horror that those ships in the ninth and tenth columns, the lines furthest to starboard and therefore nearest to the approaching torpedoes, did not change course, almost inviting the torpedoes to hit them.

Had they not seen the pennant or heard the horn? Were their commanders not concentrating on their orders, or was their focus only on the tracks of those instruments of death heading towards them.

Boddam-Whetham started to doubt his own judgement. Had he done the right thing? Was his reasoning sound?

And then the planes were over the merchant ships, and the air all around was filled with machine-gun fire, bursts from the Oerlikons and Bofors as the gunners on all the ships opened up on the Ju-88s and He-111s, trying to bring down as many as possible.

* * *

Back on the *Scylla*, Rear-Admiral Burnett realized he could do nothing about the torpedoes. Ever closer they crept towards the outer ships, and even at this distance he could see some were going to find their mark. The ships had not turned. He had no idea if the order had been given by the commodore. If so, then those in the ninth and tenth columns had chosen to ignore it; this was about to seal their fate.

The sound of a huge explosion filled the air, rising above the cacophony the aerial barrage was already producing. And then another, and another.

The ships were being hit. The torpedoes were finding their targets, just as Burnett and Boddam-Whetham had feared.

The first to be struck was the British cargo ship SS *Empire Stevenson*, the lead ship of the ninth column with a crew of fifty-nine and carrying a consignment of explosives and ammunition. The torpedo hit in the cargo holds, causing a huge explosion that split the ship apart. From his bridge on the *Scylla*, Burnett could see immediately that there was no hope for any of those onboard. A huge fireball consumed the ship and thick black smoke filled the air all around, obscuring her from view. It was as though she had disappeared in front of him, like some kind of macabre magic trick. The chances of anyone getting off the ship before she went down, if they weren't dead already, were almost non-existent.

Moments later, as the SS *Empire Stevenson* lay dying in the water, the ship sailing immediately to her rear was also hit. A Heinkel He-111 flying low over the US Liberty ship SS *Wacosta* dropped a torpedo directly into her hold, where it exploded on impact. Unlike the *Empire Stevenson*, the *Wacosta* did not look to be in immediate danger of sinking, although flames could be seen throughout the vessel. Another thick plume of smoke rose high into the sky to join that coming from the *Empire Stevenson*, mixing with the sleet and rain that was continuing to pelt the convoy.

Explosion followed explosion. Burnett looked on in horror as every ship in the tenth column looked to have taken a hit. Another Liberty ship, the SS *Oregonian*, had suffered three torpedo strikes and immediately began to capsize. Men could be seen scrambling for the lifeboats, but surely there would be no time for them to release the boats into the water; others jumped into the oil-filled icy sea, preferring to take their chances in the waters of the Arctic Ocean than go down with the ship.

Smoke was also rising from the SS *Macbeth*, sailing behind the *Oregonian*, which had suffered two direct hits and was listing badly in the water.

Burnett felt helpless as he looked on. Another two ships, the SS *Africander* and SS *Sukhona*, both sailing as the fourth ship in the ninth and tenth columns respectively, were also hit. He scanned their decks and could see rushed activity as their captains, realizing they were lost, ordered their men to abandon ship and save themselves.

This was nothing short of a disaster.

* * *

The planes were now flying between the columns, trying to avoid the anti-aircraft and small arms fire coming from all directions as gunners on the ships worked furiously, throwing everything they had at them.

Inside one of those aircraft, Major Werner Klümper fought furiously with the controls. He could hear, and feel, bullets thumping into the fuselage and prayed that none had hit either of the engines. To be brought down in these waters was nothing short of certain death.

He chanced a look to his left and through the rain-spattered canopy could see huge palls of smoke rising into the afternoon air, spreading out widely as they hit the low cloud. A black shroud enveloped the area, shielding the horrific scene from the eyes of the gods, hiding the sacrilege that had just taken place on the ocean's surface.

From what Klümper could make out, so far the attack had been a limited success. The *Goldene Zange* operation had worked to a degree, and a lot of ships had been hit, but those beyond the outer column had so far gone unscathed. And they were putting up a fierce fight.

Not only were his planes taking fire from the escort ships, they were getting hit by the guns on the merchant vessels too. As the Junkers and Heinkels moved up and down the columns, looking to release their bombs, the men on the cargo ships were giving everything they had to knock them out of the sky. Those brave sailors were fighting for their very lives and they were doing a good job of it.

To his right Klümper saw another of his planes take multiple hits, catch fire and fall into the sea. They were beginning to suffer serious losses, and Klümper knew that they could not linger too long so close to the ships or they would be annihilated, especially when the Sea Hurricanes managed to get back into the air.

* * *

Inside B turret on the *Milne*, Charlie Erswell had an uneasy feeling that things weren't going well. Above the horrendous noise within the turret he had heard the thunderous detonations taking place outside and felt the ship rock suddenly beneath him, the wash caused by the explosions causing the destroyer to bob violently in the water.

Not wanting to dwell on what might be happening out of his sight, he continued to pump the winding handles to the Petty Officer's instructions, as new targets were sought and the pointers adjusted.

Unexpectedly, the order was given to cease firing. With the planes flying so low between the columns, there was a very real danger of hitting the ships they were there to protect. Those in the turrets were left feeling impotent, and ignorant about what was going on around them.

However, those operating the short-range anti-aircraft weaponry continued to fire. Oerlikon gunners on all the ships, leaning back strapped to their guns, fired furiously at the aircraft as they flew along the channels. Those operating the pom-poms blasted their ordnance skyward in the hope of downing one of the Nazi predators.

And then something strange happened onboard the *Milne*.

Charlie could feel the ship slowing until she eventually came to a halt. Then, on receiving orders through his headset, the Petty Officer behind him informed the team they had been instructed to leave the turret and report amidships immediately. Moving quickly to carry out the order, the B turret team stepped out onto the cold and slippery deck.

It was only now that Charlie could see the full scale of what had taken place. All around, very close by, ships were burning and going down. There were desperate men in the water, fighting furiously to stay afloat, oil burning around them as they scrambled madly towards the *Milne*, hoping beyond hope to be rescued before their ship went under or the strength left them.

Quickly the order was given to throw scramble nets over the port side and drag as many men as they could from the water. Using what strength they had left, some of these oil-blackened sailors managed to pull themselves from the water. They were then hauled unceremoniously onto the *Milne's* deck and laid in a row. Many, having swallowed sea water and oil, retched violently, throwing up dirty black vomit over the snow-white deck.

However, not all could be retrieved from the sea. Some, lacking the strength to make it to the destroyer, still floundered in the water. Their ship was slowly sinking, stern first. Charlie could see half a dozen of her crew climbing the forecastle in a bid to save themselves from going under with her; they shouted and screamed wildly, desperately pleading to be saved. There was nothing anyone on the *Milne* could do to help them as the ship slowly submerged, taking them down with her.

To Charlie this was like a scene from Dante's Inferno. But then, he thought, was Hell really a hot, fiery place where the souls of the damned burned for eternity, or was it more like this, here, right now? Was the real Hell something quite the opposite of how Dante had described it? Was Hell instead a cold and miserable place on the surface of the Arctic seas and not in the bowels of the earth? He already knew the answer to that.

Putting such depressing thoughts to one side, he turned his attention to those who had made it to safety. Using cotton waste, he did his best to clean up these unfortunates, wiping the oil and grime from their shivering forms.

Some of them looked half-dead already, and he sincerely doubted they would all survive the horrendous experience. As he worked he was aware of the ship's doctor moving along the line, checking each man in turn and giving instructions to his orderlies.

After only a few minutes, and realizing there were no more sailors to be saved, the order was given to return to the gun turret, and the ship then lurched forward once more. As Charlie made his way back to B turret he glanced back. He could see escort ships from the rear of the convoy making their way forward to assist the other merchantmen that had been hit, to take off their crews before they too suffered the same fate as many on board the ship he had witnessed sink beneath the waves.

Settling back into his seat, he again focused to the task in hand and awaited instructions from the Petty Officer.

* * *

More huge explosions filled the air as two more merchantmen were struck by torpedoes. The British cargo ship SS *Empire Beaumont*, sailing at the head of the fourth column, was on fire, another pall of smoke rising high into the air and marking yet another German success. The American ship SS *John Penn*, the third ship of the seventh column, having received a direct hit in the engine room killing three of her crew, was also floundering. Gradually, as power and momentum left her, she came to a stop in the water, unable to continue.

By now the Sea Hurricanes on board the *Avenger* were ready to take back to the skies. As quickly as they could they rumbled along the flight deck and, once in the air, made for the German planes that continued to harry the ships. Fearlessly, the pilots flew towards the enemy; the danger of being hit by anti-aircraft fire from the ships was very real, yet they ignored it. They all knew that these German aircraft needed to be stopped, and they were intent on doing just that.

Seeing the Hurricanes in the air, Klümper realized now was probably a good time to leave. His planes had managed to inflict mortal damage on some of the ships, that much was clear, and with the new threat of enemy aircraft to contend with, along with the massive barrage that had been put up by the Royal Navy and merchant ships, it was time to call it a day as far as this particular attack was concerned.

He flicked the mic and gave the order to head south for home. Out of the window he could see that more of his aircraft had been damaged. Smoke trailed from the engines of some of the planes, and he guessed that all of them had been hit in some way. He looked down and could see at least two

Heinkels, having ditched, floating on the sea, their crews sitting on the wings and hoping to be rescued. One crew was hastily scrambling into an inflatable lifeboat that was a part of the aircraft's inventory, designed for situations such as this.

With the Sea Hurricanes now following behind, he pushed the throttle to maximum, pulled back on the control column and headed for the cover of the clouds. Setting a course for Bardufoss, he settled into the flight.

He did not know yet exactly how many ships they had destroyed, or how many of his crews he had lost. However, what he did realize was that the number of ships sunk was not as high as he had hoped, and he was in no doubt that they would have to come back and do this all over again. For exactly how long his remaining crews could maintain their morale, after suffering such sustained opposition from the escorts, he did not know, but he understood it was his job to ensure they were kept motivated.

He had not managed to get the aircraft carrier that Göring so desperately craved. In fact, he had not even been able to identify it at all, the ships being so numerous and the barrage so relentless. For this reason alone, he knew they would be going back, but for now he felt his job was done and he had to be content with what they had achieved.

He sighed, settled into the flight and checked the clock on the instrument panel.

The whole attack, from start to finish, had lasted no more than fifteen minutes.

Chapter 7

13 September – Afternoon

Burnett looked back at the burning ships. In little more than a quarter of an hour, the Luftwaffe had managed to destroy, or damage so as to make useless, eight of them. With the sinking of the SS *Stalingrad* and SS *Oliver Ellsworth* that morning, this meant that the SS *Mary Luckenbach*, carrying a huge cargo of TNT, was the only ship still operable from the ninth and tenth columns. The whole of the starboard section had virtually been wiped out. With this in mind, the SS *Mary Luckenbach* was ordered to move position and would now sail as the second ship of the eighth column, astern of the SS *Dan-y-Bryn* and ahead of the SS *Virginia Dare*, with the SS *Nathanael Greene* to her port side. This effectively reduced the convoy from ten columns to eight.

Orders were given to evacuate those ships badly damaged but still afloat. The minesweeper HMS *Sharpshooter*, along with the trawlers and towed motor minesweepers at the rear of the escort, were tasked with carrying this out. However, the other ships would not wait for them and continued on, leaving the rescue teams to their task. The latter were to follow later, at full speed, to catch up with the slow-moving convoy.

Burnett knew that things could have been a lot worse. With ten ships now lost, over a quarter of those that had set out from Iceland had been destroyed by German aircraft and U-boats. The convoy was now north of Bear Island and there was still a considerable distance to travel before it reached its destination. Further concentrated attacks such as the recent one would ensure the same fate as had befallen PQ17. This had to be avoided at all costs.

The Rear-Admiral had been unaware of Boddam-Whetham's order to turn. Having sailed ahead of the convoy on the sighting of the aircraft, his concentration was fully focused on the starboard columns and, seeing these ships maintain their course, he had assumed no such order had been given. In fact, he would have supported the decision for the convoy to maintain its course. He was to report later:

> The individual handling of the ships of the covering force and the screen, as far as I had time to observe, was admirable; the Commodore, to my mind perfectly correctly, made no emergency turn; such a manoeuvre

German troops crossing the Soviet border, Operation Barbarossa, June 1941. (Only two months later, the first Arctic convoy, Operation Dervish, sailed to Russia from Liverpool). (*Johannes Hähle, via wikimedia commons*)

Winston Churchill with Stalin and W. Averell Harriman (US representative) at the Moscow conference, August 1942. (*National Museum of the US Navy Lot 11596-7*)

Ships of the ill-fated PQ17 at anchor in Hvalfjord, Iceland, July 1942. The loss of twenty-four ships on this convoy caused Winston Churchill to describe it as 'one of the most melancholy naval episodes in the whole of the war'. (*IWM A8953*)

Dockworkers in Liverpool with tanks bound for Russia. Ships were loaded at ports such as this before sailing to the mustering point on Loch Ewe.

Soviet troops attack German forces, Stalingrad, November 1942. (*Hulton Archive/Getty Images*)

Rear-Admiral Bob Burnett, commander of the close escort PQ18/QP14. (*IWM A12758*)

HMS *Scylla*, the convoy flagship from which Rear-Admiral Burnett commanded the escort. (*IWM FL2932*)

SS *Temple Arch*, the commodore ship on PQ18. Her commander, Edye Boddam-Whetham, received an MBE for services during the convoy. He was to contract smallpox in Russia and died in Gibraltar in 1944. (*clydeships.co.uk*)

Group Captain Frank Hopps, senior RAF officer in Russia, who oversaw Operation Orator, the air defence of PQ18. (*IWM TR2620*)

Catalina of Coastal Command. Flying from Vaenga in Russia as part of Operation Orator, they hunted for U-boats and mines in the convoy's path. (*IWM CH2448*)

Spitfire of 1 Photographic Reconnaissance Unit. The unit carried out regular sorties over Altenfjord as part of Operation Orator. (*IWM HU29262*)

HMS *Avenger* with six Sea Hurricanes on deck. Note the arrestor cables across the flight deck which were of little use due to the location of the arrestor hooks on the aircraft. (*IWM FL1268*)

HMS *Avenger*, inside the aircraft hangar below the flight deck. (*IWM A10982*)

A U-boat of the Kriegsmarine. Operating in wolf-packs, they were the scourge of the convoys. (*US Navy*)

SS *Stalingrad*, the first ship to be sunk from PQ18 on the morning of 13 September 1942. She took less than four minutes to sink after being hit by a torpedo from *U-408*. (*uboat.net*)

Anatoly Nikolayevich Sakharov, skipper of the SS *Stalingrad*, who spent 40 minutes in icy water after his ship was sunk on 13 September 1942. He was awarded the Distinguished Service Cross by the British (pictured), for assistance in piloting ships into port. (*Jos Odijk*)

The crew of *U-408*. Responsible for sinking three ships on PQ18 including the SS *Stalingrad*, they were all killed two months later when attacked by a Catalina in the Greenland Sea. (*www.albumwar2.com*)

Major Werner Klümper, who led the 'Golden Comb' attack on PQ18, 13 September 1942 (and other air attacks on the convoy). (*tracesofwar.com*)

An He111 dropping a torpedo. With a crew of five, these planes conducted the 'Golden Comb' attack on 13 September 1942, when they successfully sank eight ships. (*Bundesarchiv, Bild183-L20414*)

Convoy under attack. An underwater detonation close to HMS *Ashanti*. (*IWM A12022*)

Ice-clearing party, HMS *Milne*. Seaman/Gunner Charlie Erswell is third from the right. (*Charlie Erswell collection*)

Charlie Erswell and shipmates clearing ice between attacks on the foredeck of HMS *Milne*. (*Charlie Erswell collection*)

German battleship *Tirpitz* at anchor in Narvik. (*US Naval Historical Center photograph NH 71390*)

A Hampden bomber of 455 Squadron. Twenty-three of these aircraft flew a 'Reconnaissance in Force' on the morning of 14 September in search of the *Tirpitz*. (*Australian War Memorial*)

Reichsmarschall Hermann Göring, commander-in-chief of the Luftwaffe, who pressed commanders to focus their attacks on the aircraft carrier HMS *Avenger*. (*Bundesarchiv_Bild_102-15607*)

German planes (circled) attacking the convoy. Seen from the aircraft carrier HMS *Avenger*. (*Mirrorpix*)

A bomb explodes close to HMS *Avenger*. (*IWM 12020*)

The SS *Mary Luckenbach*, carrying 1,000 tonnes of TNT, explodes, 14 September 1942. (*IWM A12017*)

Paul Gill, third mate on the SS *Nathanael Greene*, who raised the Stars and Stripes under fire just after the destruction of the SS *Mary Luckenbach*. (*Paul Gill*)

A Catapult Armed Merchant (CAM) ship releasing its Sea Hurricane. The CAM ship SS *Empire Morn* sailed with PQ18. (*IWM A9423*)

Flight Lieutenant Arthur Burr, who won a DFC after single-handedly fighting off fifteen German dive-bombers in his Sea Hurricane over the White Sea. (*IWM CH14107*)

Alan Scott-Moncrieff, captain of the F Class destroyer and flotilla leader HMS *Faulknor*, which sank *U-88* on 12 September 1942. He took command of QP14 on 22 September when Bob Burnett left the convoy on HMS *Milne*. (*IWM A14300*)

HMS *Somali*. After being hit by torpedoes on returning convoy QP14, she was taken under tow and sank in a storm on 25 September 1942. (*IWM FL19179*)

Skipper of *U-435*, Siegfried Strelow (right) being congratulated on his award of the Knight's Cross by the commander of the Navy Group North, Admiral Carls (left) in November 1942. *U-435* sank four ships on QP14 including the minesweeper HMS *Leda*. (*Narodowe Archiwum Cyfrowe*)

German PoWs after their surrender at Stalingrad in January 1943. The Soviet victory here eventually led to the fall of the Third Reich. (*pinterest*)

would have only thrown the convoy into confusion and would not have reduced casualties; indeed, it quite probably would have increased them.

Boddam-Whetham, on the other hand, was regretting that the ships in columns nine and ten had not made the turn as he had instructed. The reason for them not complying with his order could not be determined. Whether it was down to the speed at which the turn needed to be carried out to be effective, or the lack of experience of some of the commanders, was not clear. Boddam-Whetham was later to state:

> It is, of course, impossible to say what might have happened had all the ships obeyed my signal promptly, but the fact remains that the ninth and tenth columns either did not turn, or were far too slow. In consequence, with the exception of the *Mary Luckenbach*, they were all sunk.

However, two things were now decided. Firstly, Commander Colthurst on the *Avenger* realized that for his Sea Hurricanes to be effective they would need to wait until a large aerial assault was underway before being scrambled to intercept it. They were no longer to go up piecemeal to chase single aircraft or small groups. Secondly, due to the sheer number of shells fired during the attack, destroyer captains were to conserve ammunition as best they could. As further attacks were undoubtedly going to come, the last thing Burnett wanted was for the destroyer escort to run out of anti-aircraft shells.

To add to this, the effectiveness of the two anti-aircraft ships, HMS *Alynbank* and HMS *Ulster Queen*, had been somewhat stymied, since they had been ordered to stay in position within the merchant columns and not to move out and engage, much as the *Scylla* had done. This frustrated both commanders, and the experienced Charles Adam, captain of the *Ulster Queen*, vowed to ignore the instruction in future and come out to meet any further attacks head-on. The ship had immense firepower which had been somewhat unnecessarily held back in his view, and going on the attack would do a great deal for the ship's morale, which had been negatively affected by the 'Golden Comb' attack and their inability to repel it.

Of course, not only were the ships lost and a large number of mariners' lives cut short; the cargoes so desperately needed in Russia were also consigned to the deep waters of the Barents Sea. This would not play well with those in power, in both Britain and the Soviet Union; for the debacle that was PQ17 had been fresh in the minds of the planners when organizing this convoy.

After the failure of PQ17, the success of PQ18 had become all important. If the Nazis were to smash this new convoy, then there would have to be a total rethink regarding the feasibility of the whole Arctic route. The loss of the cargoes on that last ill-fated convoy only added to the urgency of what was to follow. In fact, Stalin was pushing for the agreed quotas still to be fulfilled, and consequently further PQ convoys were provisionally scheduled to follow PQ18 in October and November.

In a secret telegram from the Allied Supplies Executive to the Soviet government in Kuibyshev dated 4 August 1942, the British outlined their intentions for the forthcoming convoys. It was explained that PQ18 would comprise forty ships (in fact, thirty-nine merchantmen sailed, including the CAM ship), loaded in the United Kingdom and the United States. The United Kingdom was to supply vessels carrying the whole of the June quota of items produced in the UK and four new loaders carrying 'high priority cargo to be selected by Soviet authorities'. The British expected this to be 'a proportion of United Kingdom July quota of major military items; Hurricane spares on the new scale; bulk allotment of ammunition of weapons already in the USSR and other goods to secure economical stowage'. It was also stated that should conditions be favourable, then PQ18 would be quickly followed by PQ19 at the end of September and PQ20 during October; each of the latter would again consist of thirty to forty ships.

However, in a meeting of the War Cabinet on Friday, 7 August it was pointed out that the question of whether further PQ convoys could be run after September was dependent on the date to be set for Operation Torch, the Allied invasion of North Africa. The escort ships used on the Arctic convoy route would be needed for this huge and extremely important operation. At the meeting, Deputy Prime Minister Clement Attlee was invited to send a telegram to the Prime Minister, who at the time was visiting Stalin in Russia. Talks were already taking place to advance the date of Operation Torch, and around that time Churchill sent a telegram to President Roosevelt expressing the view that 'nothing is more vital' than the bringing forward of the invasion; in the same missive, he welcomed the appointment of General Eisenhower as the Allied Commander-in-Chief.

Roosevelt replied asking for the date of the invasion to be advanced by three weeks. Operation Torch would now require the Admiralty to provide resources, in the way of battleships and other naval vessels, ships that would have been much needed to protect any further voyages to Russia, particularly the planned PQ19 and PQ20 convoys. According to Churchill, both of these things should have been achievable. A telegram to Attlee, sent by Churchill from Russia, read: 'It is indispensable to run further PQs after September. I shall be asked about this and I must know. I cannot believe Admiralty resources will not admit of this as well as Torch.' Ultimately, the Admiralty would have other ideas.

A report from the Foreign Secretary on 21 August 1942 stated that the whole of the June quota and the majority of the July quota were already loaded onto ships that would make up PQ18. Although this was a significant cargo, it still fell short, due to the loss of so many ships on PQ17, of the quota agreed to be sent to Russia for that period. The remainder of the quota was to be sent on PQ19 and PQ20.

And now, with the loss of ten ships so far, much of this quota would never arrive in the Soviet Union; instead, it lay forever at the bottom of the Arctic Ocean.

* * *

On board HMS *Milne*, Charlie Erswell had been given a grim task. Stood down now that the aerial threat had subsided for the time being, he was given the grisly job of collecting the pay books and dog tags of those they had rescued earlier but who had not survived their ordeal. Working as quickly as he was able, to get it over and done with, he gathered together the items and sombrely handed them over to the Petty Officer. Seeing the down-hearted look on his face, the PO told him there was nothing any of them could have done to save the men and said he should not dwell on it too much.

Charlie was to remember this as the worst day of his life.

Before he had a chance to respond to the PO, the klaxons sounding Action Stations once more bellowed throughout the ship, and he hurried back to the turret. More aircraft had been spotted approaching from the south.

This was a group of nine Heinkel He-115 torpedo seaplanes, sent out to deal with any stragglers following the Golden Comb attack and to retrieve any downed Luftwaffe airmen. The Hurricanes, yet to land back on the *Avenger*, quickly headed in their direction to deal with this new threat.

Coming under an intense barrage from the starboard side, the He-115s split into two groups, one of three and the other of six. The group of three flew ahead of the convoy and turned to attack. Upon receiving intense fire from the covering screen, they soon realized this was an impossible enterprise, dropped their torpedoes short and turned for home.

The second group tried a different tactic. Using the cover of the clouds, they attacked from the stern but, just like their colleagues ahead of them, found the opposition too strong after coming under heavy fire from the anti-aircraft ships and a determined and alert covering screen. After dropping their ordnance too early to have any effect, they too abandoned the attack and headed away.

* * *

As the remaining ships of PQ18 continued on their journey, a huge rescue effort was being undertaken in its wake. With people still floundering in the water and others stuck on ships that would undoubtedly go down, speed was of the essence.

HMS *Sharpshooter* headed straight for the stricken SS *Empire Beaumont* and successfully rescued thirty-three of her crew, whilst fellow minesweeper HMS *Harrier* recovered the crews of the SS *Wacosta* and SS *John Penn*, 126 merchant sailors in all. The Motor Minesweeper *MMS90* picked up forty-six survivors from the SS *Macbeth* and SS *Sukhona* and successfully transferred them to the official rescue ship, HMS *Copeland*, while the other two Motor Minesweepers, *MMS203* and *MMS212*, rescued forty-seven men from the SS *Africander* and fourteen from the SS *Oregonian*, all freezing in the water as their ships sank beneath the waves.

With three damaged ships still afloat and all the crews having been evacuated, the order came to destroy them lest they fall into the hands of the enemy. HMS *Harrier* was given the order to fire at the SS *John Penn* and SS *Macbeth*, but after taking a number of shells, the two ships still remained on the surface. Using depth charges to finish the job was not considered an option, as these weapons had to be reserved for anti-submarine operations in the coming days. It was therefore decided to leave the now heavily damaged ships to the elements, as the weather was becoming increasingly inclement and it would not be long before nature itself finished off the job the Luftwaffe had started.

By now, the main body of the convoy was nine miles ahead and had disappeared from view in a snowstorm. Fearing another group of German aircraft or U-boats coming across them and finding themselves under attack again, it was decided to abandon the attempt to sink the damaged ships and to rejoin the convoy.

As the small flotilla moved away at full speed, they left behind the SS *Empire Beaumont* burning fiercely and the SS *Macbeth* slowly going down by the head. The SS *Sukhona* had been lost to sight in a snowstorm and the SS *John Penn* was floundering. However, enough had been done to ensure they all would sink in time, especially now that the weather was taking a turn for the worse.

* * *

Watching the rescue ships disappear into the intensifying snowstorm were four downed crewmen of a Heinkel He-111 who had managed to escape from their aircraft before it had sunk beneath them (this was Heinkel He-111H-6 WNr 7567 of the Squadron I/KG 26, commanded by Werner Klümper).

Managing to scramble into a small dinghy, they huddled together for warmth, hoping to God that they would be rescued. Watching the British rescue efforts taking place, they would have been more than happy to be taken prisoners of war; to be left out in the Arctic Ocean, so far away from anywhere, would mean certain death.

However, they did not have to wait long for their fortunes to change.

U-589, of the *Trägertod* wolf-pack, commanded by 34-year-old Korvettenkapitän Hans-Joachim Horrer, was at periscope depth and had also observed the rescue operations taking place. Having set out from Narvik on 9 September, the boat had been trailing the convoy. However tempted Horrer was to attack the rescue ships, he realized this would immediately give away his position, and it would be only a matter of minutes before the enemy would be upon him. He therefore decided to wait it out.

As Horrer scanned the surface, watching the warships speed away to rejoin the convoy, he noticed something on the water a few hundred yards away. He immediately recognized it as a dinghy and within it, saw four cold and shivering airmen. These could only be from the squadrons that had just attacked the convoy so bravely. He gave the order to surface and head over to them.

Ten minutes later, the four airmen were sipping hot coffee in the mess area of the submarine. They smiled and cracked jokes in their relief at being rescued, and as they warmed their hands against the tin cups, heat and morale slowly returned to their shivering forms. They could not believe their luck. They had been shot down and left for dead, all hope of being rescued lost. Now they were once again amongst their countrymen and enjoying a hot drink.

They thanked God for returning them to safety.

* * *

Although the second, smaller attack by the He-115 seaplanes had been easily repelled, one straggler continued to shadow the convoy from the cover of the clouds and was becoming a persistent nuisance. At 1645 hours a group of four Sea Hurricanes was dispatched from the *Avenger* to see him off. Seeing the British pilots approach, the German turned around and headed south, pursued by the four Hurricanes. In spite of having four British planes on its tail, the He-115 managed to escape; and as it did, its machine guns succeeded in hitting one of the Hurricanes flown by Lieutenant Taylor, the squadron commander of 802 Squadron.

Taylor's Hurricane immediately burst into flames and fell into the sea. As the He-115 disappeared to the south, the remaining three pilots headed back to the *Avenger*.

The destroyer HMS *Onslow* was dispatched to search for the downed pilot, but by the time she arrived on the scene, both aircraft and pilot were nowhere to be seen.

* * *

Aboard the ships of PQ18 there were mixed feelings among those who had survived the Golden Comb attack, combined with total exhaustion. Although the action had been brief, the intensity of what had happened had drained them all physically and emotionally. Already tired from experiencing a disjointed sleeping pattern and having to be on high alert during their waking hours, this latest battle had left a lot of men out on their feet. This fatigue was becoming a worry for the senior officers, but they understood there was little they could do to alleviate the hardships of the crews. Guns still had to be cleaned, checked and reloaded, ice had to be cleared from the decks, weapons and superstructures, and sailors needed to remain on high alert for more expected attacks. It was never-ending. However tired they were, total concentration from all the crews remained a complete necessity.

Throughout the ships, off-duty and exhausted matelots lay down anywhere they could to get some rest. Some, not having strength enough to take off their steel helmets, slumped wherever there was a space, wrapped in all available clothing to keep out the cold that was starting to penetrate the mess-decks, gangways and wardrooms. Duffel coats were pulled tightly around shivering bodies, oilskins and lammy coats used as blankets, lifejackets inflated to give more comfort, and scarves and balaclavas pulled over stubbled and bearded faces. Hardly anyone spoke, all lost in their own thoughts. Some smoked, others stared ahead, their own thoughts the only thing keeping them company.

Some shut their eyes. However, sleep did not come easy. The threat of further attacks hung over them all, and although they were resting, their nerves were on edge. This day they had seen two ships go down courtesy of a U-boat attack in the morning, and a further eight destroyed by Luftwaffe torpedoes in the afternoon. They had witnessed men dying in front of them, sinking beneath the waves with their ships or screaming for assistance that they were powerless to give. At any point either of those two predators could return to inflict still more damage, more hardship, more death.

As well as the deaths of so many sailors on those ships, the cargoes they carried were also lost to the deep. Hundreds of tonnes of materiel needed so desperately in Russia had been lost. Tanks, rails, steel, food, aircraft and medicines; the quota agreed between the two countries once again would be left incomplete.

However, twenty-eight merchant ships remained seaworthy, and there was still a very good chance they could make it to Archangelsk. Although exhausted and battered, the crews of all the ships were determined that this would happen.

Although the threat of a concerted aerial attack had abated for the time being, the U-boat danger still remained. Whereas the Luftwaffe was constrained to making hit-and-run attacks, the wolf-packs were ever-present. They shadowed the convoy almost like the escort ships did. In the confusion of battle, the sound of exploding bombs and torpedoes, and the cacophony of ships being destroyed, the Asdic was rendered quite useless, and it was not certain whether some U-boats had penetrated the outer screen and got into the convoy itself. Indeed, the crew of the US Liberty ship SS *Nathanael Greene*, the second ship of the seventh column, had reported seeing, and firing at, a periscope between the ships. With the convoy travelling at its optimum speed of 8 knots it would have by now left that U-boat behind. This sighting could very easily have been the *U-589*, the boat that had picked up the four German airmen earlier.

* * *

Klümper could see the runway ahead of him and pushed the lever to release the landing gear. It was with immense relief that he heard the whining of the motors as the wheels fell forward, but despite hearing the welcome noise, he glanced out of the canopy to make sure that it was really happening. For most of the journey back to Bardufoss he had feared the damage inflicted by the ships on his aircraft might have affected his ability to land safely.

Outside, beneath him, the ground crews were out in force to keep the runways free of ice and snow. He was leading what was left of his squadron back and, even though there were still many aircraft flying with him, he knew they had suffered considerable losses. Also, many of the planes returning were so badly damaged that they would be out of action for a while. The others would be patched up as best they could be.

Klümper knew it would take more than this first *Goldene Zange* to accomplish what Göring wanted. He was not sure how many ships they had hit, but it was clear the majority were still afloat and continuing on their journey. He understood that it would not be too long before he and his men would be back in the skies to carry on the fight; and after seeing so many of their friends and comrades shot down by the formidable firepower of the escort screen and the determination of the gunners on the merchant ships, he was not sure how long it would be before their morale was shot to pieces too.

He felt his wheels hit the tarmac beneath him. The aircraft bounced once before settling on the runway, and then he applied the brakes, slowing to taxiing speed. He sighed with relief at being back on land again and looked towards the hangars, where a ground crew waited patiently, their tools at the ready to carry out any repairs. Around and behind him, others were also coming in to land. A couple of aircraft had smoke pouring from their engines.

Once his aircraft had stopped, he cut the engines and, together with his crew, climbed out. It was now that he could take a look at the damage to his own machine. A multitude of holes peppered the length of the fuselage. It was a wonder none of the crew had been hit and no harm had been done to anything vital. All the damage was superficial and could be quite easily repaired. It would just take a little time.

He took out a packet of cigarettes from his jacket pocket and lit one. Once all the planes had landed, the crews would head to the briefing room to discuss how the attack had gone and what was to happen next.

However, Klümper already knew what was coming. They would be asked to get back into their patched-up aircraft and go out and do it all again. Go out once more to run the gauntlet. But next time, he thought, the element of surprise would not be with them. He was sure the officers on board those ships would not make the mistake of releasing their aircraft too early. Surely now they would wait until they saw the main body of any attack approaching before they committed them to the sky.

Yes, he mused, his comrades may have thought that what they had just gone through was bad, but worse was yet to come. He had no doubt about it.

* * *

Almost at the same time that Werner Klümper was arriving back at Bardufoss, there was much activity taking place at Archangelsk on the White Sea, 670 miles away as the seagull flies.

QP14, the returning convoy, was setting sail.

Commanded by John 'Jack' Dowding on the commodore ship *SS Ocean Voice*, the convoy comprised seventeen merchantmen, three oilers and a close escort covering force of sixteen warships, including two destroyers and four corvettes, as well as minesweepers and anti-submarine trawlers. The escort ships were commanded by Captain John Harvey-Forbes Crombie on the minesweeper HMS *Bramble*. The returning ships were not making the journey empty-handed. In their holds and lashed upon their decks were cargoes of timber and wood pulp.

For many sailing on this homeward-bound convoy, the journey could not have come soon enough. A lot of the ships travelling back to Britain were those that had managed to survive the notorious PQ17 over two months earlier, their exhausted sailors having been holed up in freezing temperatures in Archangelsk since then, with little to do other than wait. With winter approaching, they had feared that they might have to wait until spring before being repatriated.

In three days time, the ships were to rendezvous with the ocean escort of PQ18 near the Kola Inlet, before then heading back in greater numbers to the sanctuary of Iceland, from where they would return to British waters. It was hoped that the ships, having dropped their cargoes and being less heavily laden, would make good speed in achieving this. PQ18 itself would then head on to Archangelsk with a smaller escort but under the protection of the Russian air force and those aircraft operating under Operation Orator.

Part Two of the plan was now under way.

* * *

It was now just after 2030 hours and the light was beginning to fade. The weather, which had been considered mild for this time of year and place, was now beginning to get steadily worse. With the darkness the temperature would drop, and the ships' captains had used this lull in enemy activity to send teams out to clear ice and snow from the decks and to remove the empty shell casings that littered the gun turrets. All around, the sea was filled with ice floes reflecting like mirrors the sun as it set. At any other time and in any other situation, the view would have been one to be admired and enjoyed; and as the ships steamed ahead, pushing these sheets of ice to the sides and leaving them in their wake, the atmosphere was almost serene, even peaceful.

But that peace was about to be shattered yet again.

Picking up a number of aircraft on their radar, the escort ships on the starboard side of the outer screen called their crews to action stations once more. Exhausted men jumped to the task and the air was filled with the sound of exploding shells as a mighty barrage was put up at the aircraft: twelve He-115 torpedo-carrying seaplanes of I/903 Squadron from the Billefjord airbase coming in like a swarm of locusts.

On board the *Scylla*, Robert Hughes, having had a much-needed tea break rudely interrupted by another call to Action Stations, sat at his position in the director. With orders to shoot on sight, he spun the director to find suitable targets for the cruiser's 4.5-inch guns.

With all guns loaded and the lights showing green, he waited patiently for the range to be right.

'Oh-one-four, sir!'

'Open fire!'

Immediately, eight cannon poured their shells skyward, over the nearest merchant ships, at the enemy aircraft, merging with the barrage pouring from the other destroyers and the small arms of the merchantmen, whose gunners were giving a formidable account of themselves once more.

But still the planes came on, led by a lone He-111. Fire was concentrated at this leading aircraft, and as the bullets and shells found their target, it burst into flames and fell into the sea. On seeing this, the pilots of the He-115s banked sharply and headed for home, pursued by Sea Hurricanes that had joined in the battle from HMS *Avenger*.

As Hughes watched the He-115s grow ever smaller as they headed away, he saw another burst into flames and hit the ocean surface. Behind it, a Sea Hurricane climbed into the sky in jubilation.

This attack had been completely ineffective. Not a single ship had been hit, apart from SS *Campfire* which had been struck by 'friendly fire' from the over-exuberant crew of another merchantman. Her rigging and poop deck had been riddled with machine-gun bullets, injuring three merchant seamen, two of them seriously.

Whether the Germans had been made nervous by the loss of so many of their aircraft during the previous attack, or taken aback by the ferocity of the barrage put up by the covering force and the danger posed by the Sea Hurricanes, this attack had lacked any kind of ambition.

They had successfully wiped out the whole of the two starboard columns, but in doing so they had lost a number of aircraft and experienced pilots. Although they could be pleased with their successes so far, the sheer horror and danger of flying into the maelstrom of fire put up by the Royal Navy in its defence of the convoy was something they had not expected or experienced before.

Whether they would see another success such as that of the Golden Comb attack that afternoon was purely down to them.

Chapter 8

14 September

As dawn broke at 0210 hours on Monday, 14 September, it became immediately obvious that the weather was getting no better. Although the sky was clear and visibility good, occasional snow squalls and temperatures well below freezing added to the hardship of the crews on all the ships. Nervous mutterings hummed through the air. What would this day bring? Would there be more air attacks, similar to the day before? More U-boat contacts? Would the Germans commit their heavy surface ships that were known to be in ports not too far away? All these questions were being pondered by those tired and cold sailors trying to stay alert as they progressed further eastward. Only time would tell, they supposed. But one thing was certain, each man knew that he had to perform with the same skill and commitment he had already shown if the remainder of the convoy was to make it safely to Archangelsk.

By now, they were 115 miles north of Bear Island. At the rear of columns four, five and six were the four oilers; the RFA *Black Ranger*, RFA *Gray Ranger*, RFA *Oligarch* and MV *Atheltemplar*. Their purpose was quite simple: to provide fuel for the ships on the journey. Some of the destroyers had already broken off to refuel at Spitzbergen, but the rest would be supplied from the vast stock of oil on these four ships. Therefore, these vessels were as much a target for the Germans as those containing war materiel bound for the Red Army. It was around an hour after dawn when one of them was hit.

It was a complete surprise when a huge explosion reverberated throughout the convoy. Matelots turned their heads towards the rear to witness smoke and a huge spout of water rising high into the air. This was the last ship of the fourth column, the MV *Atheltemplar*, carrying 9,000 tonnes of fuel oil. She looked to be in terrible distress, skewing off course to starboard, and fires could clearly be seen burning fiercely on her aft decks.

On the bridge of the *Atheltemplar* herself, the ship's Master, Carl Ray, was thrown to the deck and knew immediately that his vessel had been mortally damaged. It was clear the torpedo had struck the engine room on the port side, ripping away the lifeboat positioned there and badly damaging the Bofors gun emplacement. After picking himself up off the deck Ray grabbed the ship's communications handset and attempted to call up the engine room, but the line was already dead, confirming his worst fears. As the lights on the ship flickered and then failed, the radio officer asked if he should send a distress message.

'No point', replied Ray calmly. 'They can see we've been torpedoed. Give the order to abandon ship.'

The ship was now settling rapidly by the stern and it was obvious to him that she was going to sink. The engine room and stokehold had flooded and the engines had completely stopped. It was only her momentum which carried the ship forward at all, albeit at nothing more than a crawl.

Woken by the explosion and the shouts of the crew, the Senior Second Engineer, Mr Jennings, immediately jumped from his bunk and headed to the engine room. He could hear men inside shouting for help. However, he quickly realized there was no way he could enter from inside the ship and so went on deck, to the skylight that provided the vast engine room with natural light. The only thing he could see through the skylight, other than steam and oil fumes billowing out, was that the engine room was flooded to a depth of around 25 feet, totally immersing the engines themselves. Quickly he shone his torch through the skylight to try and locate the source of the cries. Aghast, he saw that all the ladders had been completely destroyed, leaving no means of escape for those trapped inside. He turned to the side and noticed Mr Hill, the Second Officer, with a group of sailors, frantically attempting to release the starboard aft lifeboat from its housing. However, the plugs and block were frozen solid.

'Mr Hill!' shouted Jennings. 'There's still men in the engine room. We need to get them out.'

Hearing this, one of the group, Ernest Roberts, the junior Second Engineer, rushed over to assist him. Together they lifted the skylight cover.

'Hello!' shouted Roberts into the void. 'Who's down there? How many of you are there?'

'There's two of us,' came back the reply, in a voice they recognized as Broadbent's, the Assistant Engineer. 'Myself and Ridgewell.'

Harry Ridgewell was one of the firemen.

By this time the ship was listing further, with fires raging throughout the aft section. Those caught up in the firestorm, some with their clothing on fire, jumped overboard; the flames burning their bodies were immediately extinguished by the ice-cold waters of the Barents Sea, and those with enough strength swam furiously to get away from the oil that was now burning on the surface of the water.

On board, a group of sailors hastily lowered the starboard midship lifeboat, but once it hit the water it broke adrift with only three men on board. Cursing loudly, those left on board the ship headed for the lifeboat on the port side. This time they had more success, and as this lifeboat hit the surface, they were able to get into it. However, with over thirty sailors crammed inside there was a danger it might capsize. Before they could push away from the damaged ship, the order was given for them to remain alongside to await the rescue party who were still attempting to get the two stranded men out of the engine room. By now, the ship was settling further by the stern, with fires continuing to spread.

Having seen the distress the *Atheltemplar* was in, the minesweeper HMS *Harrier*, sailing immediately behind, sped forward. As she approached, her captain, Commander Alan Jay, called across to say he would take on any survivors.

Around them the sea was burning as a great oil slick started to spread outward, bluish flames dancing surreally in the morning air. Those who had taken their chances in the water were relieved to see that help was coming; they were soon picked up and taken on board the rescue ship, some of them having been burned quite severely.

Meanwhile, the rescue party, headed by Jennings, was having difficulty getting the two stranded sailors out of the engine room. They had been joined by Chief Officer James Reeves, who had come to assist in lowering the starboard lifeboat but, on seeing the group near the engine house skylight, had gone over to see what was going on. Hill and John Bailey, the assistant engineer, together with one of the DEMS gunners, Able Seaman Cross, had also joined in the rescue attempt.

Roberts had managed to get hold of a length of rope and with the assistance of the others lowered it through the skylight.

Inside the engine room Broadbent reached out for the rope, but it was immediately clear it was too short. Struggling in the oil-contaminated water, his strength was beginning to leave him; the fireman, Ridgewell, was faring no better.

'It's not long enough!' he shouted up to them weakly.

A few moments later, another length of rope splashed into the oily water near him. Wrapping it around his arms, he signalled that he was ready to be hauled up. No sooner had those on top began to pull than he slipped back into the water, lacking the strength to hang on. Things were beginning to get desperate. If they didn't get out soon they would go down with the ship. He could think of no worse way to leave this world than by drowning in oily seawater in the pitch darkness.

Then he saw the engine-house athwartship beam a few feet away. If he could make it there and climb onto it, it might be easier for those above to effect a rescue. It was around 15ft directly below the skylight.

Holding onto the ropes that were still dangling, he used them to pull himself across the water, dragging the increasingly exhausted Ridgewell with him. After a few moments he managed to climb on top of the beam, although it was already awash with the black oily water. Ridgewell, not having the strength to haul himself up, instead had to cling onto the side with what little strength he could still summon.

Up above, Hill had had an idea. Moving quickly, he grabbed one of the lifeboat embarkation ladders and brought it over. With the assistance of the others he secured it and then lowered it into the void. Broadbent, taking hold of the ladder, made an attempt to climb but once more slipped and fell back, exhausted.

'They're not going to get out without help,' said Reeves. 'They're both done in.'

Without waiting for a reply, he then climbed over the lip and, using the ladder, descended into the fume-filled engine room, those above shining their torches down to give him some light to work by. Within moments he was on the beam with Broadbent. Grabbing hold of the longer rope, he tied it firmly around the man's waist and under his armpits and shouted for those above to haul him up.

As Broadbent was lifted unceremoniously towards the skylight, Reeves took hold of Ridgewell and hauled his semi-conscious form onto the beam. Ridgewell was a very heavy man and soaked in oil, so this was no mean feat; Reeves had to use all his strength, but a mix of adrenalin and desperation seemed to do the trick, and once he had Ridgewell securely on the beam he tied the second rope around him.

Once Broadbent had been hauled up to the skylight, the rescue party manhandled him onto the now sloping deck. Soaked to the skin with freezing water and black oil, and coughing from breathing in oil fumes, he was completely spent. Another of the rescue party, Bailey, had been dispatched to procure a coat in which to wrap Broadbent's shivering form, and this was hastily placed around his shoulders.

Despite this success, Ridgewell still remained to be rescued. Reeves, having secured the second rope around him, ascended the ladder to assist with pulling him out. Summoning what little energy they had left, the men began to lift the fireman but, due to his weight, the oil that covered him and his inability to help himself, he started to slip back, his arms rising above his head. Only six feet from safety, he slipped through the loop and fell crashing back, unconscious, onto the beam.

The situation was becoming critical. If the men did not get off the ship soon they would either go down with it or be burned to death by the fires that were continuing to spread.

'We can't leave him', said Reeves and, without waiting for a reply, climbed back onto the ladder and descended once more into the darkness.

* * *

Had anyone been looking, they would have seen, not too far away, a periscope break the water. Korvettenkapitän Karl Brandenburg of *U-457* was feeling pleased with himself. Only six days earlier, he had been awarded the Iron Cross First Class following his success in sinking two ships on the previous Arctic convoy, the one that had been smashed so successfully by U-boat and Luftwaffe attacks. He had been at sea again, on this, his third U-boat patrol, for only two days and already was relishing another success.

Having penetrated the outer destroyer screen, he had been able to get off a salvo of four torpedoes at the slow-moving tankers at the rear of the convoy and scored a direct hit in the engine room of the one at the rear of the fourth column, the ship bursting into flames only moments after the torpedo struck. He could see oil burning on the surface of the sea and a couple of the escort ships moving in to effect a rescue. Whether the oiler would sink was debatable, but one thing was for certain, she wasn't going to be able to continue her journey.

Conscious that the destroyers would now be on the hunt for him, he could not risk staying at this shallow depth any longer, so, happy with all he had seen, he pulled the periscope back into the well and ordered the boat to dive deeper, his work done for now.

* * *

Upon reaching the unconscious Ridgewell, Reeves saw immediately that things were as bad as they could be.

At first he thought the man might be dead, as he was not moving at all, but on closer inspection he realized he was still breathing. To make matters worse, as a consequence of the fall, Ridgewell's left leg was now jammed between the boiler pipes and the beam itself.

The noise inside the engine room was appalling. Above the sound of the water sloshing and the fires that raged above, the *Atheltemplar* seemed to groan as the metal buckled and twisted. The fumes from the oil were getting thicker, and Reeves knew if the man was to be saved then they needed to act quickly. He did not want to leave him to die.

Again, he secured a line around the fireman, ensuring it was as tight as it could be. He could not let him slip through again. A third attempt to get him out might not be possible if the rest of them were to get off the ship alive. It was now or never.

'Okay', he called up. 'Start lifting ... but slowly.'

As those above began to pull back on the rope, Ridgewell started to rise. Quickly, Reeves grabbed his jammed leg and was relieved to see that, by manipulating and pulling it, he was able to free it from where it had been caught. Slowly, the unconscious man began to ascend towards the skylight. Grabbing hold of the ladder, Reeves made his way up alongside him.

This time they managed to get the man to the top. With Reeves pushing him from below and the rest of the rescue party pulling from above, with great difficulty and a huge effort, the second man to be rescued from the engine-room hit the deck, followed a few moments later by a very tired Chief Officer Reeves.

'I think it's about time we got off this bloody ship', said Jennings.

Carrying the two injured men between them, they made their way amidships.

By this time, HMS *Sharpshooter* had joined the *Harrier* and was lying on the starboard side, where she took the men who had escaped on the lifeboat. The *Harrier* took on board those from the midship boat, and, as the ships came together, the rescue party with the two injured men were able to successfully transfer to the minesweeper, where they went below decks and finally collapsed, totally exhausted.

Rear-Admiral Burnett, on board the *Scylla*, seeing the smoke and flames from the *Atheltemplar*, had given instructions to Commander Jay of the *Harrier* that the ship was to be sunk should she be unable to continue. Although towing wires had been attached by the *Sharpshooter* in an attempt to rescue the ship and tow her to Lowe Sound at Spitzbergen, it soon became clear that there was little chance she could be salvaged and so it was decided to scuttle her. Burnett was also aware of further U-boats in the vicinity and was not prepared to risk detaching part of the escort screen to accompany the stricken ship to Spitzbergen.

With fifty-eight of the sixty-one crew members having been rescued, *Sharpshooter* and *Harrier* headed at full speed to rejoin the convoy, which was by this time some 12 miles ahead.

The 'Tribal class' destroyer HMS *Tartar* was given the task of sinking the now abandoned oiler, dropping depth charges near her and then firing two shots into her tanks. She did not sink immediately, but not wanting to waste any more time and munitions, the *Tartar* left her to her fate, burning furiously and sending columns of thick black smoke high into the morning air that were still visible almost seven hours later.

* * *

Group Captain Frank Hopps was worried.

Sitting at his desk in Polyarny, just outside Murmansk on the Kola Inlet, he pondered the latest report he had received overnight from the Air Officer Commanding-in-Chief.

Born in Hackney in December 1894, Frank Linden Hopps had been in the military for twenty-six years. Having been commissioned as a Second Lieutenant in the 5th Battalion, King's Own Yorkshire Light Infantry in 1916, he had seen action during the Great War in France and Belgium. He later transferred to the Royal Flying Corps (RFC) and after successfully training as a fighter pilot was posted to the Western Front with 20 Squadron RFC in August 1917. When the RFC broke away from the Army to form the Royal Air Force on 1 April 1918, Hopps went with it, and graduated from RAF Cranwell in 1929. At the outbreak of war in 1939 he was the station commander of RAF Eastchurch on the Isle of Sheppey in Kent, his squadrons seeing action during the Battle of Britain.

Hopps had been in theatre now since 23 August, having been conveyed there, along with many other personnel, by the US Navy cruiser USS *Tuscaloosa*. When offered the post of Senior Royal Air Force Officer, or SRAFO, he had jumped at the chance. This was a big operation of very high importance, and the aircraft that had been put at his disposal were numerous and varied. He was confident that with these resources he could do a good job in providing early warning of surface attacks on PQ18 and cover for its safe passage. He had chosen Polyarny as his base as it had the most reliable meteorological service in northern Russia and he could liaise directly with his Soviet counterparts, keeping them abreast of British operations, and at the same time co-ordinate a response to any German surface ship attack, as the Russians themselves had many torpedo-bombers in the area.

Hopps was aware that the convoy had come under sustained attack the previous day by both U-boats and the Luftwaffe, and a number of ships had been lost. The only weapon not yet involved in attacking the convoy was the surface ships of the Kriegsmarine, the main threat of which was the 'Bismarck class' battleship *Tirpitz*.

And, if he was being honest, after reading this latest report, he had absolutely no idea where the battleship was.

The only available Catalina of 210 Squadron at Grasnaya, tasked with carrying out the daily sortie of patrolling the Norwegian coast, had experienced engine trouble and was unable to fly. Mechanics were at that very moment working hard to repair it. However, for the meantime it was impossible to keep tabs on the *Tirpitz*.

The report he was now looking at was informing him that the Admiralty had information that the *Tirpitz* was on the move. With the rest of the Kriegsmarine surface ships still in Altenfjord, was the *Tirpitz* on its way to rendezvous with them to prepare for an attack on the convoy? Hopps could not be sure.

Flight Lieutenant Fairhurst of 1PRU had reported the previous evening that the ships in Altenfjord were still there. Having flown a three-and-a-half-hour sortie himself, he had seen them at anchor and taken photographs. However, the latest sortie, flown that morning by Fairhurst's colleague, Flying Officer Furniss, had just landed, and his report was somewhat disturbing. Furniss had been tasked with flying over not only Altenfjord but also the shipping routes. However, due to bad weather, he had not been able to confirm whether the ships were still there or the *Tirpitz* was at sea and headed in their direction.

For a moment Hopps thought of PQ17 and the unfortunate decision that was made to disperse the ships, which ultimately led to the destruction of most of that convoy. On that particular occasion, the intelligence had been incorrect and the scatter order had been completely unnecessary. Was lightning about to strike in the same place again?

Back in July, the intelligence on the movement of the *Tirpitz* had been flawed, and he could not be certain if it was to be trusted this time. The last thing anyone needed was panic setting in, as it had done then. If the *Tirpitz* was indeed heading for more northern waters, then he could not sit idle and wait for the Catalina to be repaired to confirm it. He had to act immediately and he had to act decisively.

He knew what he would do. At his disposal were twenty-three serviceable Hampdens of 144 and 455 Squadrons. Their purpose in Russia was to attack any surface ships that might attempt to engage with the convoy. He would scramble them all to carry out a 'Reconnaissance in Force' and get them to fly the route the *Tirpitz* would need to take to get to Altenfjord. If the intelligence was correct and the German battleship was on the move, then he would know for certain soon enough.

He would also task 1PRU to carry out another sortie to Altenfjord to check on the positions of the major Kriegsmarine ships; and once the Catalina was repaired, he would instruct it to fly further out to sea than normal, to ensure all avenues were covered.

Without further delay he picked up the phone.

A few minutes later, at 0825 hours on 14 September, the twenty-three Hampden torpedo-bombers took off from Afrikanda on a mission that would last seven hours.

* * *

The loss of the MV *Atheltemplar* had not been a good start to the day. To make matters worse, Burnett had been informed overnight that the *Tirpitz* had left port and was likely to be heading north from her temporary base in Narvik (the ship had recently been moved from her home base at Trondheim). At that moment the Hampdens of Operation Orator were in the air looking for her, and the Distant Covering Force and Cruiser Covering Force, both operating further west, were on high alert.

This was a very nervous time for the senior officers. If it was true that the Germans were about to commit their main surface ships to intercept them, then the superior firepower of the Kriegsmarine battleships and cruisers would cause untold destruction to the convoy, despite the protection of the Royal Navy escort. After all, with the oiler's sinking earlier that morning they had now lost eleven ships, and any more losses would hit hard in terms of the convoy's success, loss of life and, as a consequence, the morale of the men.

However, if enemy ships were indeed headed their way, there was little Burnett or anybody else could do about it. There was a more immediate threat to concern themselves with. The ships, many caked in ice and snow, once again had clearing parties outside working methodically to keep their decks, weapons and superstructures free from freezing over. This was proving an almost impossible task, since water froze the moment it hit anything solid. As men worked, the moisture from their breath would also solidify, forming ice on their beards and eyebrows; balaclavas and scarves needing to be peeled carefully from their faces once back inside the mess-decks. Any exposed skin would be chapped and sore, and eyelashes, freezing solid, would snap off, causing pain and severe irritation. Most had never known cold like it; it was almost impossible to imagine.

Despite the horrendous conditions, the men still had to carry out their duties. They had to continue to prepare for the next attack that they had no doubt would come very soon. The sound of the klaxons echoing throughout the ships, bringing them to Action Stations yet again, had become almost routine now. Unlike the early stages of the voyage, when calls to arms were mainly false alarms, or triggered by the sighting of spotter planes who offered little danger, now when the klaxons blared out their irritating tones, the crews knew the danger of which they were being warned was very real. They had witnessed enough to realize they had to remain vigilant at all times, despite the fatigue that each of them was experiencing.

Swordfish crews had it much worse. Their cockpits, open to the elements, bore the full brunt of any inclement weather. Shivering inside and with the wind buffeting the light wooden frames of their aircraft, through misted and frozen goggles these men searched relentlessly for the U-boats they knew to be stalking the convoy.

It was therefore with great skill and dedication to duty that on that very morning, at 0940 hours, a crew operating in PQ18's wake spotted something on the surface six miles to the south of the convoy's position. It was the unmistakable profile of a U-boat's conning tower. Turning his plane expertly, the pilot headed over to investigate.

* * *

The skipper of *U-589*, Korvettenkapitän Hans-Joachim Horrer, had seen the British biplane at about the same time as he had been spotted. Shouting the alarm, the handful of officers cleared the conning tower and, once the hatch was sealed shut above them, Horrer ordered the crew to perform an immediate dive.

For the four airmen rescued the previous day, this represented another turn in their fortunes. Having thought they were safe after being rescued from the water following the *Goldene Zange* attack the previous day, they now found themselves once again in very real danger. The frustrating thing for them was that, whereas they had had some control over their fate when flying their aircraft, this time they were totally reliant on the skills of Horrer and his crew. They had been anxious to get back to dry land, since being incarcerated in a metal tube under the icy water was very different to flying in a Heinkel He-111. At least from the aircraft they had a view of the wider world, but life in a U-boat was very different. The lack of awareness of what was taking place above them only added to the claustrophobia they were beginning to feel.

Immediately, they headed to the crew accommodation at the rear of the boat and waited patiently on the bunks. They knew there was absolutely nothing they could contribute to evading the British ships above, and it was better for all if they just kept out of the way.

Horrer, meanwhile, knew the boat was in very real peril. He could not dive too deep, as his batteries had not been fully replenished and he would need to surface again once the danger had passed. He was sure the British aircraft would have radioed his position back to the convoy, and a ship might well have been dispatched to hunt them down. However, the British ships, some distance away, might not feel it prudent to commit their resources to chasing a U-boat that was posing no threat to them at that time. He could only hope.

Above the surface, the crew of the Swordfish had indeed radioed the position of the U-boat to the *Avenger*, dropping a smoke marker on the surface where it had last been seen. Once made aware of the sighting, Burnett, on the *Scylla*, dispatched the destroyer HMS *Onslow*, captained by 38-year-old Harold 'Beaky' Armstrong, to assist with the hunting and destruction of the submarine.

The Swordfish crew then circled the area as they waited for assistance to reach them. However, before the *Onslow* could get there, a Junkers Ju-88 appeared and immediately came in to attack. Only lightly armed, the Swordfish was no match for the German plane and, fearing being shot from the sky, the pilot turned away and headed back towards the safety of the convoy, all the time followed by the German torpedo-bomber, which fired its cannon at the soft-sided biplane, its bullets flying narrowly wide.

All the time this was taking place, a Luftwaffe BV138 seaplane circled the Swordfish menacingly but did not move in to join the attack, leaving the Ju-88 to its task.

Aware of the situation, the escort screen opened fire on the German planes as soon as they were within range, forcing them to turn away and allowing the Swordfish to land safely back on the *Avenger* some minutes later.

Horrer had kept his boat at periscope depth. After watching the Ju-88 see off the biplane he quickly scanned the surface and, seeing no ships in the vicinity, gave the order to surface once more in order to continue recharging his batteries. The danger over, he breathed a sigh of relief. The four airmen now resting in the crew accommodation felt good fortune had once more smiled on them.

No sooner had the *U-589* surfaced, and Horrer and his officers climbed to the conning tower, than he realized he had made a fatal mistake. Coming over the horizon and bearing down upon them fast was the unmistakable sight of a Royal Navy destroyer.

* * *

Heading in the direction reported, HMS *Onslow* sighted the smoke marker dropped by the Swordfish crew at a range of 14,000 yards. 'Beaky' Armstrong on the destroyer's bridge then received a call from the masthead lookout reporting that he could see the conning tower of a U-boat, and a couple of minutes later Armstrong himself could see the same thing, as the German submarine, now alert to this new threat, was hastily diving.

On *U-589*, the elation at having escaped the attention of the Swordfish was quickly replaced by a feeling of despair in Horrer and his crew. Although still some considerable distance away, the British destroyer would no doubt sweep the area with its Asdic. Horrer had to get his boat as deep as possible and carry out evasive manoeuvres. There was still hope this would end well, as long as he had luck and God on his side.

Armstrong knew that finding and destroying the U-boat would be down to the decisions he made over the next few minutes. However, he was a very experienced and confident seaman, having contributed to the sinking of the German battleship *Bismarck* in May 1941 as commander of the 'Tribal class' destroyer HMS *Maori*. With almost six miles of water to scan in all directions, he knew the chances of finding the boat now that it was submerged, and with such a large area to cover, would be about one in four.

Despite these odds, it was only a few minutes later that a firm contact was reported by the Asdic operators. The submerged U-boat was showing 1,900 yards away. Estimating the track the slow moving submarine would follow, Armstrong ordered the *Onslow* to run along its probable course. As the contact grew stronger, he knew he had judged it right and ordered the depth charges to be prepared.

Immediately, the depth charge teams set their charges to explode at 50ft and, once it was judged the *Onslow* was more or less over the U-boat, they launched them into the sea. A few moments passed before the sea was violently disturbed by an eruption of seawater and spray as the charges exploded.

Armstrong called for a report from the EWO room and was informed the contact was still there and as strong as it could be. He knew now that he was almost directly above his prey and it would be only a matter of time before the U-boat would be destroyed.

* * *

Below the surface, things were extremely tense.

Horrer was cursing his decision to resurface so early following the Swordfish contact. He knew now that had he stayed submerged for longer, the destroyer above him might not have been able to locate them. As the sweat trickled down his neck he dared not look at his crew, who were all maintaining the silence necessary if they stood any chance of survival. Their lives were in his hands, but he had misjudged the situation completely.

As for the four airmen who had been rescued and had presumed they were now safe, the feeling of dread and despair they had felt whilst in the dinghy the previous day had returned. The irony of being shot down, left for dead, then rescued, and now facing death for a second time, was not lost on them.

And then the U-boat was rocked violently as a charge exploded close to its hull, throwing the crew violently around the boat. Then another explosion was followed by a third. As the injured men slowly got to their feet they knew the chances of escape were remote.

With all engines now cut, the *U-589* was a sitting duck, and there was nothing Horrer or any of his crew could do about it. The only thing left for them to do was to pray, but, in his heart of hearts, he knew that looking to God for help was likely to be useless.

* * *

'Beaky' Armstrong knew he had the boat exactly where he wanted it. He had so far seen eleven ships taken out by the Germans, and if the rest of the convoy was to get to Archangelsk unscathed, then neutralizing the U-boat threat was of paramount importance.

And so, depth-charge run followed depth-charge run, the sea being hurled into the air almost to a rhythm as the underwater explosions continued to reverberate. After the fifth attack, diesel could clearly be seen at the surface, indicating beyond doubt that the hull of the *U-589* had been breached. For the forty-eight men sailing in her, this would be their last day on earth.

Despite the presence of oil signalling that the U-boat was doomed, Armstrong continued the attack. After the seventh run, a huge explosion lifted a mountain of seawater into the air, and once it had settled again, there were signs of debris amongst the oil-covered seawater. Wooden gratings and food supplies that would now never be consumed mixed in with other detritus floating on the surface.

Still not totally content that the job was complete, Armstrong took the *Onslow* for a final depth-charge run, and once the sound of the explosions had faded, he asked for a report from the EWO room. This time, the Asdic operators informed him that all contact was now lost with the U-boat; it had broken up and sunk to the bottom.

With only a handful of depth charges still remaining, Armstrong ordered the ship to make good speed back to the convoy, which, he now heard, was once more under aerial attack.

It was now a few minutes after 1300 hours. As the ship hastened to take up her position back at the far starboard side of the convoy, she passed the wreckage of a downed He-111 from the previous day. Sitting atop the wreckage were its five crew members. Having neither the time nor the inclination to pick them up, the *Onslow* sailed past, leaving them to their fate. Had they been spotted by the now destroyed *U-589*, as their colleagues had been the day before, they would have suffered the same end. Out on the water, at least they still had a chance of survival.

* * *

Half an hour before Armstrong turned his ship away to return to the convoy, PQ18 came under another huge aerial attack. This time, the first wave was led by Klaus Nocken commanding twenty He-111s of Squadron III/KG26. He and Klümper, who was to follow in the second wave, were under express orders from Hermann Göring himself that the sole focus of this attack was to be the aircraft carrier HMS *Avenger*. Should opportunity arise to hit other ships after the main objective was secured, then the anti-aircraft ships and other large escorts could be attacked too.

However, all was not to go to plan. As the planes approached, the *Avenger* steamed ahead, all the time sending her Sea Hurricanes into the air. The mistake of using these aircraft too early the previous day, leading to them still being refuelled and re-armed when the Golden Comb attack came in, was not going to be repeated. At the same time, Captain Adams on the anti-aircraft ship HMS *Ulster Queen* defied his instructions to keep in formation and also headed out to meet the oncoming force, freeing up his vast array of weaponry to its full advantage. Having been frustrated at his ship's lack of effectiveness the day before, he was determined to ensure his guns were put to better use now.

For Charlie Erswell in B turret on the *Milne*, this was yet another test of his skills. Although exhausted from lack of sleep and being on constant alert, and suffering cold that was now becoming unbearable, he knew he had to focus completely on doing his duty. Called to Action Stations as soon as the planes appeared on the radar, he was ready for what might come, hands firmly gripping the training handles. As soon as the planes came within range, the order was given to open fire.

Turning the training gear handles, he spun the turret to match up the pointers as the loaders and gun layer to his side pumped the shells into the breech and raised and lowered the barrels. The noise inside became horrendous, the rate of fire fast, the constant boom of the 4.7-inch shells being fired from the twin barrels deafening. Methodically the team worked, firing shell after shell into the air to explode amongst the Ju-88s and He-111s that were determined to wreak havoc upon the slow-moving ships.

For Robert Hughes on the *Scylla*, things were equally frantic. Their eight 4.5-inch guns firing salvo after salvo at the oncoming aircraft caused the ship to shudder. Constantly having to recalculate and adjust the ranges as the cruiser sped out to meet the attack meant he had to have his wits about him, the adrenalin coursing through his veins keeping him alert and effective.

It quickly became clear that the Germans were focusing on the aircraft carrier, but with the Sea Hurricanes now in the air, and the effective barrage being fired by the destroyers and anti-aircraft ships, the attack was proving fruitless; the German pilots dropped their bombs and torpedoes short and then had to turn away lest they got hit.

The German aircraft were taking casualties, many more than on the previous day. With small arms fire coming from all the merchant ships as they passed over, the concentrated flak barrage from the destroyers and the skills of the pilots of the Sea Hurricanes, plane after plane began to crash into the sea.

For one such British pilot, things were a little frustrating. On board the CAM ship SS *Empire Morn*, Flying Officer Arthur Burr could only look on as his fellow pilots from the *Avenger* fought back against the Luftwaffe. He looked longingly at the single Sea Hurricane sitting prepared and ready on the catapult at the bow of his ship and longed for the order to be given to throw it into the fight. Still, no matter how much he wanted it, the order was not forthcoming. This plane might be needed more once the *Avenger* and the Fighting Destroyer Escort left them at the Kola Inlet in a couple of days' time to take up their role with the returning QP14. The convoy would then be left with minimal air cover to see it through to Archangelsk on the White Sea. Although Burr knew this made sense, as he watched the aerial battle taking place above him he could not help but wish to be a part of it.

Up in the air, things were going well for the British. With Göring's express order to make the sinking of the *Avenger* the priority, the merchant ships were largely being left alone. Nevertheless, some torpedoes were dropping dangerously close to the freighters, so Boddam-Whetham gave the order to carry out a 45° turn, exactly as he had done the day before. Whereas not all of the ships had carried out his instruction then, this time all of them complied, and the move was carried out perfectly.

For some German pilots the whole thing became too much. Seeing their comrades' aircraft bursting into flames, they dropped their ordnance at random, sometimes far too early to have any effect at all, and then turned and headed away from the battle, not willing to endure the fire being put up by the escort ships. With this first wave of attack now over, Nocken and his crews turned about, their mission a total failure.

For Werner Klümper, failure was not an option. Commanding the second wave of twenty-two He-111s, along with eighteen Ju-88s of Squadron III/KG26 commanded by his comrade, Major Bloedorn, he spotted what he thought was the *Avenger*. He had received a report from Nocken on the way that the aircraft carrier had steamed out ahead of the convoy. What he was unaware of, however, was that the *Avenger* had by this time once again moved position and was operating on the convoy's starboard quarter with four Sea Hurricanes circling above to provide her with added protection. The ship Klümper was now preparing his planes to attack was, unfortunately for them, the *Scylla*, with its immense firepower.

Leading a group of twelve He-111s, Klümper moved in for the kill.

He gave the order for the twelve aircraft to split into two sections to attack the ship from both the bow and the stern and, as they banked away to carry out his instruction, he was forced almost immediately to withdraw it. A fierce barrage opened up on them, coming from the very ship he was moving in to attack, and coming at them from behind were the four Sea Hurricanes that were providing protection for the *Avenger*.

Ignoring the vicious barrage put up by their own ships, the British pilots began firing at the German planes. As the Heinkels started to take evasive action, Klümper, realizing he had mistaken the cruiser for the *Avenger* and seeing the aircraft carrier to the starboard side, flicked his mic once more and ordered them to turn to attack it instead.

However, some of the German aircraft were already committed to the attack on the *Scylla* and, although they tried to break off and swing away towards the *Avenger*, it proved to be too drastic a change of plan so late in the attack. Feeling the full force of the *Scylla*'s guns, a number were shot down, crashing in flames into the sea.

For Robert Hughes, in the *Scylla*'s blue director, targets were everywhere. No sooner had one salvo erupted from the guns then another target was selected and the cannon blazed once more. As the planes drew closer, the short-range weapons, the Oerlikons, Bofors and machine guns, took over, hurling deadly metal into the approaching enemy aircraft. The Germans were taking a battering, and thus far, not a single ship had been hit with anything bigger than machine-gun fire.

By now the German planes were flying the channels between the eight lines of ships, the DEMS gunners on the merchants throwing more ordnance into their paths. More planes, meeting fierce resistance and being pursued by the exuberant Hurricane pilots, burst into flames and fell from the skies.

Yet some of the German aircraft managed to release their torpedoes, some spinning hopelessly head over tail to land and sink immediately, whilst others sped through the water with no defined target. One was headed at that moment for the *Scylla* and was on track to score a hit. Captain MacIntyre, on being made aware of it, ordered an immediate turn, and as the ship moved it passed harmlessly by, exploding on hitting the wake caused by the ship's turn and spraying nothing more than seawater and blocks of ice high into the air.

Klümper was now determined to get his torpedo away at the correct target. Having made the turn away from the *Scylla* in time, he and his wingman were the only two pilots who had managed to get into a suitable position to fire torpedoes at the aircraft carrier. However, Commander Colthurst, alert to what was taking place, was quickly able to turn the *Avenger* away from their tracks, and they too fell harmlessly into the deep. As the German pilots now realized their attack on the *Avenger* was another total failure they began to extricate themselves from the fight. The Sea Hurricanes following and harassing them were not without casualties. Heading bravely into the same barrage that was intended to shoot down the Heinkels and Junkers, it was inevitable that some friendly fire would hit them. At around 1415 hours, the first of the British fighters was struck by shrapnel, forcing the pilot to ditch into the sea, and only a minute later, a second was downed. Ten minutes later, a third Hurricane was also shot down by friendly fire. All three pilots were, however, quickly rescued by passing ships.

On board the US cargo ship *Nathanael Greene*, the second ship of the seventh column, the track of a torpedo was seen heading in their direction off the port bow. The ship's commander, Captain Vickers, immediately ordered a turn to port and, as the quartermaster spun the wheel to carry out the order, the ship's crew held their breath. Luckily for them, the missile passed them by, missing by only a few feet. However it was now heading in the direction of another merchant ship.

The SS *Mary Luckenbach*, carrying a cargo of 1,000 tonnes of TNT, had been the only surviving ship in the far two starboard columns after the Golden Comb attack the previous day, and as such she had quickly been given the nickname 'Lucky'. Boddam-Whetham, not wanting to leave the ship isolated, had repositioned her to the eighth column after that action.

As those on the *Nathanael Greene* looked on in horror, a Heinkel He-111 flew over and dropped a torpedo which headed in the direction of the *Mary Luckenbach*.

What happened next shook the convoy to its core. Every person sailing on PQ18 felt the tremendous shock wave as the *Mary Luckenbach* exploded. The ship had been hit in the cargo hold, instantaneously detonating the whole load of TNT she was carrying. In an instant the ship was blasted apart, causing a massive pall of smoke and debris to hurtle skyward. For a second the world seemed to stop as, within the plume of smoke, more explosions shot out flames of red and yellow, like some macabre firework display. What was left of the ship was covered by the twisting smoke plume, and as the thick black changed to dark grey, it was as though she had become invisible. It was quickly realized that the reason the wreck could not be seen was because the ship simply did not exist anymore. There was nothing left of her to sink.

What those sailors looking on had witnessed was the vaporization of the ship and all onboard. In a fraction of a second, forty-one crew members and twenty-four US Navy Armed Guard gunners had perished before their eyes, wiped from the earth as though they had never existed.

As the smoke continued to spurt skyward, the Heinkel that had flown over it was seen to crash in flames into the sea beyond. Whether it was the torpedo from this plane that had destroyed the ship, or the one that narrowly missed the *Nathanael Greene*, or a combination of the two, could not be determined. But that was immaterial now, for another ship of the convoy had been destroyed, with a significant loss of cargo and life.

On board the *Nathanael Greene* there was panic.

Sailing close by and caught in the blast, the US ship was momentarily lifted from the sea, falling back down with such violence that Captain Vickers assumed she too had been hit by a torpedo.

As the smoke began to clear, it was evident the *Nathanael Greene* had suffered considerable damage. Her rigging was torn to shreds and the chains that lashed the tanks and trucks to the decks had come loose. The crates containing planes destined for the Russian Air Force had also been broken up by the vacuum following the blast, and the clothing of those caught outside was ripped and torn.

Compounding this damage, the debris from the destroyed *Mary Luckenbach* was now starting to rain down on the decks: shrapnel, metal shards, burning embers. On seeing the damage to his own ship, Vickers immediately called for her to be abandoned and for the crew to make their way to the lifeboats. It was clear to him that staying on board was now untenable.

As the smoke cleared further, the sound of the pipes calling the crew to boat stations filled the air, mixed with the noise of the battle that was continuing to rage all around them. Hastily, the men did as directed, their ears still ringing from the recent massive explosion. As the crew started to fill the lifeboats with the wounded, it was noticed that the ship had not been flying its ensign. The third mate, Paul Gill, rushed off to correct this error in naval etiquette, taking the Stars and Stripes from its locker and raising it aloft. Those observing broke out in cheers, their morale lifted by this solitary display of patriotism.

Before the boats could be lowered into the sea, Vickers paused. On second thoughts, the ship might not be in mortal danger after all. Stopping the engines, he ordered a quick survey to be carried out of the general state of mechanical equipment and the ship's seaworthiness. He was now of the opinion that the damage to the ship had been caused solely by the explosion of the *Mary Luckenbach* and not by a torpedo or any other enemy action.

It was quickly determined that the ship's hull had not been breached and she was still fine to sail; the call to abandon ship had been an over-reaction. Revoking his initial order, Vickers instructed his crew to return to their stations. Those who had been injured were taken to the sick bay, and a working party was dispatched to secure the loose deck cargo. Meanwhile, those operating the guns were sent back to continue the fight.

And so, badly shaken, their clothes torn and bodies battered, in the wind, sleet and freezing temperatures, the men of the *Nathanael Greene* manned the guns and took up their positions once more, the ship holding its station and her crew ready for action.

* * *

As the sound of the *Mary Luckenbach*'s explosion dissipated and the shock waves died down, the huge plume of smoke hanging over the convoy showed no signs of fading. It hung over the convoy like a great black cloud, in places blocking out any light from the early afternoon sun.

There was a brief respite in the aerial attack as the remaining German planes flew to the south to regroup.

Robert Hughes, on the *Scylla*, was then to witness something that caused him great concern. From his position in the blue director he could see a downed Junkers Ju-88 in the water between two of the columns. Sitting on the wings was its crew of four airmen. Despite these men having just attempted to sink the convoy's ships, there was no denying the courage it had taken for them to fly through the barrage thrown at them. Although Hughes was not sorry they had been shot down, he could not help but respect their bravery.

Then suddenly, from one of the merchant ships, a long arc of tracer fire crept steadily towards the men on the downed aircraft. Below him, someone called out for this to stop, but his shouts of protest went unheard, or were ignored. The machine-gun fire continued to be directed at the airmen and after a moment was joined by small arms fire from other merchantmen, until eventually all four were knocked from the wings into the sea, the plane on which they had taken refuge floating calmly down the convoy lane.

The respite from aerial attack did not last long. A little after 1430 hours, eighteen Junkers Ju-88s returned but this time kept their distance, not wanting to subject themselves to the bombardment their comrades had experienced earlier. Using the clouds for cover, they occasionally dropped their bombs through any gaps, while one or two summoned up the courage to venture below cloud level and carry out a dive-bombing run. Having been refuelled and re-armed, the Sea Hurricanes went out to meet them, driving them back where they could. This attack lasted an hour before, having had no success, the German planes turned and headed back to their airfields in Norway.

Captain Colthurst on the *Avenger* was doubly pleased. The defence of the aircraft carrier had been a complete success despite the best efforts of the Luftwaffe to destroy it. A combination of anti-aircraft fire, from its own guns and those of the destroyers, and the valiant efforts of the pilots of the Sea Hurricanes had boosted the morale of the crew. To add to this, the quick rescue of the downed pilots meant anyone unlucky enough to get hit and having to ditch in the water was now reassured that he would soon be collected and returned to the *Avenger*.

Having fought solidly for a number of hours and only lost one ship to an essentially lucky shot by the Germans, there was now a feeling amongst the crews that PQ18 could yet succeed. Losing only one ship as compared to so many the previous day, and having downed many German aircraft, today's battle could be seen as a victory. However, this did not detract from the sense of loss felt by everyone as a result of the destruction of the *Mary Luckenbach*. It showed just how dangerous these convoys could be.

By 1520 hours the only aircraft that could be seen were the spotter planes that persistently shadowed the convoy, but these were now little more than an irritation; the only problem they caused was being able to keep the Kriegsmarine abreast of PQ18's exact position.

This lull in enemy aerial activity gave time for the crews to take meals and get some rest. However, as the temperatures were continuing to plummet, the ice and snow fixed solidly to the superstructures, decks and equipment had to be cleared, and so working parties once more attached themselves to hawser lines, hammers, mauls and picks in hand, and chipped away at the ice.

It was relentless, never-ending work.

* * *

In Bardufoss, Klümper sat in his office smoking a cigarette. In the nearby hangars ground crews worked on patching up those aircraft still serviceable and wrote reports on those that would have to be written off. Resting in the common rooms down the corridor from his office were the remainder of his squadron. Exhausted and demoralized pilots lounged about, smoking cigarettes, writing letters home or snatching some well-earned sleep.

Today had been a disaster. The order to focus on one ship alone was a crazy idea. There were so many targets out there, but Göring had been absolutely insistent on attacking just the aircraft carrier. In a way, Klümper could understand his thinking, but it was like the Battle of Britain all over again: gain air superiority at all costs, and once that's achieved then you can pick off the ships at will. Just like Operation Sealion, this too had ended in failure.

But then, this convoy was protected like no other before it. The sheer firepower of the British escort ships was something he had never experienced or expected. To add to this, the gunners on the merchant ships were showing equal skill. Even if you took the Sea Hurricanes out of the equation, it would still have been an extremely difficult job.

The *Goldene Zange* attack the previous day had brought much success. They had left so many Allied ships burning. Had they been allowed to do the same thing today, there might have been a similar outcome. Instead, they had managed to destroy just one ship and had paid a massive price for it. At least thirteen planes had been shot from the sky and many others had returned with major damage. The initial reports of the ground staff suggested Klümper only had eight serviceable planes left, and it might be several days before more could be made airworthy again. Even with so many of his comrades left out there to die in the Arctic Ocean, he still did not have enough machines for the crews he had left.

And the aircraft carrier was still afloat, with most of its Hurricanes still able to fly.

He sighed. He knew that he would have to go out again, but he needed more planes. A request for more aircraft would probably be met with a frown, but he was sure they would nevertheless be forthcoming. But how quickly they could be supplied, he did not know.

With each passing hour, his belief that PQ18 could be stopped was fading. The loss of so many aircraft was not sitting well with his men. Would they fly again so bravely into the barrage put up by the escort ships? It was a lot to ask of them.

And was he himself able to go through the trauma of it once, twice, maybe three times more? He could only hope that he was strong enough.

* * *

Frank Hopps was a lot happier now than he had been a few hours ago.

The Hampdens he had sent out on the Reconnaissance in Force mission in search of the *Tirpitz* had returned at 1555 hours to report that they had sighted nothing of any interest. He had also received, some hours earlier, the report of Pilot Officer Walker, who had flown the second PRU sortie to Altenfjord to check on the dispositions of the heavy German battleships and cruisers anchored there, telling him they were still in situ. Walker had had to fly low, at no more than 2,000ft, and through the haze he had observed all the ships still at anchor and showing no signs of movement. All this was welcome news.

The Catalina that had been dispatched to fly further out to sea also reported no sightings of the *Tirpitz*. With all this information now gathered, Hopps was more than confident that the threat of enemy surface ship attack had diminished and the *Tirpitz* was more than likely still at anchor in her current base of Narvik.

He was aware that the convoy had again come under another sustained attack from the Luftwaffe and U-boat wolf-packs. At that moment he had Catalinas carrying out cross-over patrols across the whole of the north of Norway. Very soon, as the convoy sailed south towards the Kola Inlet, they would come closer to the extreme east of the Catalina patrol zones. Hopps was sure that as the ships got closer to this air screen, the protection he could offer them from the danger posed by the underwater threat would be greatly increased. As far as the RAF's role in this convoy was concerned, he was more than happy so far with its performance.

Soon the operation would move to the next phase. In two days time, the Russia-bound convoy PQ18 was due to pass the homeward-bound ships of QP14, near to the Kola Inlet north of the port of Murmansk. At that point, aerial protection of the ships heading to Archangelsk would be taken over by his Russian counterparts, and Operation Orator's focus would switch to giving protection to the vessels returning to Iceland.

He had much still to prepare.

* * *

With so many rescued crews scattered throughout the ships, Burnett wanted to use the lull in the fighting to get them better organized.

Rather than leave some of those men on the ships bound for Archangelsk, where they would possibly spend months stranded in poor conditions waiting for a return berth home, and having more room on the *Scylla* itself to accommodate them, he and Captain MacIntyre came up with a plan.

HMS *Sharpshooter* and HMS *Harrier* now both had many seamen on board whom they had rescued from the various merchant ships that had been sunk.

It was clear that the two minesweepers did not have room to accommodate them all, and so the order was given for them each to come alongside the *Scylla* and transfer the men. The official rescue ship, SS *Copeland*, had already taken on many, some being transferred from the Motor Minesweepers that had been so effective in rescuing the survivors of the *Stalingrad*, *Oliver Ellsworth*, *Sukhona*, *MacBeth*, *Oregonian* and *Africander*. The majority to be transferred from the two Royal Navy ships were those who had survived the attacks on the *Atheltemplar* and *Empire Beaumont*. Those rescued from the Russian ships SS *Stalingrad* and SS *Sukhona*, along with those too injured to move, would remain on the rescue ships and be taken to Archangelsk for repatriation.

Unable to stop to effect the transfer, and travelling at a speed of around 8 knots, the first to pull alongside the cruiser was HMS *Harrier*. All available hands were called to the forecastle to assist with getting the men over the gunwales, some of whom were quite seriously injured.

One of those assisting was Robert Hughes. As the ships came alongside, he noticed that heaving lines and hawsers were already laid out on deck ready to pull the two vessels together. Without slackening speed, the quartermasters on the two ships skilfully guided them closer until they were only a couple of feet apart. Expert hands then threw across the lines and hawsers, pulling the ships together until they were separated only by inches. Hughes could see that the decks of the *Harrier* were crowded with very many survivors, making it hard for the crew to work around them. There were well over a hundred at least, all eager to make the crossing to the heavy cruiser. It was evidently clear that there were far too many of them for the smaller craft to cope with.

There was a surge as the survivors pushed forward to make the crossing, and with the call of 'Over you go!' from an officer onboard the *Harrier*, they started to effect the transfer. Grabbing hold of a young seaman, Hughes pulled him over, and no sooner was he on board than he moved away, freeing up room for Hughes to assist another. All along the gunwale these men were helped onto the *Scylla*, and it wasn't long before the majority had been successfully transferred.

For a brief moment the ships drifted apart a few inches before coming back together with a thud, chipping the paintwork and causing some minor damage, before the transfer of men resumed. One of the last to cross was a seaman who held on to the guardrail with one hand whilst holding the other protectively over his coat. For a moment, Hughes thought the man was wounded, but after he was safely across he opened his coat to reveal a small puppy.

The survivors were taken below deck to receive refreshment and were allocated somewhere to rest. For the remainder of the journey they would be the guests of the Royal Navy and would have to keep themselves out of the way of the crew, especially during Action Stations.

The merchant seamen now resting on board the *Scylla* had been dealt a very bad hand by fate. The loss of their ships meant their pay would automatically be stopped. The way the owners looked at it was this: why pay the crew of a ship that no longer exists? Of course this would have a knock-on effect on those they cared for back home, wives and families to whom they could no longer send any money. The only real option open to them was to return to Britain and find a position on another ship as soon as possible. And so, having endured the terrors of sailing on a Russian convoy in the harshest of conditions, then suffering the horror of being torpedoed and fished from freezing waters, perhaps with quite serious injuries, their only reward was to have their livelihood removed. This seemed quite wrong to the men, and their Royal Navy colleagues were in complete sympathy with them.

No sooner had the last survivor stepped onto the *Scylla*, than the hawser and heaving lines were let go and pulled on board. Now free, the *Harrier* moved away to port to take up her position again at the rear of the convoy.

Next up was the *Sharpshooter*, with ninety-five more survivors to transfer. Again, with expert seamanship from both crews, the two vessels were bound together, and these men too crossed over successfully.

With the main German force now repelled, and the worry of an immediate threat from the *Tirpitz* having diminished, the convoy was subjected to only sporadic attacks by small groups of aircraft. The SS *Empire Baffin*, with pennant number 11 (the lead ship of the first column), came under one such attack from three Junkers Ju-88s. However, against another strong anti-aircraft barrage, their only success was to spray the ship's deck with icy sea water as their bombs exploded harmlessly close by, the water freezing on impact as it hit the steel and adding to the ice that already needed to be cleared.

With the ironically named Hope Island, a barren and desolate place, being sighted off the port bow at 1800 hours, the convoy now started to make its turn south towards the Kola Inlet.

And so, as the light began to slowly fade on Monday, 14 September, a huge sigh of relief seemed to emanate from the ships. Apart from the horrific loss of the SS *Mary Luckenbach*, the rest of the ships, still a large number, had come through the day unscathed despite sustained aerial attack from the Luftwaffe. To add to this, the Germans had been given a seriously bloody nose, losing a U-boat and at least twenty-two aircraft, with possibly more left unserviceable.

There was now growing confidence that the worst was over and PQ18 would be the success that Churchill and Stalin both craved.

Chapter 9

15–16 September

Charlie Erswell looked at what seemed like the thousandth corned beef sandwich he'd been served since leaving Iceland. Sitting in the mess-deck with his good friend Charlie 'Robbo' Robinson, after waking from a couple of hours of snatched sleep, he bit into the thick and tasteless bread. He had been so tired earlier that as soon as he'd curled up into a ball and got himself comfortable, he fell into a very deep and dreamless sleep, oblivious to the noise and activity taking place all around him.

Although he knew there was not much that could be done about it, the food was beginning to get him and his crew-mates down. Even with the restrictions of food rationing back home, he had always managed to eat pretty well. However, this endless stream of sandwiches, with absolutely no variety in filling, was beginning to grate. When comments and jibes had been made to the cooks in the galleys about the lack of choice, those who had spent endless hours preparing them had not taken it too well. You got what you got, and that was that. When Charlie had asked if they could do some kind of stew with the corned beef instead, he had been shown a potato and asked what exactly they could do with it. At first he thought it was a joke, that he had been handed some kind of strange-looking sponge, but it was quickly explained that because of the way the potatoes had been delivered and stored on board they were now completely inedible.

At least there was always the kye, that chocolate drink the sailors on all the ships seemed to enjoy. Full of flavour and served hot, sometimes with a thick skin on top, it was a welcome luxury that somehow seemed out of place in the hell that was the Barents Sea.

So, sighing to himself, Charlie chewed on the sandwich and counted his blessings. Compared to others on the convoy who had experienced a lot more hardship, he could only agree with the cooks and consider himself lucky.

The weather seemed to be getting worse, if such a thing was possible. He didn't mind the cold so much; after all, he had spent his early years in Berwick-upon-Tweed, officially the coldest town in England. He had very fond memories of the place, including swimming in the cold water of the North Sea as a 10-year old. But these temperatures were something quite different. Wiping condensation from the nearest porthole, he looked out.

Snow and sleet hit the window, smearing the glass as it slid down. The waves were beginning to get higher, as the ship bounced off the water, throwing spray and foam into the air which crashed onto the deck, before sloshing into the scuppers and back out into the sea. He could see already that more clearing parties would be required as the day wore on; the ice and snow were beginning to build up on the spots from where they had been cleared the previous day.

It was now obvious that the ships were starting to make their run towards Russia, having passed Bear Island and taking a more southerly course. The previous day, the loss of the *Mary Luckenbach* notwithstanding, had been successful as far as the defence of the convoy was concerned. Charlie was aware that many German planes had been shot down, and he would be very surprised if they were to attack in the same manner again. He was quite proud of the part he had played in repelling the attack. He had done everything asked of him and had not been found wanting.

For many on the ships, personal hygiene had been forced to take a back seat. Most had not changed their clothes in over a week and were beginning to smell. Itchy rashes were breaking out on unwashed skin, adding to the general discomfort. To prevent their skin from cracking in the cold, men sometimes applied lard or engine oil, which did not help with the irritation. Venturing outside, their very breath froze to their beards, making it painful to breathe. With hats low and scarves pulled up to the bridge of the nose, only their eyes could be seen as they took shallow breaths to avoid the pain of the ice-cold air hitting their lungs.

As Charlie sat in the mess-deck eating his bland sandwich, drinking his kye and waiting for the order to go out on yet another ice-clearing duty, the convoy was enjoying a period of respite. Those not detailed to clear ice seized the opportunity for some well-earned rest.

When it came to clearing ice and snow, those on the merchant ships had it considerably worse. With smaller crews than their Royal Navy counterparts, and in most cases a bigger surface area to clear, men were called upon more often to carry out this essential task. Throughout the convoy, matelots attached themselves to hawser lines and once again went through the routine of cracking the ice and sweeping it overboard. With the freezing wind blowing snow and sleet into their tired faces, they went about their labours robotically, all the while conscious that the enemy could return at any moment. It would be ironic to have avoided the German bombs and torpedoes, only for their ships to capsize due to the weight of ice.

Charlie, having finished his lunch, once again found himself with a hammer in hand, smacking it against a large chunk of ice on the *Milne*'s foredeck.

As the wind howled around him he called out to the petty officer who was sweeping a large chunk into the sea.

'Hey, PO. Any chance of getting a couple of deck-chairs out here so we can enjoy this weather properly?'

'I'll ask the captain,' shouted back the petty officer. 'Maybe you can get your bathing suit on too and take a dip in the sea.'

And then he broke into the first verse of 'Oh, I do like to be beside the seaside', which was taken up by the whole working party.

Keeping a sense of humour was important for the morale of the men. They knew they were in a situation which was out of their control and they just had to make the best of it. This display of jollity amidst the most horrendous of conditions was commonplace throughout the ships. If you let things get on top of you, that was when you would start to fail. Friendships were being made, bonds created, that would last their whole lives.

* * *

At around 1245 hours planes were sighted off the starboard bow. Immediately, the klaxons calling the ships to Action Stations sounded, and once again gunners pounded the skies with their ordnance.

It was instantly clear that the Germans had learned their lesson of the previous day and were not attacking in nearly the same force. They headed for the safety of the clouds, all the time pursued by fire from the destroyers and the anti-aircraft ships *Ulster Queen* and *Alynbank*. Without delay, a group of Sea Hurricanes took to the skies from the *Avenger*'s deck and climbed to attack them.

There was little that those below could fire at, since the cover of the clouds made it impossible to fix on a target; and with the fear of hitting the Hurricanes, the anti-aircraft fire dropped to sporadic bursts as and when the German planes came into view. Trying to avoid the Hurricanes, the Germans could not conduct an organized attack and were reduced to dropping their bombs and torpedoes through gaps in the clouds where they splashed harmlessly between the channels, the only damage being caused to the ice floes.

Every now and again a single Ju-88 or He-111 would break cloud cover and attempt a more purposeful run at the ships, but once they met the intense flak and tracer fire from the Royal Navy ships they soon retreated back to the relative safety of the clouds, only to be harried once more by the Hurricanes. Those manning the weapons with only a limited range on the merchant ships had to wait until aircraft were very close before unleashing their fire.

As a second wave of Hurricanes took off from the *Avenger*, the German aircraft jettisoned their remaining bombs, again scoring no hits on any of the ships, and headed south away from the fight, leaving behind three more of their number.

As the enemy aircraft disappeared over the horizon they were almost immediately replaced by a second wave heading towards the convoy on the starboard side. Again a huge barrage was sent up by the ships of the outer screen, firing shell after shell at the tightly packed formation of torpedo-bombers. As the planes got closer they split up, each seeking an individual target.

This second wave was a lot more controlled and organized. There seemed to be more of a plan this time, as each of the planes sought out a merchant ship on which to unleash its torpedoes and bombs.

Despite the intense fire being put up by both the escort ships and the gunners on the merchantmen, this new attack continued, the German planes blasting their machine guns at the ships as they flew through the channels, ripping bullet holes in the superstructures and hulls. Tracer fire criss-crossed the columns as the DEMS gunners trained their Oerlikons and machine guns on the low-flying aircraft, desperate to stop them inflicting further damage on the convoy. As bullets flew all around, ricocheting off the metal of the ships, men ducked and dived to keep from being hit.

This was a brave and purposeful attack, of that there was no doubt, but as quickly as it had started it seemed to end, the German aircraft taking to the clouds to avoid the terrific firepower they had just faced. The Hurricanes again climbed above the clouds to chase and harry them. It seemed that the majority of the aircraft had now left the battle; only a few still attempted to avoid the British aircraft and drop their bombs through gaps in the clouds, much as the first wave had done earlier.

And then, almost out of nowhere, a single Heinkel He-111 decided to mount a lone attack, coming at the convoy from the rear to strike at the middle column. Concentrating solely on the ships ahead of him, the pilot seemed to have tunnel vision, the danger of the guns on the merchant ships to both sides of little concern to him. Careless of their proximity, he continued with his run.

Just as it looked as if this attempt was about to have some success, the guns of the merchant ships opened up on him. At such close range they couldn't miss. Immediately realizing the futility of his action as the bullets tore into his tail and engine, the pilot was forced to break off the attack, pulling hard on his control column to get away. With smoke pouring from his engine, and realizing his part in the mission was over, the pilot made the sensible decision to turn for home, trailing a line of thick black smoke behind him as he went.

Ahead of the merchant ships, another He-111 decided to carry out what was little more than a suicide mission. Flying from starboard to port, the pilot seemed hell-bent on making his mark, heading for a destroyer on the port side. As he flew directly for the ship, the other nearby destroyers turned their guns upon him, flak bursting all around and tracer fire winding its way almost snake-like towards him.

Heedless of this, the pilot continued on his deadly mission. However, the intended target, aware of the threat, also had her own weapons trained upon him and, waiting until the He-111 was so close they couldn't miss, the gunners opened up. Hit by such intense fire at such close range, the German aircraft disintegrated, exploding in a massive ball of flame, the sound of the blast echoing throughout the whole convoy. One second the plane was there, the next it had disappeared; the debris, both material and human, was scattered over the sea, leaving only a small patch of burning oil to mark the spot where the plane had ceased to exist.

The remaining German aircraft, all confidence and morale now spent, turned to the south, their futile attack over.

For Rear-Admiral Burnett it was clear the Luftwaffe pilots were now starting to become battle-weary and unhappy. The ship had been picking up chat between the pilots, who were becoming increasingly worried at being harassed by the Hurricanes and having to resort to dropping their bombs either blind or through breaks in the clouds. One had also expressed his frustration that so many ships were still afloat and that their efforts had done little to stop the convoy.

This was music to Burnett's ears. With the morale of the Germans dropping and that of his own forces rising, he realized that in the absence of another German success like that of the 13th, when the ninth and tenth columns had been destroyed, the enemy could quickly lose the will to fight. For them now it was all about survival as much as stopping PQ18 from completing its journey.

With only the odd spotter plane in the air and posing no real aerial threat, the atmosphere relaxed somewhat throughout the convoy. With the Luftwaffe once again having been repelled with no loss to shipping, and no sign of them coming back for a renewed attack, this lull in enemy activity was extremely welcome. The convoy had been at sea for two weeks now, and under intense pressure for the last days. Any respite, no matter how fleeting, was received with open arms.

However, the threat from the deep remained ever-present. Signals from the Admiralty were keeping them informed of the activity of the wolf-packs known to be operating in the area, and those escort ships on the outer screen, no matter how weak the contact, would conduct depth-charge runs as soon as anything was picked up on the Asdic. This activity put the fear of God into those working below decks. Hearing the nearby blasts as the underwater explosions produced shock waves that spread to the other ships, causing some to rock violently, the sound amplified in the engine rooms, men made frantic calls to the bridge. After receiving reassurances that they were in no danger, they would then get back to work. The fear for any stoker or fireman was being caught in the bowels of a ship when she was hit, cut off from above and with no way of getting out. They therefore needed an early warning if they were to save themselves, should their ship be struck by a torpedo. Otherwise, it would mean an unfortunate and untimely end for those unlucky to be working in these places when a ship was hit.

It was mid-afternoon when the destroyer HMS *Opportune*, bringing up the rear of the outer screen on the port side, was dispatched to investigate smoke that had been spotted on the horizon. Fearing this could be from enemy surface ships, she set off to investigate. As she drew closer, it became clear that instead of German cruisers and battleships, this was in fact a pair of U-boats sailing line abreast and trailing the convoy.

Upon spotting the destroyer bearing down on them, the nearest boat carried out an immediate dive and was quickly out of sight. However, the *Opportune* was able to fire four salvoes from her front two gun turrets at the second, before it too vanished beneath the waves, at a distance of around 10,000 yards.

Heading to the spot where the submarine had submerged, Commander Lawrence Manley ordered a depth-charge run, zig-zagging along the route he expected the submerged U-boat to be taking.

Meanwhile, the second submarine, which happened to be the *U-457*, the very boat that had sunk the MV *Atheltemplar* the previous morning, let off a salvo of two torpedoes in the direction of the *Opportune*. This time, the missiles passed harmlessly wide and, cursing his luck, skipper Karl Brandenburg ordered his crew to take the boat deeper lest they too came under depth-charge attack.

As the run was being carried out, a German BV138 spotter plane came over to investigate and was immediately subjected to fire from the guns of the *Opportune*. Realizing it could do nothing to assist the hunted U-boat, and fearing for its own safety, it turned away.

After a number of runs, and with no indication they had hit anything, Manley halted the attack and ordered the *Opportune* to return to the convoy, which by now was fast fading from sight.

Throughout the evening and into the night, the wolf-packs probed the convoy. Asdic contacts appeared on screens throughout and then quickly disappeared again, none of the U-boat commanders being prepared, just yet, to play their hand and attack. And so, with the sun fading below the horizon for what would be another very short period of darkness, as 15 September drew to a close, the ships of PQ18 plodded on, their final destination coming steadily closer.

* * *

The morning of Wednesday, 16 September would prove to be eventful. With the aerial threat gone for the time being, and all indications showing that the Kriegsmarine were not prepared to commit their surface ships to break up the convoy, the only threats were the U-Boat wolf-packs and the increasingly bad weather.

And at that moment, at 50ft below the surface, *U-457* was once more on the prowl.

Flushed with confidence after sinking the *Atheltemplar* and coming close to hitting the destroyer HMS *Opportune* the day before, Fregattenkapitän Brandenburg still had a complement of nine torpedoes and he was determined to make them count.

With great expertise he had managed to evade the Asdic of the outer screen and now lay in wait on the port side of the convoy, close to the first column. He knew that now he was amongst the ships, as they were about to pass overhead, it would be even more difficult for them to get a contact on his boat, as the noise of their own propellers would cause the sonar to be less effective at such short range.

He looked at his watch. It was getting close to 0300 hours. He felt a little tired, not having slept for some considerable time, and paused for a moment. Should he risk raising the attack periscope? If he did, there was a danger of it being spotted by an eagle-eyed lookout. If he didn't, then he would have little chance of scoring a hit, and what was the point of getting into this position if he was not going to attack? He was here to do a job and was intent on doing just that.

However, Brandenburg's belief that the Royal Navy's Asdic was too temperamental to discover him so close to the convoy was ill-founded. At the same time as he was contemplating raising the attack periscope, a faint echo was picked up by the nearest destroyer, HMS *Impulsive*, commanded by 32-year-old Lieutenant Commander Edward Roper, which at the time was 800 yards away. Realizing how close the possible U-boat was to the merchant ships, he headed to the area and commenced an immediate depth-charge run, with orders for the charges to be set at 50ft. As the charges exploded in the destroyer's wake, the Asdic contact was lost due to the sound of the explosions and the propeller noise from the merchant ships which were also approaching the position.

Beneath the waves, Brandenburg knew immediately that he had a problem. Without any kind of warning and unable therefore to take evasive action, the boat was violently rocked by an explosion in the water extremely close to the hull, throwing the crew around the central control room. Before they had chance to pick themselves up, more explosions came in rapid succession, tossing the boat from side to side.

Seawater immediately began to pour in, and the lights started to flicker. Seeing a look of complete horror on the faces of those around him, he knew, as did his crew, that there was nothing they could do to fix this. The hull had clearly been breached, and to have any chance of survival they would have to surface and either put themselves at the mercy of the British, or try to fight them off with the deck gun. In his heart he knew there was little chance of coming out of this alive should he decide on the latter course.

Realizing he had no other option, he gave the order to surface while there was still a chance. Composing themselves, the crew proceeded to carry out his instruction.

Above the waves, the *Impulsive* was turning back to carry out another run. However, in order to come round in an arc, the destroyer was now sailing between the SS *Kentucky* and SS *Charles McCormack*, the second and third ships of the first column. The first ship of the column, the SS *Empire Baffin* was now almost directly on top of where the destroyer had dropped its charges.

From that ship, something was spotted in the water. Seamen working on the foredeck could see a long, dark, cylindrical shape slowly rising in front of them. Shouting excitedly to the bridge, they pointed to the spot. Alfred Grossmith-Mason, the ship's gunnery officer, was in charge on the bridge and gave the order to head for it at full speed.

Brandenburg had by now resigned himself to the fact that his war was over. As commander of *U-457* he had sunk three merchant vessels totalling over 24,000 tonnes of shipping in the two patrols he had carried out. This was a haul to be proud of, he thought, since many U-boat commanders had yet to score any hits at all. Now that his time as a U-boat skipper was ending, whether as a prisoner of war or as a more permanent statistic, he felt immensely sad. He was a skilled submariner and still had a lot to offer.

His thoughts were immediately interrupted as the U-boat struck something in its ascent, so sharply that everyone was once again thrown to the floor. And then the boat began to roll over, again and again, tossing Brandenburg and his crew around like rag dolls as she broke in two and seawater engulfed what was left of her. Death had come quickly to all forty-five men on board, as what was left of *U-457* sunk to the bottom of the Barents Sea.

Had any of the U-boat crew managed to stay alive a few seconds longer, their days would have ended to the sound of cheering from the *Empire Baffin*. As the U-boat was about to break the surface, the huge British merchant ship had struck her, rolling her over and causing her to spin and break up, before what was left of the wreck sank beneath the waves.

Moving back into position, the *Empire Baffin* sailed on, leaving Lieutenant Commander Roper on the *Impulsive*, now following behind, to confirm the kill after sighting oil and debris rising to the surface at the spot where he had dropped the depth charges.

* * *

In Bardufoss, Werner Klümper looked out of his office window and lit a cigarette. The weather was becoming increasingly bad, and he knew that flying today would be impossible. Rain and sleet were lashing the panes, and he now had a report in front of him that thick fog was predicted to envelop the ships of PQ18 later in the day.

With the morale of his men at an all-time low, and with so many aircraft out of action, this came as something of a relief. His remaining crews would get the day off and, should the bad weather continue, this break in operations might last longer.

Klümper did not know what to feel. The success of the *Goldene Zange* attack on the 13th had not been repeated. Had the squadrons been allowed to press home their advantage and repeat this tactic, he was convinced that they could have inflicted heavier damage on the convoy. However, Herman Göring had not allowed this, ordering them instead to focus on sinking the aircraft carrier. Was this a good tactic, he wondered? Well, it had its merits, because the Sea Hurricanes had been an incessant problem, but surely the aim was to stop the merchant ships making it to Archangelsk to unload their cargoes? Was the sinking of the carrier merely to satisfy Göring's personal pride? To give him something to brag about in Berlin? Maybe. But to focus on this ahead of the main objective would surely come back to haunt them. The cargoes on those ships were ultimately destined for Stalingrad, a battle that simply had to be won if Germany was to gain victory in this war.

So many of his men were now gone. Some very good men. Friends of his. Shot down by the impressive firepower of the Royal Navy, not to mention the skill of some of the gunners on the merchant ships themselves. Flying into those barrages had been horrendous. Most of his men had acted bravely, facing the flak and avoiding the British aircraft without regard for their own safety. Some had quickly dropped their bombs and turned away, without really pushing home the attack; he was convinced of it. But who could blame them? The chances of coming back from a sortie were diminishing each time they took off.

And so, as the rain and sleet continued to lash his window panes, he stubbed out his cigarette in an ashtray on his desk and stood up. He would go to the mess and get some breakfast, then put his feet up for a while. As far as he was concerned, he deserved it.

* * *

The sinking of *U-457* did not deter the other boats of the wolf-pack in any way. Just after 1030 hours, the captain of the destroyer HMS *Offa* sighted a U-boat around five miles away. Together with HMS *Opportune* she set off to investigate, but on seeing the two ships approaching, the U-boat submerged and, despite a number of depth-charge runs, proved to be elusive. The attack was called off, and the ships returned to their positions in the outer screen.

By this time convoy PQ18 was only 300 miles from the Kola Inlet, and it would take the ships just over one more day before they crossed over with the returning QP14, which had now been at sea for three days, heading towards its rendezvous point with the Fighting Destroyer Escort.

The fog that had been expected now descended on the ships, cutting visibility down to almost nil. The only vessels that could now be seen from any of the bridges were the white and pale green warships as they patrolled the columns. Navigation lights were turned on and chip floats were launched. These were flattish boat-shaped buoys, slightly raised at the bow and approximately 6–8ft long dropped from a ship's stern; as they were dragged through the water they would fling up spray and a miniature bow-wave to show the next ship in line how far she was from the one ahead. This was done to eliminate the danger of collisions in foggy conditions.

Burnett was now preparing for the second phase of the journey, escorting the returning QP14 back to safety. Not wanting to draw attention to the fact that as well as the *Scylla*, the whole of the Fighting Destroyer Escort, HMS *Avenger* and one of the anti-aircraft ships were leaving PQ18, he gave the order for them to do this in stages. For the remainder of the journey, PQ18 would receive air cover from Russian-based Soviet fighters and the single Sea Hurricane on the CAM ship, SS *Empire Morn*. Operation Orator's Catalinas would also continue their anti-submarine sweeps, since the Swordfish were no longer available.

First to leave and take up escort duties with the returning ships would be *Scylla* herself, accompanied by a single flotilla of destroyers and followed shortly after by a further two flotillas and the anti-aircraft ship HMS *Alynbank*. Finally, the *Avenger* with two more destroyers and the final flotilla would follow soon after.

Burnett would have liked to have taken PQ18 all the way to Archangelsk, but this was not possible. The orders were to provide the same cover for QP14 as for the outbound convoy and, with many of the men and ships having gone through the hell that had been the disastrous PQ17 a few months earlier, it was the least they could do for them. However, this left only two destroyers and one anti-aircraft ship, the *Ulster Queen*, along with the trawlers, corvettes and minesweepers, to take PQ18 on the final leg. They would also be supported by Soviet destroyers, which would come out to meet them from their bases in northern Russia. For the remainder of the journey to Archangelsk, the escort ships would be under the command of Commander Archibald Russell of the Admiralty-type destroyer HMS *Malcolm*.

* * *

Having experienced a few initial problems, QP14 had set sail nearly seven hours later than planned on the 13th but had managed to make up the lost time en route to the rendezvous point. At that moment, they were on course to meet the outgoing ships as planned, but due to the heavy weather conditions and fog and snow squalls reducing visibility to a minimum, it would be some time later than intended before Burnett was to put his plan into practice.

Fearing enemy air attack en route, Captain Crombie, the close escort commander on HMS *Bramble*, had had a nervous time of it. With no air cover to speak of, a single Ju-88 had been circling around the ships, keeping tabs on them. Two Soviet fighters were also seen in the skies above but made no attempt to engage the German aircraft. Crombie feared a concerted attack could be launched at any moment against the seventeen merchantmen he was to protect until reaching the rendezvous with Burnett and the Fighting Destroyer Escort; but these anxieties proved ill-founded as no attack materialized, more than likely due to the losses the Luftwaffe had sustained in its attacks on PQ18.

The sooner he sighted the destroyers and, more importantly, the aircraft carrier, the sooner he would feel a little safer.

* * *

With temperatures at an all-time low, more working parties were sent out to clear decks of ice and snow. The threat of air attack had by now virtually completely disappeared, but everyone knew that once the skies were clear again, the Luftwaffe would be back.

The closer the convoy got to Russia, the more support it was receiving from Hopps and the aircraft of Operation Orator. Catalinas were now carrying out constant anti-submarine sorties and mine sweeps in the path of the approaching ships; and although it was known that wolf-packs were in the area, they were keeping themselves to themselves for the time being. This respite from enemy activity was welcomed, but at the same time every man on the ships knew full well that this was just a lull; the enemy would be back again soon enough.

On board the *Scylla*, the loudspeaker crackled and a familiar voice rang out throughout the ship:

'We will be leaving the convoy shortly and steaming north to escort the homeward-bound convoy ... our present convoy is now within short steaming time ... well within range of Russian fighters.'

This gave Robert Hughes a feeling of great achievement. The convoy had covered hundreds of miles, under constant attack, but the majority of the ships were now on the final run to the White Sea to deliver their cargoes to the Russians. They had lost a lot of ships – too many – but when he looked back at the vast array of vessels they were leaving behind he could see that the job had been done, and done well.

After sending messages of good luck, the *Scylla* moved away, with the remaining escort ships closing up to fill the gaps left by those departing. Hughes hoped they had done enough. There was still a few hundred miles to cover before the ships of PQ18 would finally anchor at the dockside in Archangelsk. Their journey was by no means over.

It did not seem too long before QP14 came into sight. Hughes could see they were not lying as low in the water as the ships they had just left, mainly due to their being filled with ballast instead of heavy freight. Some had substantial deck cargoes of timber and wood pulp, part payment for the war materiel that had been delivered. This convoy was a lot smaller than PQ18, less than half its size, and he was determined to protect them as well as he had those that had been escorted to Russia. The men on these ships had been through enough already and they just needed to get home safely.

And so, with two convoys now at sea, one approaching Russia and the other heading for home, the Germans had to decide which one was the most important to destroy. They did not have much time left if they wanted to stop PQ18; it would not be long before its ships reached port. With air cover now reduced and the Fighting Destroyer Escort gone, would PQ18 be a much easier target than it had been earlier?

Flying Officer Arthur Burr, the Sea Hurricane pilot on the SS *Empire Morn* who had been so frustrated at having to watch his colleagues take to the skies over the last few days and not being able to join them, might yet see the action he so craved.

Chapter 10

17– 18 September

As the Fighting Destroyer Escort settled into position around the seventeen returning ships of convoy QP14, Russia-bound PQ18 continued its journey eastwards towards the White Sea.

With the weather worsening, the chances of air attack on either of the convoys was almost zero, the only planes braving the weather being the huge Blohm and Voss BV138 seaplanes used for tracking and reconnaissance. They had been ever-present, almost as much as the U-boats. Although this lack of enemy air activity was welcomed, the threat of storms and heavy seas took its place as the immediate hazard.

With the much reduced escort under the command of Commander Russell on HMS *Malcolm*, PQ18 ploughed its way through the wind and sleet and the huge waves and squalls that battered the ships as they doggedly ploughed ever closer to the White Sea. It was with relief that, early that morning, two Soviet destroyers, the *Gremyashchi* and *Sorushitelni*, were sighted to the south heading in their direction. These had been sent to give the convoy added protection now that the cover had been depleted and also to guide them into port. Upon reaching the convoy they settled on each beam.

On board the rescue ship SS *Copeland*, Anatoly Sakharov, the captain of the ill-fated SS *Stalingrad*, the first of the merchant ships to be sunk in the early hours of 13 September, had now made a full recovery from the forty minutes he had spent in the icy waters of the Arctic Ocean. He had been treated with much compassion by those on board the British ship, and now he was fully recovered he wanted to do more to assist the convoy. Although he would have much preferred to bring his own ship in to dock at his home city, he knew the waters of the Dvina River well and offered his services as a pilot to those that had been more fortunate in making it to Archangelsk.

Having lost his own ship which, like the city, had been named for the Soviet leader, he had no idea how he would be treated once ashore. Not only had the ship been sunk with the loss of twenty-two people, but all the cargo had gone down with her, and this loss of materiel would be considered more important to those in power than those poor souls who had perished. Maybe if he contributed to the safe passage of the other vessels, the loss of his ship might be looked on with greater sympathy. After all, there had been absolutely nothing he could have done to prevent it. The death of so many of his shipmates and passengers, some of them his friends, was still weighing heavily upon him.

As the morning wore on, PQ18 was hit by south-easterly gale-force winds, making it almost impossible for sailors to work on deck to clear the ice. However, this essential duty still had to be performed, as temperatures of -20°C froze water on impact to decks and superstructures, adding to the already thick clumps of ice that covered all exposed areas. Inside mess-decks, anything that could be stored away was secured in lockers and cupboards, and men hung on for dear life as their ships were thrown about in all directions, waves surging over the decks as the hulls were battered by this sheer force of nature. For those on lookout duties this experience was even more extreme; being higher up, they felt the sway of the ship more keenly, whilst the icy wind blew more fiercely into their faces.

The storms continued throughout the day with no let-up. For a short period a group of Ju-88s was spotted, but due to the weather conditions they did not come in to attack and instead circled the convoy for a few minutes before deciding to head for home. At around midday, two more Soviet destroyers joined the convoy and took up position, one ahead and the other astern. These were the *Listenev* and *Luzhkov*, two huge but dated ships. The sight of them riding the waves, each carrying four 5-inch guns and two 3-inch anti-aircraft weapons, was most welcome; apart from the few remaining destroyers and the *Ulster Queen*, the anti-aircraft capability of the convoy had been severely reduced when the destroyers left the previous day.

At 1530 hours another pleasing sight appeared on the horizon. A Catalina of 210 Squadron, part of Operation Orator, was seen in the sky above carrying out its anti-submarine patrol. With the Swordfish no longer available, it was now up to these large aircraft to carry out this essential duty. After passing visual signals it sighted a German aircraft shadowing the convoy and set off to intercept. However, the German pilot, refusing to engage, turned and headed away, leaving the Catalina to resume its search for the dreaded U-boats.

The rest of the day passed without any further contact with the enemy, and the convoy was left to concentrate on simply staying afloat. Now the Germans had decided to leave them alone for the time being, Mother Nature herself had taken over in trying her damnedest to stop the ships from reaching port.

* * *

The weather on the morning of the 18th was much the same as the previous day. Storms and high seas again battered the ships as they struggled onwards, inching closer and closer to Archangelsk. However, unlike the previous day, as the morning wore on, the storms and rough seas abated somewhat, meaning that the threat of air attack returned.

At 1000 hours a spotter aircraft was again sighted. Fearing an enemy air assault and concerned by his lack of substantial protection against it, Commander Russell ordered the anti-aircraft balloons to be raised from the ships. The *Ulster Queen* had now taken up a position at the rear of the convoy, as an attack from the north had been considered most likely; the convoy was sailing south between the desolate Kanin Point to the west and the land mass north of Archangelsk to the east.

A group of Ju-88s had by this time appeared above the clouds, using occasional gaps to rain down bombs at the ships below. As gunners turned their barrels skyward to deal with them, yet another threat was at that moment heading their way, led by a man who had seen much action over the past few days. Twenty-five minutes after the barrage balloons were sent aloft, twelve more enemy planes were spotted approaching, astern of the convoy.

* * *

Werner Klümper believed this was going to be his last chance to stop PQ18. Now having only twelve serviceable aircraft in his squadron with which to attack the convoy, he had given the order to hit it from the rear in another *Goldene Zange* formation. The convoy was at the very limit of the planes' range, so this had to be a quick strike; they could not linger long in the area.

This was also to be the first of a two-wave attack. His own squadron would come in from the rear, followed by another group of fifteen coming from the west. Meanwhile, ahead of him, the Ju-88s of III/KG30 Squadron, led by Captain Hajo Herrmann, were already harrying the ships by dropping bombs through gaps in the clouds, hopefully diverting their attention from his approaching *Goldene Zange* torpedo run.

This attack was supposed to have been a joint effort by the Luftwaffe and the nearby U-boat wolf-pack, but the submarines had not been quick enough to get themselves into position, so it was up to the planes to carry out the mission on their own.

The loss of so many of his aircraft over the past few days weighed heavily upon Klümper. The initial successes had not been repeated, and he considered this an opportunity missed. Concentrating on sinking the aircraft carrier when the convoy was there for the taking had been a mistake which still rankled with him; but now that the threat of enemy fighter aircraft had diminished and the majority of the destroyers had been diverted to protect the returning convoy, his chances had improved. However, with most of his squadron either destroyed or unserviceable, he was under no illusion that any success against so many ships would be severely limited.

He dropped his He-111 to 50ft above the waves and looked to his sides to see the other eleven planes do likewise, spreading out in line abreast to attack. Ahead he could see the guns on the ships firing into the clouds, trying to hit Herrmann's Ju-88s as they appeared in the gaps. There was also a mass of barrage balloons swaying in the wind on their steel cables; these would need to be avoided once the planes had released their torpedoes.

As the flight came nearer to the ships, the air around was suddenly filled with exploding shells spraying fragments of shrapnel in all directions, as the gunners on the escort ships, now placed at the rear to repel the kind of threat he was posing, turned their attentions to his squadron. It was an intense barrage which rocked his plane from side to side as the bursting shells caused massive turbulence all around. He cursed as he saw many of his crews prematurely dropping their ordnance and pulling away, unwilling to fly through another intense barrage.

It was far too soon for the torpedoes to have any effect. They would be seen coming from far away, giving any ships in their path ample time to take avoiding action. Whether this was nerves, fear or a miscalculation on the part of his pilots, he did not know, but he could not think about that just yet. However, given the fire being aimed at the squadron, he could hardly blame them.

And then his and the remaining aircraft were within range. With the ships 600 yards away, the pilots released their torpedoes and immediately pulled back on their control columns to gain height, as the anti-aircraft shells from the big guns were now joined by smaller-calibre weapons as they got closer to the ships. With the momentum of the flight taking them amongst the convoy, the He-111s let loose with their cannon, strafing whichever vessels were in their path; but with the returning fire being so strong, and wishing to avoid the steel cables that stretched into the sky above them, Klümper decided the situation was becoming too dangerous to continue. Ahead of him, one of his squadron had succumbed to the determined combined firepower of the convoy, taking multiple hits before crashing in flames into the sea.

With his torpedoes now released and realizing that to continue the attack from this height was foolhardy, he gave the order for the squadron to turn for home. As far as he was concerned, his job was done. He had made a supreme effort to stop PQ18, and many of his men had made the ultimate sacrifice and perished in the attempt. However, as he looked back at the huge number of merchant ships still afloat and steaming towards Archangelsk, in his heart of hearts he knew that the attempt had again fallen short and that PQ18 would deliver most of its cargo to the Soviets.

He turned in his seat and looked out at the remaining aircraft of I/KG26. He counted only eight more besides his own. Another three gone. Another three crews almost certainly dead and fifteen more men lost in this battle. In the space of less than a week his squadron had been virtually wiped out.

* * *

As Klümper and what was left of I/KG26 turned away and headed for home, one of the torpedoes they had loosed found its mark.

Sailing as the second vessel in the port column, the American cargo ship SS *Kentucky* was struck amidships and immediately caught fire. The captain had seen the approaching torpedo only when it was too late to avoid, but he had enough time to give a warning, allowing the crew to move away from where it was likely to hit. The resulting explosion almost completely destroyed the bridge on the port side, and thick, acrid smoke enveloped the whole of the ship as fires quickly spread along her deck.

With orders to abandon ship, the crew made their way to the lifeboats. The minesweeper HMS *Sharpshooter* and the trawler HMS *Cape Mariato* headed towards them to effect a rescue. However, seeing the ship away from the main body of the convoy, in distress and listing, two Ju-88s of Herrmann's III/KG30 Squadron descended from their cloud cover to drop bombs and finish her off. As the crew frantically rowed the lifeboats away from this renewed attack and towards the safety of the rescue ships, the bombs hit home, leaving the ship burning furiously.

However, the SS *Kentucky* was not to sink so easily, and it was a further forty-five minutes before she finally succumbed to her injuries and sank beneath the waves.

Their fuel running low, the remaining planes of III/KG30 also made a turn for home. Having destroyed only one ship, and having lost a number of aircraft, it was now up to the second wave of He-111 torpedo-bombers, coming up from the west, to deal the convoy a mortal blow.

The time was now 1130 hours. A request had been put in earlier to release the Sea Hurricane from the CAM ship SS *Empire Morn*, but due to her position, some technical problems and the sea conditions at the time, it had not been possible to launch it. However, that situation had now changed.

* * *

17–18 September   121

Flying Officer Arthur Burr was sitting in the cockpit of the single Sea Hurricane on the bow of the SS *Empire Morn*. He had been there since 1015 that morning. If there was a time when his services were needed, then this was surely it. There were no Soviet fighters in the sky to protect them, and if the German pilots were skilled and determined, the anti-aircraft balloons swaying in the wind on their steel cables were not going to stop them. A request had been put forward for Soviet air support, but as yet no Russian planes had shown themselves. Burr's was the only available Allied fighter aircraft.

On first sighting the German planes earlier that morning, he had made his way to the Hurricane and climbed into the cockpit. He had looked on in frustration, unable to do a thing about it, as the He-111s of the first wave and those above in the clouds had attacked the ships. The position of the *Empire Morn* and the sea conditions had been the reasons he was given for not being released into the sky. However, a launch at that time would not have been possible due to the plane having suffered a complete electrical failure. This problem had been thankfully short-lived; the mechanics had simply changed the battery and soon all was well again.

Now, as a second wave of torpedo-bombers had been sighted to the west, he was given the order to stand by and prepare himself to take to the skies. This was his time and he was ready for it. Checking the instrument panel again, he saw that everything was as it should be. The aircraft was good to go.

As was routine, the trolley receiving bar had been released at dawn and the aircraft was already warm, having been started up at intervals by the supporting airmen. At once, the master ordered the international flag, code F, to be hoisted, indicating to the other ships that the CAM was about to launch the Sea Hurricane.

Burr took a breath. This was it. Over the past week he had watched impatiently, eager to join the fight, as the pilots on the *Avenger* had regularly flown to take on the He-111s and Ju-88s. However, with these colleagues gone, he was now on his own, and the odds did not look good. At least fifteen torpedo-bombers were approaching fast, and he would have to try and repel them alone.

He looked down to the foredeck. One of the airmen had removed the pins and was showing them to him. He nodded an acknowledgement and watched as the man took the pins to the Catapult Duty Officer (CDO). With the pins now released, Burr set the flaps to 30° and the rudder a third to the right.

Turning to the bridge, the CDO raised the blue flag above his head, indicating to the master on the bridge that the plane was ready for take-off. Immediately, the master ordered the ship to be turned into the wind and, after positioning himself and his officers on the starboard bridge to avoid any backfire from the launch rockets, he raised his blue flag in response, authorizing the launch.

Burr looked out and saw the CDO now waving his blue flag at him. This was the final signal to tell him that authorization had been given and to prepare himself to be catapulted into the sky. He raised his left hand in acknowledgement and then, using his right, he opened the throttle to full, tightened the throttle friction nut, pressed his head back into the head-rest and his right elbow tightly against his hip. Taking a deep breath, he brought down his left hand, telling the CDO he was ready to go.

Counting to three, the CDO waited until the bow of the ship was raised, then hit the switch to fire the catapult rockets.

Burr was instantly forced back into his seat as the rockets ignited with a deafening roar, jetting out a streak of flame and smoke against the port side of the bridge, leaving dark scorch marks on the grey metal. Immediately the Sea Hurricane was blasted into the sky, Burr pulled back on the control column to gain height. The CDO and ground crew on the *Empire Morn* had done an excellent job; he couldn't have asked for a more perfect take-off. Gaining height quickly and settling into the flight, he banked away from the ship and glanced at the deck. He could see the crew waving at him, wishing him good luck, and he raised his hand in acknowledgement.

However, now he had to focus. After so long cooped up on the *Empire Morn*, it felt good to be in the air again. But he knew he had an essential job to do. How long he stayed in the sky was up to him and the skills he had acquired as a pilot with the Royal Air Force.

All at once he came under fire, but not from the fast approaching enemy planes. Some gunners on the merchantmen, not expecting to see a British aircraft in the air so close to the ships, opened fire with their machine-guns and Oerlikons, believing it was an enemy. Burr weaved the Hurricane from side to side, hoping to throw off this friendly fire. Not realizing their mistake, the gunners continued to fire at him until he was out of range.

Not to be put off by this idiocy, and turning his attention to the west, Burr pushed forward on the throttle to meet the oncoming threat. Ahead were fifteen Heinkel He-111s, determined to sink those ships beneath him. He looked down at them. It was only now that he was in the sky that he could appreciate the sheer size of the convoy: eight columns of huge ships, plodding steadily through the ice, en route to deliver their much-needed supplies to the Red Army. It was now he understood fully just how important his mission was. The planes he was about to face were hell-bent on sinking as many of those ships as they could – maybe one last attempt to stop the thousands of tonnes of cargo from reaching port.

But Burr was equally determined to stop them. It was a daunting task, he knew. Just how effective could a single British fighter be against over a dozen formidable and battle-hardened German pilots?

With instructions to climb to an altitude of 700ft and to set out to the port quarter, Burr at once saw the Heinkels below him, flying in at only 50ft above the waves in line abreast.

Ignoring the odds, he pushed forward on the control column and dived down upon them, like a falcon hunting its prey, the gap closing with each passing second. Fixing one of the He-111s in his sights, he flipped the lid of the column with his thumb and, when he determined he was within effective range, pressed down hard, firing a long burst from the 7.7mm Browning machine guns on the outer wing panels.

The Heinkels immediately fired back, but Burr ignored the tracer flying around his small aircraft, his mind totally focused on what he had to do. At once, he saw his bullets hitting their mark, smashing into the engine and nose of the target plane. Smoke began to issue from the He-111's starboard engine.

All around him flak was starting to burst as the destroyers and *Ulster Queen* opened up against the formation. Now having to dodge the fire from the escort ships along with the Germans' machine guns, Burr expertly manoeuvred the Hurricane into another attack position, coming around again to run at the damaged Heinkel from the starboard side.

Burr opened up once more, firing a long burst into the stricken German aircraft. As he flew over it he saw it was now in flames; unable to control his aircraft any longer, the enemy pilot could do nothing to avoid crashing into the sea. Moving to avoid the mortally damaged aircraft, another He-111 pilot attempted an evasive manoeuvre, but he too was unable to stop his aircraft hitting the water, where it cartwheeled, one of the wings separating from the fuselage.

Burr felt exhilarated. In the matter of only a couple of minutes he had downed a He-111 torpedo-bomber and caused another to crash into the sea. Disturbed by Burr's success, the rest of the German formation was beginning to break up. Quickly he checked his weapons and saw that he had spent all his ammunition on the two attacks.

And then the Fighter Direction Officer, Lieutenant Carrique, came over the radio.

'Patrol to the starboard side, Arthur. See what you can do.'

'I'm out of ammo,' he replied. '... but they don't know that.'

Burr pulled back on the control column and turned to where Carrique had instructed. Observing the remaining He-111s attempting to form up again, he flew directly at them.

Seeing the Hurricane coming round again and heading directly towards them in an aggressive manner, the pilots of the He-111s again broke formation and headed for the safety of the clouds. They had just seen two of their colleagues fall into the sea and had no desire to join them.

Burr headed into the clouds after the He-111s and continued to buzz them, preventing them from launching any kind of coordinated attack on the ships below. After a few minutes he checked his fuel gauge. Seventy gallons left. It might be enough to save the aircraft if he made land, and he didn't much fancy ditching into the icy waters of the Arctic Ocean.

He flicked the mic.

'Can you give me the distance and vector of the nearest airfield. I may be able to save the kite.'

After a few moments, Carrique's voice sounded in his ears.

'Keg Ostrov is 240 miles south-south-east, across the river from Archangelsk. Head for that . . . and well done!'

Burr turned the aircraft in the direction given and headed away from the convoy. He had done all he could. He had managed to break up the attack and downed two He-111s in the process. After flying for fifteen minutes he hit a fog bank. Flying at altitudes of between 200 and 2,000ft, he sighted landfall and was able to pinpoint his position. As he approached Archangelsk he fired off his recognition flares; the last thing he needed was to be shot down by Soviet fighter planes or anti-aircraft guns.

At 1415 hours, with five gallons of fuel left in his reserve tanks, equating to only six minutes of flying time, Flying Officer Arthur Burr landed successfully at Keg Ostrov airfield. He had managed to single-handedly repel the second wave of He-111s which, after being harassed by him, had been unable to launch any kind of attack on the ships and had turned for home lest they run out of fuel.

However, the Ju-88s remained in the clouds until just after midday, when they too turned for home, leaving the ships of convoy PQ18 only a couple of hundred miles away from the sanctuary of the Dvina River and the port of Archangelsk.

* * *

It was only after the Ju-88s had left the area that the Russian planes finally arrived. At 1315 hours two Soviet MB biplanes circled the convoy a couple of times before heading back to their airfield. This was purely to count the number of ships heading towards Archangelsk so that the logistics of how they were to be unloaded could be arranged.

However, although the planes had left the area and the U-boat threat seemed to be diminishing the closer they got to the bottleneck that was the entrance to the White Sea, the weather decided that it had not yet done with the ships of PQ18. With the light fading and the wind starting to pick up once more, it was surprising to see a number of Ju-88s returning late in the afternoon to carry out more bombing from the clouds. Again, as earlier in the day, they had no success and did not hang around for long, clearly deciding that the increasingly bad weather and fading light was not conducive to a productive attack.

Now the ships were heading south, darkness came earlier. By 1700 hours the sun had fallen below the horizon, and going out on deck to clear the ice and snow was decidedly trickier, but still it had to be done. In gale-force winds, men who had spent the best part of the day fending off enemy air attacks were once again called upon to carry out this laborious task.

As dusk was starting to fall, land was sighted to starboard. This was Cape Gorodetski, a significant point on the run into the White Sea. Boddam-Whetham ordered the convoy to break from its eight columns and form into just two, in order to negotiate their entry into the White Sea more easily. Once inside its waters, they would then head down to the entrance of the Dvina River, where they would be met by Russian boats which would provide pilots to take them into Archangelsk itself for unloading.

They were nearly there.

But the weather wasn't done with them just yet. Coming from almost nowhere, the strong winds turned to gale force, whipping up the waves to a height of 30 or 40ft, the rain coming down by the bucket load. As the ships attempted to negotiate these treacherous waters, the rain became a blizzard, throwing hail, sleet and snow at the ships as they tried to stay in line.

It was not long before visibility was down to zero, requiring the ships' navigation lights to be turned on and their chip floats again thrown from the sterns.

And so, as 18 September drew to a close, the sailors who had endured another day of almost constant battle were once again subjected to a night of horrendous sailing conditions. But with the assurance that port would be reached in the next day or so, they supposed they could put up with a little more of it if they were to get there safely.

Chapter 11

19–20 September

The gale force winds and blizzards continued throughout the night without let-up, whipping the sea into a frenzy. It was now impossible for the ships to keep the two-column formation, and consequently, when day broke on September 19, they were scattered far and wide. With the seas still throwing waves 30 and 40ft high, and snow and hail pounding the ships' bridges, visibility was again down to almost nil. There was nothing the sailors could do other than brave it out.

The only saving grace was that the likelihood of either a Luftwaffe or U-boat attack was also down to zero. There was no way war could be waged in these atrocious conditions.

However, it wasn't only the Germans who were grounded by the weather. The Catalinas of Operation Orator, which had continually swept the seas north of Norway from their base in Grasnaya, were also out of action, having been forced to abandon their sorties when the weather became too hostile. The convoy was now left totally alone to fight its way through the storm and get into position for the final run in to port.

With only a few miles left before they hit the mouth of the Dvina River and from there the docks at Archangelsk, the captains were mentally preparing themselves for the end of the voyage. The previous day, Boddam-Whetham and Commander Russell had agreed to send the minesweepers ahead to ensure the waters they were approaching were free of enemy mines. German planes had been sighted in the area over the last few days, and although the Russians had been patrolling the waters, Russell thought it prudent to make sure, in his own mind, that this threat was no longer a concern.

For the men on the ships it seemed to be one thing after another. Thoroughly exhausted from having to fight a continuous battle for the last week, along with lack of sleep and the absence of hot food, the journey had taken its toll on most of them. They slept wherever they could find a vacant spot, the motion of the sea throwing them around and waking them every few minutes. Their eyes bloodshot from lack of sleep, their clothes stinking, their beards ragged, they were a motley band. But they had done their duty and done it well. They could tidy themselves up once they were in a place of safety.

The loss of thirteen ships was a heavy price to pay, but it looked now as if the majority of those that had set out were going to make it through. It would take an almighty effort from the Germans to stop them now; their own losses seemed to have been equally heavy, and time was running out. An untold number of planes had been blasted from the sky, evidenced by the depleted numbers that returned each day, and the sinking of three U-boats had ensured that those still out there were hesitant in committing themselves to attack. But on 19 September, due to the state of the ocean, there was very little chance of that happening.

With navigation a problem during the night because of the weather, and radio beacons alone being insufficient to steer by, one of the minesweepers was stationed at the entrance to the Dvina River to act as a marker, with the others set at three-mile intervals to mark the safe route. The convoy was then to lie at anchor near to the fairway buoy and wait to be called in. Boddam-Whetham tasked the Motor Minesweepers with assisting the five Russian pilots to take the freighters in to Archangelsk, but with the weather so bad, these men had to return to port, leaving the ships to brave the storm at anchor until such time as it was safe for them to return.

As 19 September drew to a close, this is where the ships of PQ18 remained, stuck at anchor in a howling gale, with the destination they had fought so hard to reach only a few short miles away. They could see it; to the south, the huge landmass that was Russia was waiting for them, as desperate to receive their cargoes as they were to give them up.

Through the early hours of 20 September it was all the ships could do just to stay afloat. As the wind, rain and hail pummelled them, it was inevitable that some would suffer real damage, and it was not long before a number experienced serious problems.

HMS *Harrier*, having been forced to head out to sea, lost power to her steering engine and had to be hand-steered in atrocious conditions. It wasn't until early afternoon that a repair was carried out and she was able to rejoin the convoy.

The trawlers *Cape Argona* and *St Kenan*, two of those ships that had performed so heroically in rescuing stricken sailors from the sea a few days previously, had suffered major movement of their ballast; the latter almost capsized; the storm tearing away a lifeboat that had been made ready in case the ship needed to be abandoned, at the same time damaging the davits.

The larger ships were faring no better. The US freighter SS *Exford* lost both of her anchors, and one of her lifeboats was swept out to sea. With no way of remaining stationary, the captain requested a pilot be boarded to take her to safety down the channel that had been swept by the minesweepers. The request was duly complied with, and a pilot bravely boarded the ship.

However, after an hour they came across three more merchantmen that had been grounded, and the wind swept the ship towards them, narrowly avoiding a collision and in the process becoming grounded herself. After an attempt was made to refloat her, she again ran aground, and it was there that she stayed for the remainder of the night.

Further ships hit trouble in the course of the night and into the following day. More ran aground as the storm continued without let-up, having to remain motionless and exposed to the elements until the tide rose and refloated them. Others, like the trawler HMS *Daneman*, narrowly avoided collision with the bigger ships and needed to be towed to safety. It was mayhem.

This had not been the end to the journey that anyone had expected. It was to everyone's great relief that late in the day on 20 September the weather started to ease, and the convoy was again able to put itself back into some kind of order; they now waited for the pilots to come in and take the ships into port, with Anatoly Sakharov, the former captain of the ill-fated SS *Stalingrad* and native of Archangelsk, adding to their number.

With the storm abating, exhausted seamen found themselves once more out on deck clearing the ice that had formed during the extreme weather. And just like the storm that had battered the convoy over the last thirty-six hours, this task was relentless. As they chipped the ice from the superstructures they glanced southward. With Archangelsk now in sight, the end of the line was nearly there. It was almost within touching distance. Sanctuary was close, and maybe a chance to finally get some proper rest, a decent hot meal and a shower.

For by God did they need it.

It wasn't long after the storm subsided that the familiar sound of klaxons calling the men to Action Stations reverberated around the ships. Approaching from the west was a group of Junkers Ju-88s, on one final mission to cause as much damage as they could before the ships made port. However, with the anti-aircraft ship HMS *Ulster Queen*, in position at the mouth of the River Dvina, opening up a steely barrage, joined by the guns of the Royal Navy and Russian destroyers, the German pilots would not have it easy.

Dropping bombs from the cover of the clouds, some of which narrowly missed the ships still grounded and waiting to be refloated, it was not long before the planes were intercepted by Russian P-53 fighter aircraft. Realizing they were on a hiding to nothing, the Germans abandoned the attack and headed for home, three aircraft fewer than they had set out with.

And so, with the German planes disappearing from sight, it looked like the remaining ships would finally make it to Archangelsk after all.

* * *

While the spirits of the men on PQ18 were being lifted by the successful repulsion of this latest air attack, things were not going quite so well for those travelling on the return leg to Iceland with QP14.

Having made good progress after the rendezvous with HMS *Scylla*, HMS *Avenger* and the Fighting Destroyer Escort four days previously, the ships were now 300 miles north-west of Bear Island, having passed Spitzbergen, which now lay 200 miles to the east. The weather had been relatively calm compared to what their colleagues on PQ18 had endured, and they had not come under any attack from the skies, the Germans clearly focusing on the Russia-bound convoy.

The time was a little after 0600 on the morning of 20 September and, to the south of the approaching convoy, U-boat *U-435* was lying in wait.

Thirty-one-year-old Korvettenkapitän Siegfried Strelow was a career sailor, having joined the Kriegsmarine eleven years previously. Already a recipient of the Iron Cross (First and Second Class), this was Strelow's fifth patrol, having transferred to U-boats in April 1941, when he was given the command of *U-435*. In March 1942 his boat had successfully sunk the US freighter SS *Effingham* and on 13 April had hit and destroyed two ships of the returning convoy QP10 – the British freighter *Harpalion* and the Panamanian-registered *El Occidonte*.

But now, as he patrolled the waters of the northern Norwegian Sea stalking the returning ships of QP14, he had been somewhat frustrated. The destroyer screen around the merchant ships was keeping them well protected; to attempt to break that cordon and go in for the kill was tantamount to suicide. He therefore decided to change tactics; instead of hitting the freighters, he would target something quite different.

In his sights right now was a British warship. And he was determined to send her to the bottom of the sea.

Strelow ordered the torpedo tubes to be made ready and then took hold of the attack periscope.

* * *

The men on the seventeen returning merchant ships of QP14 had waited a long time for this journey and had been relieved at finally setting sail from Archangelsk a week ago. Most, having endured the infamous voyage that was PQ17 that summer, had undergone weeks of boredom in the cold of northern Russia, where they had constantly dreamed of home. Since meeting the escorts detached from PQ18 near the Kola Inlet it appeared that, despite the weather, they were making good progress. There had been heavy snow squalls and thick patches of fog, and on occasion they had had to alter course slightly to avoid icebergs that seemed to materialize out of the darkness and fog like long-forgotten Norse gods. The bad weather had caused two ships, the SS *Troubadour* and the SS *Winston Salem*, to fall behind and lose contact with the convoy.

Burnett had decided to sail as far north as was possible to avoid any chance of torpedo-bomber attack and hopefully to keep out of the U-boat patrol areas. He wanted to avoid another attack like that of 13 September, when the Golden Comb formation had sunk eight ships within only a few minutes. However, his fears were unfounded, as no attacks by the Luftwaffe were forthcoming; they were instead using what was left of their depleted resources to focus on PQ18, now hundreds of miles away. The only threat he had to consider, besides the weather, was that of the U-boat wolf-packs. With three Swordfish operating from the *Avenger*, and the Catalinas of Operation Orator carrying out patrols ahead, the convoy could not have been better covered.

It was around 1700 hours on 18 September that Burnett's attempts to avoid German submarine contact were scuppered, when one of the patrolling Catalinas spotted two U-boats some distance away to the north-west. Immediately, Burnett dispatched HMS *Onslow* to investigate, but the destroyer returned having found nothing.

As the convoy had approached Spitzbergen, the original aim had been to detach the destroyers to refuel at Bell Sound; but now, fearing that the depletion of his resources might tempt the U-boats to come in and attack, Burnett instead gave the order for one of the two oilers, stationed there as part of Force P, to join the convoy and refuel them at sea. Consequently, HMS *Fury* and HMS *Impulsive* were sent to collect the fleet oiler RFA *Oligarch*.

A further U-boat contact was made later on the 18th, when a patrolling Swordfish sighted one on the surface 20 miles to the rear of the convoy. Upon seeing the approaching aircraft, the submarine carried out an emergency dive and managed to avoid a depth-charge attack by the small aircraft; the biplane returned to the ship some time later.

On 19 September, the two lost stragglers made an appearance. The *Winston Salem*, after briefly causing a scare when she was mistaken for a German surface vessel, had managed to find the convoy again by simply following the ice-line, its captain correctly presuming that Burnett had taken the ships as far north as he possibly could. The *Troubadour*'s return to the fold, on the other hand, had been a little more dramatic; she had come under U-boat attack 70 miles to the south of the convoy, requiring Burnett to send HMS *Onslaught* and a Swordfish to assist in bringing her back to the safety of the convoy.

The fear of a U-boat attack was now growing. Many had been sighted over the last few hours, and with German spotter planes also being seen in the grey skies above, it seemed inevitable that QP14 would at some point have to defend itself from this 'scourge beneath the sea'.

* * *

On the morning of 20 September sailing conditions were quite different to that of the previous few days, with a gentle breeze wafting over the surface of a very calm sea and visibility now being excellent. However, ahead were grey skies that threatened more snow and storms, and despite this lull, nobody expected the good weather to last.

With no Luftwaffe or U-boat attacks, and the convoy now about to turn south for the final few hundred miles to Iceland, the feeling among passengers and crews was more optimistic. They had only a few days left to sail, and with the dream of home coming ever closer to being realized, it was something of a shock when, at a little after 0630 hours, a loud explosion was heard to starboard.

Carrying eighteen passengers along with her crew of 116, HMS *Leda*, a Halcyon class minesweeper sailing astern of the convoy, appeared to be in trouble. Black smoke was pouring from her funnel and fires were breaking out throughout the ship. The feared U-boat attack had now occurred

Siegfried Strelow, deep underwater in the control room of *U-435*, was feeling pleased with himself. He had let off three torpedoes and had seen two strike the British minesweeper, one hitting the forward boiler room. It was inevitable that this would sink the ship. Immediately, he ordered the U-boat to dive deeper and turned his attentions to evasive manoeuvres, since the commander of the convoy would now undoubtedly order his anti-submarine ships to seek him out and destroy him.

* * *

On *Leda*, things quickly became chaotic.

As fires raged all over the ship, those sailors unable to reach the lifeboats were jumping into the icy seas to escape the flames or avoid breathing in the thick, black, acrid smoke that now engulfed the decks.

Almost as soon as it was realized what had happened, nearby ships headed in *Leda*'s direction to pick up survivors, including the trawler HMS *Northern Gem* which was positioned on her port bow. Ordering his crew to throw scramble nets over the sides, the captain, Lieutenant William Mullender, had, within only a couple of minutes, brought his vessel alongside the stricken minesweeper to rescue as many men as he could, careful not to hit anyone already in the water. As those in the water swam frantically towards the nets, and those who were able jumped across to the safety of the *Northern Gem*'s decks, a destroyer pulled up alongside to starboard.

A voice called across to the *Northern Gem* through a loudhailer.

'Stop what you are doing and return immediately to the convoy. You are not to pick up survivors. This is to be left to the designated ships.'

Mullender was incensed. They were in the best position to help these men, who were by now piling onto his ship's deck in considerable numbers, to be greeted by comrades eager to help them. There were still men in the freezing water, and there was no way he was going to leave them there.

Grabbing his own loudhailer, Mullender put it to his lips.

'Respectfully... fuck off! I am in a position to assist and am doing so. I will return when my duty here is concluded.'

The use of such language did not go down well with the destroyer's captain, who threatened to report him when back in port. However, Mullender was not bothered one iota by this threat; there were men in severe distress who needed his help, and to delay providing it would undoubtedly mean a greater loss of life. He was in the right and he knew it. If the man was offended by his choice of words and disregard of naval etiquette, he really could not care less; he would deal with the consequences later.

By setting the engines on slow and manoeuvring gently in the water so as not to hit anyone still trying to make it to safety, the *Northern Gem* was able to pick up more survivors. They were quickly taken below decks, where they were treated for their wounds and given a tot of rum. Once all had been picked up, the trawler turned hard to starboard and headed back to its designated station. A short while later, the *Leda*, succumbing to her injury, turned onto her starboard side and slid beneath the waves, taking down with her anyone still be trapped on board.

For many of the survivors taken on board the *Northern Gem*, this was the second time they had found themselves in the icy waters of the Arctic Ocean in only a few months. Nine of them had been on the SS *Navarino* and the SS *River Afton*, two of the ships that had been sunk on convoy PQ17. Unfortunately, three of those plucked from the water, having been wounded by the explosion on board the *Leda*, died within minutes of being rescued. All in all, HMS *Northern Gem* rescued eighty-one people.

* * *

The U-boats were not quite done with QP14 just yet. Sensing more scalps, they probed the lumbering convoy, searching for any further opportunity to wreak havoc upon it.

19–20 September   133

Throughout the day, the convoy encountered a number of U-boats who were harassing the ships like a pack of hyenas, seeking any opportunity to strike. Swordfish crews from HMS *Avenger* worked tirelessly, constantly patrolling the skies around the convoy, seeking any sign of a periscope or the track of a torpedo. It quickly became clear that at least five U-boats were somewhere in the vicinity, with more probably on the way as the position of QP14 was transmitted by B-Dienst to all the packs operating in nearby waters. Ironically, now that the ships were getting closer to Iceland, the two British submarines (*P614* and *P615*) that had travelled at the rear of the convoy with PQ18, and had also joined the returning QP14 at the Kola Inlet, were due to depart shortly to return to their base at Lerwick.

Rear-Admiral Burnett on the *Scylla* saw this departure as something of an opportunity, and ordered the destroyer HMS *Opportune* to escort the two submarines to patrol 20 miles astern of the convoy, in the area he suspected some of the U-boats to be stalking.

With the weather taking another turn for the worse, it was in a heavy snow storm that, at 1517 hours, the commander of *P614*, Lieutenant Denis Beckley, sighted an unsuspecting U-boat on the surface only 1,000 yards away, after hearing the distinctive sound of the German submarine's diesel engines. Immediately, he ordered the torpedo tubes to be armed and turned in to attack.

* * *

Reinhard von Hymmen stood on the conning tower of *U-408* and pulled his collar up against the snow that was now driving hard into his face. He had so far had a very successful patrol, sinking two merchant ships in the early morning of 13 September and then coming across a burning tanker that had capsized the following afternoon, the British destroyers having failed to scuttle her after she had been torpedoed by *U-457*. He had ordered his crew to open fire on her with the 88mm deck gun, and after a few rounds the large ship had finally succumbed to her injuries and sunk beneath the waves. This was the British oiler *Atheltemplar*. Technically, by finishing off the huge abandoned tanker, he could claim a third kill. With the arrival of the returning QP14 in these northern waters, von Hymmen saw an opportunity to add to his tally.

Putting his binoculars to his eyes, he began to scan ahead. He knew the convoy to be some miles away and felt secure at being on the surface while they were so far ahead. Surely the main focus of the convoy commander was to get his remaining ships back to port successfully, and von Hymmen sincerely doubted any destroyers would leave their protective stations to patrol this far from them.

The only thing he was concerned about was enemy planes. Those outdated biplanes that had run constant patrols, buzzing above like irritating mosquitoes, had come to haunt every U-boat commander on this run. Although they were small in both number and size, and flew at very low speeds, they each carried a torpedo and a couple of depth charges, any of which could sink his boat if they got lucky. With the ships getting ever closer to Iceland, the Catalinas of the RAF Coastal Command would also come into play, their range being quite extensive. They too could cause immeasurable problems if they spotted the U-boat. It was therefore on the sky that he focused his attention.

He turned around, looking in all directions, but could see nothing in the air to worry him. But with this new snow storm came low-lying grey clouds, and should an enemy plane be directly above him, it would be difficult to spot.

And then, as he lowered the binoculars, something caught his eye on the surface around 1,000 yards to the south. It was the conning tower of a submarine. At first he thought it was another member of the wolf-pack, but there was something about it that made him pause for a second. This unidentified U-boat did not appear to be moving along the correct bearing. Instead of travelling in the same direction as his own boat, that is, towards the convoy, this submarine was heading directly for *U-408*.

And then his eyes were drawn down to the water. To his horror, he could see the tracks of a number of torpedoes.

They were all heading for him!

* * *

Beckley had made an instant decision. After sighting the U-boat in a clear patch in the snow storm he had turned to attack, firing four torpedoes in quick succession. From his vantage point on *P614*'s conning tower he watched patiently as the torpedoes closed in on the target. From what he could see, he had got the trajectory right and he was confident at least one of them would score a hit.

* * *

For a fraction of a second von Hymmen froze. This was completely unexpected. To be attacked by an enemy submarine on the surface was an irony he could not yet fully appreciate. Now he knew what those sailors on the merchant ships must have felt as they watched his own torpedoes close in on their ships. The fear was instant and immense.

'Alarm!' he shouted, pushing the two officers with him towards the open hatch.

As they slid down the ladder, he quickly followed, shouting orders to carry out an immediate crash dive. As the crew jumped to the task, he spun the wheel to seal the hatch and held his breath.

* * *

Beckley held his binoculars to his eyes and watched as the German officers rapidly evacuated the conning tower. Moving his focus lower, he could see the tracks of the torpedoes getting ever closer to the target. Just like von Hymmen was doing 1,000 yards away, he held his breath. He could only admire the speed at which the U-boat commander and his crew had reacted to the threat.

By now *P614* was around 600 yards from the U-boat. The sound of an explosion filled Beckley's ears, and a few seconds later, two more carried over to him as seawater erupted high into the air. Ahead he could see the stern of the enemy boat rise in the water in a flurry of foam and then disappear beneath the waves.

Fearing the explosions may have been heard by other U-boats who might be surfaced in the vicinity, Beckley ordered the conning tower cleared and, once inside the command room, gave the order for the submarine to dive. He had seen enough.

As far as he was concerned, he had successfully sunk an enemy U-boat and would inform the convoy commander of his achievement as soon as possible. There was no need to surface to search for debris to confirm this. He had seen the submarine hit and sink beneath the waves. It could not have survived such an attack.

* * *

However, Lieutenant Beckley was completely mistaken.

U-408 was very much still alive and active. The speed and skill with which von Hymmen and his crew had carried out the crash dive and evasive manoeuvres had ensured the boat's survival. The first torpedo had detonated before it had hit, possibly due to premature ignition of one of the warheads, with the other two exploding beneath the boat as they dropped deeper, having reached the limit of their range. The fourth had simply missed and fallen harmlessly to the bottom.

With his heart still beating faster than it ever had, von Hymmen ordered the boat on a southerly course. He knew he had been extremely lucky. Things could have gone very wrong for him and his crew, and it was partly due to his own lack of vigilance in assuming no attack would come from the sea so far away from the convoy and its escorts. To be attacked by another submarine was something he had never expected, an utterly ridiculous possibility. And this surprise attack had come very close to ending it all for him. He was determined not to make the same mistake again.

* * *

Twenty miles ahead, the convoy steamed on.

The spotter planes in the air to the south were now a constant irritation. There was no getting away from the fact that QP14's position would be relayed back to the wolf-packs. Although they knew they had no chance of hitting them, the gunners nevertheless fired occasional bursts from the anti-aircraft weapons to keep the spotters at bay, a token gesture to warn the pilots that the convoy was still able to defend itself and not to come any closer.

At around 1830 that evening Robert Hughes on HMS *Scylla* was disturbed by a siren wailing from a US Liberty ship sailing on the starboard side of the convoy. The captain of the ship, the SS *Silver Sword*, was telling the rest of the convoy they had sighted a torpedo in the water and it was headed in their direction.

Almost immediately, streams of tracer could be seen shooting towards the track of the torpedo, as the gunners on the merchant ships nearest to it opened fire in an attempt to destroy the torpedo before it could hit them. They were quickly joined by the *Scylla*'s Oerlikon, which was housed just below the blue director, the gunners pumping shell after shell into the water, desperate to detonate the cigar-shaped missile before it hit the merchant ship.

The *Silver Sword* appeared clumsy in the water, swaying from side to side as she tried to avoid this instrument of death, her deck cargo of timber and wood pulp giving the vessel an ungainly appearance. However, the efforts to stop the torpedo striking the ship were ultimately unsuccessful; only a few moments later, an enormous column of water erupted violently on her port side, catapulting huge planks of wood into the air as the deck cargo was blasted high into the sky. The ship had been hit in the bow, severely damaging the front section of the bridge.

And then it seemed as though she had let out an almighty cough, as thick black smoke erupted skyward from her funnel. A second torpedo had struck the ship in the stern, ripping off the stern post, propeller and rudder. A moment later, the aft magazine detonated, causing yet more damage to the superstructure and effectively leaving the ship dead in the water.

Without further ado, the captain gave the order to abandon ship and, wasting no time, the ship's crew and passengers headed for the lifeboats. Within moments, the two designated rescue ships SS *Rathin* and SS *Zamalek* raced to the scene to pick up survivors who had quickly clambered into the lifeboats and pulled away from the stricken vessel.

A few hundred yards away, the captain of *U-255*, Reinhardt Reche, lowered the attack periscope and gave the order to his crew to take the boat deeper and maintain a speed of only two knots. He also called for total silence. His work done for now, he needed to avoid the destroyers that were at that moment dropping depth charges anywhere where they could get the faintest of Asdic signals. However, it was as though the whole of the Royal Navy's Asdic had stopped working, since none of the depth-charge runs carried out by the destroyers came anywhere near his boat; after an hour or so, the convoy had moved further away and the danger of being hit by an underwater charge had greatly diminished.

* * *

Throughout the rest of the afternoon, numerous sightings of U-boats were made by Swordfish crews and destroyers sent out to engage them. Each time they returned to the convoy having been unsuccessful in their attempts to destroy the boats.

With the wolf-packs operating so close to the convoy, and the U-boats treating every ship as a target, be it merchant or military, Bob Burnett now had a decision to make. The *Scylla* and the *Avenger* were now serious targets for the U-boats, and he realized that the destruction of either would have a negative effect on the morale of the British, and conversely give a boost to the Germans. With the *Scylla* also carrying scores of survivors from ships sunk earlier in the voyage, he could not risk her being hit; too many lives would be lost. He had to give consideration to ensuring both ships made it back to port safely. With the convoy fast approaching the area in which Coastal Command could carry out anti-submarine sweeps from its bases in Iceland and Sullom Voe in Shetland, in place of the Swordfish, and with the Sea Hurricanes now quite redundant due to the threat of air attack having gone, it made sense to send both these ships back to Iceland at full speed.

However, there was no way he could personally leave the convoy just yet.

He gave orders to contact Ian Campbell, captain of Force B's flotilla leader, HMS *Milne*, which at that moment was sailing on the port side of QP14.

* * *

It was a little after 1830 hours on 20 September when Charlie Erswell heard a familiar voice over the loudspeaker. It was the *Milne*'s skipper, Lieutenant Commander Campbell.

'All available hands are to make their way amidships. The *Milne* is to receive a very special visitor. Admiral Burnett is to join the ship for the remainder of the journey. This is a great honour for all on board. It is an opportunity to show him what an excellent and professional crew we are.'

Having been stood down from B turret, Erswell and his good friend Charlie Robinson immediately headed amidships as ordered. Upon arrival, they found the deck was heaving with seamen kitted out in all manner of apparel to keep the chill at bay, each of them eager to see just how they were going to transfer the Admiral from one ship to the other.

The ships came together at a combined speed of 14 knots. Seen from the *Milne*, the *Scylla*'s decks looked the same, full of sailors keen to help with the transfer, or to watch as it was conducted. It seemed to Charlie that for the first time in a long while the morale of the ship was rising. Smiling and waving to each other across the short distance between the two ships, there was much merriment as the sailors exchanged greetings and banter. As Charlie waved to his colleagues on the *Scylla*, returning his wave and that of the others was Robert Hughes. The officers, looking down from the cruiser's bridge, were also smiling, this being a welcome respite from the more serious duties they had been engaged in since leaving Iceland nearly two weeks earlier. Charlie could see Burnett amongst them, wearing a heavy greatcoat and a dark cap on his head.

A rope was quickly thrown across from the *Milne* to the *Scylla*, where a couple of sailors attached a hawser line. Once fastened, all available hands hauled the hawser across and it was quickly attached to the *Scylla*'s crane. Next, a metal bosun's chair was secured to the hawser, and Burnett, seeing all was ready, bade farewell to the officers on the bridge and made his way down to the deck, cheered along by all on both ships.

Charlie was struck by the joviality of the man. He had such a burden upon his shoulders; the safety of everyone on the convoy was his responsibility; yet he bore that weight with amazing good cheer and professionalism. Charlie could not fail to be impressed.

Once safely secured in the chair, Burnett gave a wave to indicate he was ready to be moved and instructed them to 'Haul away'. At once he was lifted into the air and out over the gap between the two ships, the cap on his head amazingly staying put despite the wind. Waving to all around, he hung precariously over the water.

Charlie found the sight extremely comical and he couldn't help but laugh. At one point, the ships hit a swell and the Admiral was lost from his sight for a brief moment, the chair seeming to dip to only a few feet above the waves. However, he quickly came back up and, as the waves rose again, the crane swung him over the deck and onto the *Milne*, where a group of sailors released him from the chair to the sound of the boatswain's pipes.

In line with naval etiquette, the Rear-Admiral's flag was raised at the masthead, and the *Milne* broke away from the *Scylla* to resume her station. With Burnett now firmly ensconced on the *Milne*, the pennant on the Scylla was duly removed, command having successfully been transferred to the flotilla leader.

The day wore on monotonously. Slowly the convoy steamed ever southward across a now calm and peaceful sea. Late in the afternoon, the *Avenger* and her escorts, the destroyers HMS *Fury*, *Wheatland* and *Wilton*, turned away from the convoy and headed away at full speed for Iceland, their contribution to QP14 now over.

As the ships sailed away, Charlie pondered the decision made by the men in charge. Watching the ships slowly disappearing over the horizon, he was not altogether comfortable with what was taking place. The departure of the Swordfish, with their anti-submarine capability, was surely not a good thing. The responsibility of providing anti-submarine air cover now rested solely with Coastal Command who, as far as he was aware, were already stretched in providing cover for the ships of the Atlantic convoys as they approached the Northern and Western Approaches.

But then, he thought, he was merely an Able Seaman with less than a year's service. What did he know? He was sure those in charge knew exactly what they were doing, and he and his shipmates had to put their faith in them.

What Charlie was unaware of was that the focus of Operation Orator was now fully on the returning ships of QP14; the ships of PQ18 now at anchor on the Dvina River waiting to be taken into Archangelsk for unloading were no longer in need of anti-submarine sweeps along their path.

It was not long after the *Avenger* had parted company with the convoy that another U-boat was sighted by the Tribal class destroyer HMS *Ashanti*, which immediately proceeded in its direction to engage. However, on seeing the huge ship bearing down on him, the skipper of the submarine ordered a dive; and despite a number of depth-charge runs, the boat looked to have evaded the danger. Eventually, the destroyer gave up the chase and returned to the convoy, which by then was almost 20 miles away.

* * *

The departure of HMS *Avenger* had not gone unnoticed by the U-boat wolfpack that was currently lurking around the convoy's edges. She was moving at too great a speed to be a viable target, but it was with huge relief that the skippers of the submarines watched her disappear, taking with her those cursed Swordfish biplanes that had been such a pain in their collective necks for the past few days.

One such U-boat, the *U-703*, commanded by 26-year-old Kapitänleutnant Heinz Bielfeld, was not about to waste the opportunity provided by this lack of air cover. Giving orders to proceed with caution, he took hold of the navigation periscope and sought out a suitable target.

* * *

It was now time for the *Scylla* to take her leave. Robert Hughes, observing from the bridge, looked on as the destroyer HMS *Somali* moved across the *Scylla*'s starboard bow to take up the *Ashanti*'s position; the latter needed to be refuelled following her unsuccessful hunt for the U-boat. As the *Scylla* moved away he was shocked to see the *Somali* shudder and then come to a stop, a great tower of water soaring high into the air over her.

The destroyer had been hit by a torpedo which struck her amidships, causing extensive damage. Her torpedo tubes were ripped from their housings and blown over the side, and all the main stringers on the port side were severed, meaning the ship was now only prevented from splitting in two by the upper deck and starboard side, as far as the keel, remaining intact. The port engine was also heavily damaged and fell through the bottom of the ship.

Immediately, the nearest ship, the trawler HMS *Lord Middleton*, moved over to take off survivors, and as they were filling the lifeboats and being lowered into the water, Lieutenant Commander Colin Maud, the *Somali*'s captain inspected the damage. With the fires being quickly extinguished by the swift action of the crew and the fire control system, he was able to see that if the leaking bulkheads on both sides could be quickly shored up and the seawater pumped from the engine and gear rooms, it was entirely possible the ship could be saved. After giving a damage report to Rear-Admiral Burnett on the *Milne*, it was decided to leave a party of eighty on board to carry out first-line repairs and try to keep the ship afloat.

A steel tow-line was to be attached from the *Ashanti*, and the *Somali* would be taken under tow by her sister ship for the remainder of the journey to Iceland. However, this meant that the already slow-moving convoy would need to slow down further, to a snail's pace of around 7 knots.

And so, with orders given to the remaining crew not to go below deck unless for essential work, a tow-line was rigged between the two ships and a generator set up to provide light and power to the bilge pumps at work in the flooded engine room.

An electrical line was also rigged from the *Ashanti*. However, with the sections of line only available in strips 50 yards long, six had to be connected together and waterproofed. This required three men (an officer and two leading seamen) in a motorboat to strap the electrical lines to the tow cable, a job which took them four hours in freezing temperatures. Eventually, the cable was hauled aboard and hooked up. For this action, the officer, Sub-Lieutenant Terence Lewin, was awarded the Distinguished Service Cross, and the two Leading Seamen, Payne and Wylie, were both awarded the Distinguished Service Medal.

Slowly the ships plodded on, the calm sea remaining ideal for towing and for spotting any periscopes that might break the surface.

As dusk turned into night, the ships of QP14 continued south at reduced speed towards the sanctuary of Iceland, which now lay approximately 700 miles away. Sunday, 20 September had been a most eventful day, that was for sure, and the journey was by no means over.

The officers and men looked on as the sun slowly sank beneath the horizon, all acutely aware that there was still a long way to go before this journey would come to its end.

And who knew what tomorrow might bring.

Chapter 12

21–22 September

Almost 1,200 miles away, most of the ships of PQ18 were still lying at anchor in freezing temperatures at the entrance to the Dvina River, patiently waiting for pilots to take them upstream to the docks for processing and unloading, whilst gale-force winds pulled their anchor chains taut and rocked them violently upon the waves. In the distance, explosions could be heard and brief flashes of light illuminated the sky as the Luftwaffe turned its attention to bombing the city, the dull boom of anti-aircraft fire carrying back over the water as the Russians fired anti-aircraft shells at their attackers.

In the pitch dark of early morning a total blackout was in force in the city, and Boddam-Whetham ordered the same thing for the ships. The anti-aircraft ship HMS *Ulster Queen* had positioned herself close to the three freighters still aground, in order provide some protection should they be spotted by the Germans and come under attack. She was later joined in this task by a Russian destroyer and the minesweeper HMS *Britomart*.

The day slowly dawned and the pilots began to arrive. Very slowly, the task of taking the freighters and some of the escorts to the docks at Ekonomia and Bakharitsa began. Anatoly Sakharov, the former master of the SS *Stalingrad*, was now using his knowledge of the area and his skills as a pilot; his first task was to guide HMS *Harrier* to Krasny Quay, where twenty-four survivors of his ship could be disembarked. After watching them make their way down the gangplank and back onto Russian soil, he felt immense sadness that, although he had finally brought these people home, so many others had perished along the way.

As the ships moved slowly up the Dvina River and pulled up at the various quaysides, sailors could now finally take a look at the place they had battled so hard to reach. Each bank of the river was covered with trees and lengths of timber in enormous stacks. The water was full of huge logs drifting peacefully, almost serenely, downstream, and the occasional raft could be seen of logs lashed together for the workers to use as platforms.

To most of the seamen the area looked bleak, desolate; the last place God made. The quays, in the main, were wooden-decked with concrete facings. A rusting double-tracked railway line ran the full length of the docks, but there was no sign yet of any rolling stock. There was general puzzlement as to just how the cargo was to be taken away, but as far as the sailors were concerned, that was something for the Russians to worry about. Behind the railway line, row upon row of derelict-looking wooden huts stretched far back to a high brick wall that cut off any view of what lay beyond, if indeed anything did. Along the top of this wall was a thick coil of barbed wire to stop anyone from climbing over. Snow and ice covered almost everything, and the cold Arctic wind howled and whistled as it blew between the iron and steel cranes that would soon be put to work to take off the freight. Spaced out upon the docks, large loudspeakers could be seen which continuously broadcast deep voices in Russian, presumably motivational speeches. Between these dreary monologues, the distinctive sound of traditional Russian music could be heard, tinny and distorted.

Why anyone would wish to live in such a desolate and dreary place was beyond any observer's understanding. Many looking on from the ships reluctantly had to accept that this inhospitable and bleak location would be their home for the next few weeks as they waited for the ships to be unloaded and an escort to become available to take them home. Exactly when that would be, nobody knew.

As the day wore on, the weather started to improve, and at 1545 hours two Junkers Ju-88s, seeing the grounded ships, decided to spring a surprise attack. Immediately, the gunners on the *Ulster Queen* opened up on them but, ignoring the severe barrage, the German pilots managed to drop a stick of bombs amongst the stranded freighters. However, fortune favoured the mariners, no damage was done, and the planes eventually turned away.

By now the skipper of the *Ulster Queen*, Captain Charles Adam, was conscious of the fatigue of his men who had been fighting a constant battle against the Luftwaffe and the elements for two solid weeks. It was high time they all had a proper rest, he thought. Now that this attack was over and another seemed unlikely, he weighed anchor and moved further upstream towards Archangelsk, stopping at a spot eight miles closer to the city.

As the merchantmen now started to vacate their anchorage and move into the docks, it looked as if their journey had finally come to an end.

* * *

For some of the ships of QP14, progress had now become a slow crawl.

Unwilling to leave the *Ashanti* and the damaged *Somali* adrift, unprotected and vulnerable to another U-boat attack, Rear-Admiral Burnett had detached a number of escort ships to provide them with protection; these put up a close ring around them, their Asdic operators' eyes glued to their screens for any sign of nearby enemy activity. With this protection in place, the remainder of the convoy carried on, leaving them to bring up the rear as quickly as they were able.

However, wanting to see the damage to the *Somali* for himself, Burnett ordered the *Milne* to be moved closer to the crippled destroyer so he could take a better look. Standing at the gunwale, Charlie Erswell looked on as the ships approached each other. Even from some distance away, Charlie could see the destroyer was in a bad way; it was nothing short of a miracle that she was still afloat. There was a large gaping hole in the hull, through which he could see men working hard to repair the damage and save their ship. It was evident to him that the destroyer had no chance of making it to port without the assistance of the surrounding ships Burnett had allocated to the job. Although the weather was still quite calm, it was only the hard work of the men on board, and luck, that kept the *Somali* from sinking beneath the waves.

No sooner had the *Milne* left the struggling *Somali* in her wake to return to the main body of the convoy, than Action Stations sounded once again. As Charlie raced to B turret he looked to the skies, expecting to see a squadron of He-111s or Ju-88s bearing down on them. The sky was, however, devoid of torpedo-bombers, so he assumed it was another U-boat sighting. Fixing himself into position at the turret trainer, he awaited instruction. Maybe this time the submarine was on the surface and they might be able to get a shot off at it before it dived.

A U-boat had indeed been picked up four miles away on the Asdic, and for an hour or so they hunted the sea around where the contact had been made before finally giving up, the U-boat commander having successfully evaded the destroyers once more.

* * *

With HMS *Avenger* and her Swordfish now safely back in port in Iceland, it was up to the Catalinas and Liberator aircraft of Coastal Command to conduct anti-submarine sweeps in the track of QP14.

One such Catalina, Z/330 from 330 Squadron (RAF) based at Akureyri in Iceland and crewed by exiled Norwegian airmen, was on patrol to the south of the convoy, 150 miles north of Jan Mayen Island on the lookout for U-boats, when it sighted something on the surface.

The pilot, Lieutenant Carl Stansberg, turned his aircraft to investigate, and as the seaplane lost altitude and flew closer, the unmistakable outline of a U-boat's conning tower was clearly seen. Still some distance away, Stansberg put the throttle forward to increase speed, but by the time the Catalina was over where it had been sighted, the U-boat had vanished. The plane circled the area a couple of times, but by now its prey had well and truly disappeared.

Not wishing to waste any more time, the pilot headed north, and some time later, the ships of QP14 came within view. There was also a German Blohm and Voss BV138 seaplane circling the convoy; it had been stalking the ships for the past few days.

Stansberg immediately flew in to intercept, but on seeing the approaching RAF plane, the pilot of the BV138 turned his aircraft and headed away, refusing to engage in aerial combat.

With the time now approaching 1100 hours, Stansberg again turned south to continue his patrol and seek out any U-boats that might be operating in the area.

* * *

Twenty-seven-year-old Kapitänleutnant Dietrich von der Esch had been in the Kriegsmarine since the age of nineteen. He was by now a seasoned U-boat commander, having completed four patrols in *U-586*, and was a recipient of the Iron Cross (First and Second Class). Having been asked to take temporary command of *U-606*, he had been on patrol in the Norwegian Sea for the last seven days and was eager to put his skills as a commander to the test. He knew where the convoy was and had positioned his boat ahead, waiting for it to come closer. However, it was still some distance away, and he therefore felt confident in remaining surfaced. The batteries could be charged, he could receive signals as to the exact position of the British ships and, with the weather being quite mild, the crew could get some fresh air; after being cooped up in the submarine for the past few hours, many of them were now sitting on the deck below him.

He was also aware that the aircraft carrier had left the convoy and the only threat in the air came in the form of the Catalina seaplanes and Liberator bombers that operated mainly out of Iceland.

For the moment he felt safe.

* * *

Carl Stansberg and his crew of eight in Catalina Z/330 were also feeling confident.

Having forced a U-boat to carry out an emergency dive and sent a BV138 skulking away, the patrol had so far been something of a success. It was not totally necessary to sink enemy submarines or shoot down aircraft, as long as they were kept at bay, allowing the ships to return safely to port.

Stansberg checked the clock. It showed 1114 hours, and he was currently nearly 200 miles north of Jan Mayen Island, flying just below the clouds.

Sitting at his side, Per Devons, Z/330's navigator, nudged him and pointed to the south. 'Carl ... there ... U-boat.'

Stansberg looked where his colleague was indicating and there, just as Devons had said, was a U-boat. And more importantly, there was no rushed activity taking place on the conning tower to indicate to him that they had been spotted.

He called out to his crew.

'U-boat below. Set depth charges to 25ft. Four should do it. We'll drop at 60ft intervals.'

As his crew set to work, he pushed the throttle forward and reduced altitude, setting course directly for the unsuspecting submarine.

* * *

By the time van der Esch heard the droning of the Catalina's engines he knew it was too late to get everyone safely inside the boat and carry out an emergency crash dive.

Looking up at the sky, he could see the large seaplane coming in for the kill, appearing bigger the nearer it got. Although he could not take the boat beneath the waves he might just have enough time to get someone on the guns and put up some resistance.

Shouting orders to man the 20mm anti-aircraft cannon and the machine gun, situated just behind the conning tower, he knew he would have to fight this one out. There was nothing else for it.

* * *

Stansberg could now see activity on the U-boat below. Not to be put off, he continued on his course and, when he was within range, ordered the four 450lb depth charges to be dropped.

As the barrels of amatol fell into the sea and detonated, he could see that they had landed 30–40ft away from the U-boat's starboard beam, the water from the explosions sprayed high into the air. Whether they had been close enough to cause any significant damage, he was not sure; he might have to turn and carry out another run.

As he was contemplating this, the machine gun and 20mm cannon of the U-boat opened fire. Whoever the gunners on the submarine were, it was immediately apparent that they were good.

Stansberg felt the aircraft shudder as rounds from the German guns found their target, ripping into the fuselage and shattering the perspex of the cockpit. He was horrified to hear screams as Devons to his side was hit, along with one of the fitters behind him.

"Per . . . are you all right?' he shouted above the noise.

'I'll live, Carl,' came the reply, through gritted teeth.

After determining the fitter's injuries were also not life-threatening, Stansberg looked out of the shattered window and could see the aircraft had taken a significant battering. The port engine looked to be damaged, and the petrol tank had clearly been hit, aircraft fuel spraying behind them as he banked to check on the U-boat.

More fire was being sprayed at the Catalina as he now approached the submarine head-on. If he was going to be shot down, which seemed quite likely given the damage already suffered, he was not going to go down without a fight.

* * *

On the tower of the *U-606*, van der Esch could see that his gunners had done well.

Smoke was issuing from the seaplane's port engine and, from what he could make out, there was further damage to the aircraft. It could probably not withstand more hits like this.

His men had reacted quickly to the threat, and for that they should be proud. The enemy's depth charge run had been unsuccessful, the explosions merely rocking the boat from side to side, and he was confident no significant damage had been caused.

As he looked on, the plane started to bank towards them once more, and it was with horror that he saw its front guns open fire.

With bullets ricocheting all around the conning tower, he threw himself to the deck, whereupon he heard screams of agony from some of his crewmen. Two had clearly been mortally wounded, both falling from the conning tower, one of them splashing into the sea.

However, the gunners continued to spray bullets in the direction of the Catalina which, having carried out this latest run, finally turned and headed away, a trail of black smoke streaming from the port engine as it did so.

Van der Esch now realized this was the time to make his escape. No doubt the captain of the aircraft, which was slowly receding from view as it headed northwards, would be radioing their position to the destroyers of the approaching convoy, which would be upon them shortly if they didn't leave quickly.

Ordering everyone inside, and closing the hatch behind him, it was with a deep regret that he had to leave the bodies of two his men outside for the sea to claim.

* * *

Van der Esch had been wrong.

The crew of Z/330 would not be radioing back the position of the *U-606*. This was because the radio had been smashed to pieces by German bullets and was now totally inoperable.

Losing fuel and flying on only one engine, Stansberg had quickly realized that he could not make it safely back to Iceland and so had turned the plane north, to find the convoy once again and ditch the aircraft where he knew he and the crew could be picked up.

And so, only a few minutes later, on sighting the ships steaming south towards him, he took the Catalina down and made a safe landing near one of the destroyers. Collecting the log books and anything else that was salvageable, the seven able men assisted their two wounded colleagues, and a short while later they were picked up by the destroyer HMS *Marne*.

After making his report, a second Catalina made a search of the area where *U-606* had been engaged, but by the time it was over the site, van der Esch had taken the boat beneath the waves.

A little later in the day, a Liberator on patrol 85 miles north of Iceland spotted two more U-boats, one of which was fully surfaced and another at periscope depth with half the conning tower visible. The aircraft was virtually over the two submarines when they were sighted, but as it turned to make an attack run, they disappeared beneath the waves.

The threat the U-boats posed to QP14 was becoming extremely serious. They had already caused a significant loss to shipping and since they were being routinely sighted in the convoy's path, it was clear they were not done with the ships just yet.

* * *

In Archangelsk, things were going equally slowly.

It was taking the Russians a while to get organized, and those ships that were currently docked at Ekonomia and Bakharitsa were at that moment lying idle, whilst the remainder of PQ18 still lay at anchor waiting to be called in to be unloaded. Each dock had at that moment eleven ships tied to its quayside, all waiting for the Russian dockers to arrive and unload their cargoes.

Across from the docks, the city of Archangelsk was under sustained attack by the Luftwaffe which continued into the night. The area the Germans were attacking was vast, from the city itself all the way up to the island of Mudyugskiy, just off the mainland to the north in the White Sea.

For those merchant seamen now waiting at anchor, this was extremely disheartening. They had thought that, once tied up at the quayside, their journey over, they would get some respite from the German bombers. Alas, this was not to be.

However, what did make for a lot of head-scratching was that although the enemy were at that moment attempting to flatten Archangelsk, the docked ships, vulnerable and poorly protected, were not targeted despite their being brightly illuminated by parachute flares and containing thousands of tonnes of war materiel, much of which was bound for Stalingrad. It was suggested that those attacking might actually be Finnish and not German, the Finns having been at war with the Soviets ever since they were invaded by Russian forces in November 1939, and they did not want to hit any American ships. Whatever the case, the ships were largely left alone during this air raid, much to the relief of those waiting on board.

* * *

Whilst the men of PQ18 waited patiently for their cargoes to be unloaded, those travelling on QP14 were now allowing themselves dreams of home. By the morning of Tuesday, 22 September, the convoy was just 50 miles northwest of Jan Mayen Island, with the ports of Iceland only 350 miles to the south. It would not be long before they were safe again and could enjoy warm food, hot showers and a chance to relax.

For those on HMS *Milne*, the end to this Arctic run was to come sooner than others. After establishing the position of HMS *Somali* and handing over command of the convoy to Alan Scott-Moncrieff on HMS *Faulknor*, Rear-Admiral Burnett ordered the ship to proceed at full speed to Seydisfjordur to rendezvous with the *Scylla* so that he could be transferred back to his own ship.

To Charlie Erswell, this was very welcome. With the convoy having been pretty much left alone for the past day or so, and now being well within range of the aircraft from Coastal Command, which could provide increased air protection, he presumed that Burnett was of the opinion that the rest of the journey would be routine.

As the ship broke away and steamed at full speed ahead, leaving QP14 in her wake, he felt a real sense of achievement. This had been his first voyage and it had been extremely eventful. Although some merchant ships had been lost, he understood that it had been something of a success. The convoy had got through to Archangelsk and the ghost of PQ17 might now have been laid. Would this mean more Arctic convoys in the future? He was guessing it would, but what part he would play in them, as yet he had no idea.

As the mountains of Iceland came into view, he sighed to himself. For the first time in nearly three weeks he felt safe again.

* * *

For those following the *Milne*, trouble was by no means over. Not by a long chalk.

Having sunk the minesweeper HMS *Leda* two days previously, Siegfried Strelow, commander of *U-435*, was determined to add to his tally.

As HMS *Milne* was heading away, Strelow was at that very moment attempting to penetrate the convoy's outer screen. After dealing the death blow to a Royal Navy ship, he had managed to dodge detection and, once clear of the convoy and aware no destroyers had followed him, he had ordered the boat to the surface and raced ahead, to lie in wait again and seek out an opportunity to inflict still more damage on the ships.

This he had expertly done and had approached the convoy on its starboard side. Successfully evading the outer screen of destroyers which passed by overhead, he raised the attack periscope to seek out new targets.

Immediately, he could see a line of merchant ships dead ahead. He had earlier given the order for the torpedo tubes to be armed, and the crew in the torpedo room had more underwater missiles at the ready, to re-arm the tubes once the first salvo was let loose. He was ready, and from what he could see, those ships sailing above had absolutely no idea of what he was about to unleash upon them.

The time was a little after 0715 hours. Without further ado, lest his periscope be spotted, he gave the order to fire, and as soon as the torpedoes had left their tubes, heading at speed towards the lumbering merchant ships, he gave the order to arm and fire again. In total, *U-435* released five torpedoes in quick succession.

Lowering the attack periscope, Strelow stepped out into the main command room and looked at the hydrophone operator, who stared back at him, listening for the sound of explosions on the surface. It was not long before he raised his hand indicating a successful strike, followed shortly after by another.

In total, three of the merchant ships above had been hit by Strelow's attack; the first was the United States cargo ship *Bellingham*, carrying mineral ore and skins, which was hit in the number four hold on the starboard side. Seeing the damage was fatal, the skipper, Soren Mortensen, ordered the ship to be abandoned, and quickly the crew evacuated on the lifeboats; all seventy-five of them were picked up later by the rescue ship HMS *Rathlin* and some nearby destroyers.

At almost exactly the same time as the torpedo exploded in the *Bellingham*'s side, the commodore ship SS *Ocean Voice* carrying Commander Dowding and a cargo of timber and wood pulp was hit. It quickly became apparent that this ship, too, needed to be abandoned, and the eighty-nine men on board, including twenty-five Soviet passengers, took to the lifeboats to be picked up by HMS *Seagull* and the rescue ship *Zamalek*. Safely taken on board the *Seagull*, Commander Dowding decided to stay on the ship for the remainder of the journey, passing the commodore responsibilities to his subordinate, Captain Walker, on the *Ocean Freedom*.

The third ship to suffer in Strelow's attack was another of the fleet oilers. The RFA *Gray Ranger* now endured the same fate as her fellow tanker *Atheltemplar* had on PQ18 to Archangelsk. The sinking of an oil tanker was a big prize for the U-boats. The more they sank, the more stretched the Royal Navy would be in refuelling their ships whilst on convoy duties. And now two had been lost in two weeks.

On board the tanker, fires raged as the ship started to break up. As on the other two ships hit in the attack, the order was quickly given to abandon ship, the wounded being aided to the lifeboats by their shipmates. However, some had been killed, and of the crew of sixty-five only fifty-nine made it onto the lifeboats and boarded HMS *Rathlin* a little later.

Strelow had by now taken the U-boat deep underwater and was carrying out evasive manoeuvres as the British destroyers dropped depth charges wherever they could get any kind of contact. He was extremely pleased with his morning's haul. Three ships in one attack run was something to be proud of, and this had taken his total to four confirmed kills in a matter of only three days. He would be going back to port content that he had done his duty.

Watching two of the ships disappear beneath the waves, while the third, the *Bellingham*, was also slowly going under, Scott-Moncrieff on the *Faulknor* gave orders for the screen to be tightened up. At all costs he had to avoid another attack on the ships, many of which contained men who had already undergone so many hardships and privations over the last few months.

Hastily reorganizing the set-up of the outer screen, he placed his own ship at the head, with the other destroyers spread out across the face of the convoy as an advanced screen. He also arranged for depth-charge runs to be carried out during the night, at intervals of a mile, to keep at bay any other U-boat commander wanting to make a name for himself. Using HMS *Worcester* to patrol across the rear of the convoy at an increased speed of 16 knots, and the *Impulsive* and *Middleton* to carry out random anti-submarine patrols on the flanks, he had done as much as he could do to provide the remaining ships with the protection needed to take them safely back to port.

As the day wore on the weather started to deteriorate, becoming more blustery with sleet and snow showers. With the *Somali* still being towed by the *Ashanti* and held together by little more than steel cables, there was now a worry that the ship might not make it back to port after all. With her speed further reduced to prevent her from breaking up, it seemed that Iceland was further away the closer the ships got to it. With only a few miles left, the weather and the U-boats of the Kriegsmarine were still a major headache for Scott-Moncrieff and Captain Walker.

At that moment, lying in the convoy's path was yet another enemy, the *U-253*, on its very first patrol and commanded by the enthusiastic 28-year-old Kapitänleutnant Adolf Friedrichs, keen to score his first kill.

However, the men of RAF Coastal Command might yet have something to say about that!

Chapter 13

23–27 September

Flight Sergeant J. Semmens and his crew of eight had set out on what they thought would be a routine patrol at 2330 hours on 22 September. Taking Catalina U/210 to patrol the track of the approaching QP14, which was due to arrive in Iceland within the next couple of days, they quickly settled into the flight, scanning the sea 600ft below for any signs of enemy activity. These flights had become run-of-the-mill now and could last many hours, as they had a vast area to cover; and since the aircraft's range was over 4,000 miles, they could stay in the air for the best part of the day.

Semmens had heard that the ships were being harassed by U-boats and had suffered significant losses. With the Swordfish of the *Avenger* having left them some time ago, it was now up to 210 Squadron operating out of the airbase at Sullom Voe to provide as much protection as possible.

They had been flying for well over seven hours when Sergeant Langdon, Semmens' navigator, sitting beside him in the cockpit, tapped him on the shoulder and pointed to the sea below.

'U-boat!' he exclaimed. 'Port side, approximately three quarters of a mile away, I'd say.'

Semmens looked to where Langdon was indicating and, sure enough, its dark hull standing out against the clear sea, was the unmistakable form of a German submarine. It was fully surfaced and seemed unaware of the Catalina's presence, making no attempt as yet to carry out an emergency dive. He glanced quickly at the clock and saw the time was 0653 hours. They were currently flying around 120 miles north of Iceland.

Semmens spoke into his mic.

'Okay, gentlemen, U-boat ahead. Prepare six depth charges. Set to 25ft.'

Immediately, the crew got to work, following instructions, and a few moments later reported they were ready.

Banking the aircraft to port, Semmens took it down to only 50ft and came in to attack. He could feel the blood pumping around his body and the adrenalin starting to kick in as the large seaplane skimmed over the waves. This switch, a rather mundane patrol turning in an instant to combat operations, was something that could never be replicated in a training scenario. The feeling of euphoria was intense, excitement and fear in equal measures.

In a few moments time he would be above the U-boat and could hardly miss. It was a sitting duck.

* * *

Adolf Friedrichs, standing on the conning tower of *U-253*, heard the drone of the Catalina before he saw it. Turning in the direction of the sound, he was horrified to see the huge twin-engine seaplane bearing down on them and for a moment he froze, before screaming the alarm and rushing to the open hatchway. Shouting orders to dive as quickly as possible, he spun the wheel to seal the hatch and jumped into position in the central control room.

Within seconds, U/210 was above them, and as the U-boat slipped beneath the waves, periscope still visible, Semmens dropped the six 250lb Torpex depth charges at 35ft intervals, the bombs straddling the disappearing hull.

As the charges detonated and water erupted into the sky, Semmens could see that two of the bombs had exploded almost on top of the desperate submarine, no more than 6ft from it on either side. He immediately took the Catalina higher and banked to come around for another run.

However, Semmens could see that dropping more charges would be a waste of ammunition. An even larger body of water burst into the morning sky, right in the centre of the stick of six charges he had just dropped. As he watched, five seconds after the explosion, the tail end of the U-boat rose out of the water and hung there for a while before falling back beneath the waves. Anyone on board would have been thrown around violently, and if they had not yet been killed, then what was to come in the next few seconds would surely finish them off.

The U-boat sank beneath the waves once more before rising again, rolling over and sliding back beneath the water for one final time.

It was clear to Semmens and the rest of the crew that it had been destroyed and the chances of anyone making it out alive were non-existent. He circled the area for a few more minutes, but when nothing else was sighted he turned away to continue the patrol, landing at Reykjavik at 1755 hours after nineteen hours and twenty-five minutes in the air.

The *U-253* had been sunk, on what was her first patrol, with the loss of forty-five men.

* * *

For the remainder of the day further Catalina and Liberator patrols were undertaken by Coastal Command, with a Liberator from 210 Squadron coming under attack from an unidentified aircraft before shaking it off and continuing its mission. With the U-boats harassing the convoy doggedly for the past few days, it was increasingly necessary to undertake as many sorties over the track of the oncoming ships as possible, to ensure they arrived back in Iceland safely.

Scott-Moncrieff's decision to close up the escort and carry out almost continuous depth-charge runs in the convoy's track, together with the continuous patrols of anti-submarine aircraft even further ahead, was having the desired effect. U-boat commanders were now keeping their distance lest what happened to the men on the *U-253* became their fate also. After all, QP14 did not have the same importance as the Russia-bound PQ18, containing mainly cargoes of timber and raw materials with nothing as yet bound for the front line.

For the rest of 23 September and all the following day, QP14 continued at a snail's pace towards Iceland. Although spotter planes could be seen occasionally in the skies above, they offered no threat, and no U-boat commander penetrated close enough to attempt another attack. By 2000 hours on the evening of 24 September the main body of the convoy was only eighty miles north of Iceland.

However, the following morning, as Iceland came plainly into view, that other adversary, the weather, decided to have a go at stopping them.

Still some 170 miles from land, trailing behind the main body of the convoy, was the heavily damaged destroyer HMS *Somali*, being towed by her sister ship HMS *Ashanti* and protected by a detachment of destroyers.

For the last few days the fate of the *Somali* had been hanging in the balance. So far, she had been towed for around 420 miles. After rigging steel cables to prevent her splitting in two, and attaching umbilical electricity lines along towing cables from the *Ashanti*, the 102 men now on board the ship, including her captain, Lieutenant-Commander Colin Maud, had managed to keep her afloat, working tirelessly to do so. Thus far they had been assisted by good weather and calm seas, and confidence was growing that the ship could make it safely to port, where repairs could be undertaken to save her.

However, in the early hours of 25 September, disaster struck.

A storm, appearing as if from nowhere, struck the small group of ships. The weather that had been so calm over the last few days turned suddenly, and within minutes the sea was throwing up 30ft waves, a severe gale roaring out of the darkness and bringing with it thick, blinding snow.

On the *Somali*, things became chaotic. The cables now pulled taut as the ship was forced further from the *Ashanti*. It was no surprise that after only a few minutes the tow line and electricity cable snapped, throwing sparks in all directions to light up the black sky like an unearthly fireworks display.

A searchlight was quickly brought to bear from the *Ashanti* on the crippled ship. What it illuminated was horrific. The ship was folding in half, her stern and bow rising into the air. The deck plating, which had played a huge part in keeping the ship together for the last few days, finally snapped, causing the bulkheads to collapse, effectively splitting the *Somali* in two.

It was too late for anyone to launch the lifeboats, and those left on board had only one option, to jump for their lives into the icy waters of the Norwegian Sea.

Now separate, the bow of the ship rose vertically into the air whilst the stern, quickly filling with water as the sea raged all around it, capsized and quickly sank. The bow bobbed for a few moments longer in the water then slowly disappeared beneath the surface as the huge waves crashed all around it. Finally, HMS *Somali* was gone forever.

In the water desperate men fought to stay afloat. As efforts were made by the surrounding ships to pluck them from the water, it was soon clear that not all were going to be saved; their screams for help were drowned out by the roar of the storm.

One of the men in the water was the *Somali*'s captain, Colin Maud. Having no choice other than to entrust his fate to God by throwing himself into the sea with his men, he had struggled desperately in the water until consciousness left him. The next thing he was aware of was being hauled aboard the *Ashanti*, where he was quickly revived by eager deckhands who took him immediately into the shelter of the sick bay, along with others they had managed to save.

What Maud did not know at that time was that he had been pulled from the sea by Leading Seaman William Goad, who had gone into the water to rescue him. Seeing him unconscious, Goad had been given permission to go over the side tied to a line in an attempt to rescue him. Although there was a very real risk of being washed away by the breaking seas, or swept under the bilge keel of his own ship, which was rolling heavily in the heaving water, Goad nevertheless saw a man about to die in the water and was prepared to do all that he could to save him.

Whilst Maud and thirty-four other men were plucked from the rolling sea, the remainder of those who had stayed on board the *Somali* were not as lucky; sixty-seven of the crew died in the water, tragically only a few hours from safety.

With no merchantmen to protect, this small group of escort ships now headed directly for Scapa Flow, arriving there at 2115 hours on 25 September.

* * *

HMS *Somali* was to be the last ship lost on the returning convoy. Ahead of the group that had provided protection for the destroyer, the main body of QP14 had made it safely back to Iceland, the Royal Navy escorts breaking off and heading back to Scapa Flow, their duty done. After twenty-five days at sea, the sailors on the escort ships could now relax for a short while, enjoy some hot food, clean themselves up and shave off the beards they had grown. However, it wouldn't be long before they were back in action, many of the ships heading off to the Mediterranean to take part in Operation Torch, the invasion of Vichy-controlled North Africa.

Now that their mission was over, the planes of Operation Orator based in Russia were starting to head home. After having to turn back due to bad weather on 25 September, a Catalina of 210 Squadron was involved in a brief skirmish with a Junkers Ju-88, 70 miles north of Russia. The seaplane was hit with machine-gun fire, killing its captain, Tim Healy, but the heavily damaged Ju-88 crashed into the sea some time later, killing all of its four-man crew. The Catalina was able to make it back to Grasnaya with no other casualties.

Force P, those vessels that were sent to Spitzbergen to provide a refuelling station for the escort ships en route, arrived back in Scapa Flow on the 27th, having been escorted by aircraft from Coastal Command, the final ships to arrive back in port.

However, the final casualty of the expedition was not one of those who had perished when the *Somali* went down in the early hours of 25 September. Flying a sortie over Altenfjord on the 27th, Pilot Officer Gavin Walker of 1PRU was unable, due to heavy cloud, to give a positive report that the German heavy ships were still in dock. Taking his Spitfire (BP889) below the clouds to get a better look, he was immediately hit by small arms fire from the ground, his aircraft crashing a few minutes later, killing him on impact. He was just twenty-four years old.

For the men who sailed on PQ18 or QP14, these were voyages that none of them would ever forget. The memories would live with them forever.

Winston Churchill described the Arctic convoys as undertaking 'the worst journey in the world'.

He was not wrong. He described them well.

Epilogue

Out of the thirty-nine merchant ships that set out from Iceland on 9 September 1942, twenty-seven arrived in Archangelsk twelve days later to deliver their cargoes, supplies that were so desperately needed by the Russians in their struggle against the Nazis. Despite problems early on in regard to the pace of unloading, it soon picked up, and all of the ships had been unloaded by 20 October, just under a month after the convoy's arrival.

Almost as soon as cargoes were taken off the ships, the materiel was rushed by rail south towards Stalingrad, where the battle for the city was still raging.

For the men left in Archangelsk, there was now going to be a considerable wait before they could go home. Their freight delivered, there was not a lot for them to do other than enjoy the somewhat mixed hospitality that Soviet Russia had to offer and wait for orders on just how and when they were going to undertake the return journey.

For those in power, PQ18 had been a success, albeit a limited one. Enough ships had made it through, enough war materiel delivered, to justify keeping the Arctic route open. The Germans' attempts to stop it, although meeting with some success, especially the Golden Comb attack on 13 September, had largely failed, and they had suffered severe losses in aircraft and U-boats. The failure of PQ17 had thankfully not been repeated, although at times the fate of PQ18 had hung in the balance, and things might not have ended so well had the Germans employed different tactics.

There were many factors that came together to ensure that the majority of the merchant ships made it through. This was emphasized in Rear-Admiral Bob Burnett's report after the convoy had concluded.

Although the weather had been extremely harsh at times, at others it had been relatively calm, allowing the ships to progress at a steady pace. The sinking of the fleet oiler *Atheltemplar* meant that immediately available fuel resources were reduced by 25 per cent. Had any of the other three oilers been sunk, then the covering force would have had to be withdrawn, leaving the merchantmen unprotected, much as they had been on PQ17.

Burnett was also of the opinion that any delay in refuelling Force B at Spitzbergen on 12th/13th would have resulted in those ships, including the *Scylla* and the six destroyers that accompanied her, not being involved in the action of the 13th. Had they not been there, more than eight merchant ships might have been lost in the massed attack that took place that afternoon.

Also contributing to the convoy's success was the inability, or unwillingness, of the Germans to continue with the tactics used on the 13th. Had the Golden Comb attack been repeated (instead of the Luftwaffe focusing on trying to sink the *Avenger*) and combined with a concentrated U-boat and surface-ship attack, they might very well have dealt a decisive blow to the convoy and prevented any more from sailing.

The presence of an aircraft carrier, as part of the close escort, also proved pivotal in the defence of the convoy and in ensuring the majority of the ships arrived safely. Although dated and somewhat antiquated, the Swordfish aircraft and their unflappable crews had proved their value on many occasions and were a deterrent to U-boat attack. Likewise, the part played by the pilots of the Sea Hurricanes in breaking up torpedo-bomber runs can also not be underestimated. Rear-Admiral Burnett said of them in his report: 'I shall never forget the reckless gallantry of the naval fighter pilots in their determination to get in among the enemy, despite the solid mass of our defensive fire of every type.'

It seems very strange that despite having so many powerful surface ships available to them very close by, the Germans were not prepared to commit these to action. The reasons for this are numerous.

Firstly, the success of their attack on PQ17 that summer was misinterpreted. The Germans were unaware that the scatter order came about due to fears of the *Tirpitz* being at sea, believing instead that it was purely because of attacks by the Luftwaffe and the U-boat wolf-packs. They believed the job could be done without surface ship involvement. Had they known the truth of it, they might very well have either ordered the ships into action, or conducted operations nearby to try and cause a similar panic in the Admiralty.

Secondly, the British had submarines patrolling near the Lofoten Islands and would have been able to engage with the *Tirpitz* had she left Narvik, only a few miles away. Along with Operation Orator's two squadrons of Hampdens waiting for such a moment, and the Cruiser Covering Force and Distant Covering Force patrolling the Norwegian Sea, a heavy attack could have been mounted upon her, resulting in a major sea battle that the Germans might well have lost.

Thirdly, the sinking of the *Tirpitz*'s sister ship *Bismarck*, in May the previous year, was still fresh in the minds of the Nazi hierarchy. The destruction of the battleship with the loss of over 2,000 men had hit German morale very hard. Hitler was not going to let the same thing happen again, and so committing

Tirpitz to battle against a heavy Royal Navy force was not something he was prepared to do.

For Churchill, PQ18 was a success; so much so that he was keen to get two more organized for October and November with the codenames PQ19 and PQ20. He had promised Stalin that the agreed quotas would be fulfilled and he was determined to keep that promise.

However, Operation Torch, the invasion of North Africa, was just around the corner. The date had been brought forward by Eisenhower to early November, and the Admiralty argued that they could not provide the escort ships needed for both Torch and the proposed PQ19 and PQ20 convoys. Churchill was of a different opinion and saw no reason why they couldn't be. However, he was to lose the argument, and Operation Torch would take priority, this being the first ever combined operation between British and American forces.

And so, instead of another convoy of the size of PQ18 being sent, merchant ships would sail independently without escort cover, leaving at twelve-hour intervals to space them out and hopefully avoid detection by the Luftwaffe and U-boat wolf-packs. This mission was codenamed Operation FB. In fact, the merchant ships still in Archangelsk would use the same tactic to return home. However, only five of the thirteen ships that took part in Operation FB reached Russia; five were sunk and the other three returned to Iceland, proving this was not an effective way of transporting freight to Russia. In December the convoy system was resumed, once the ships from Operation Torch became available.

The Arctic convoys provided approximately 20 per cent of all weaponry used on the Eastern Front during the Second World War. Considering the scale of the fighting on that front, this represented an enormous amount of equipment and supplies. The Battle of Stalingrad was eventually won by the Russians after they managed to trap and encircle the German Sixth Army in late January 1943. This defeat was to be the beginning of the end for the Third Reich. The Germans never recovered on the Eastern Front, and the Red Army forced them all the way back to Berlin, where they eventually surrendered in May 1945.

Just how much the supplies delivered by PQ18 contributed to the overall victory at Stalingrad can be debated, but there is no doubt that the outcome of the battle, for a long time, could have gone either way. The arrival of weapons and the replenishment of ammunition at the very least kept the Russians in the fight.

Whatever the opinions, Churchill was keen to keep the Arctic convoys running, and this they did until the end of the war; the last sailed a couple of days after the armistice was signed. In total, seventy-eight convoys sailed the route, either going to or returning from the ports of Murmansk and Archangelsk, delivering an assortment of war materiel as well as food, medicines and raw materials, supplies that kept the Soviets in the war.

At a 'Welcome Home' luncheon for survivors of QP14 in Glasgow on 28 September 1942, Philip Noel-Baker, Under-Secretary to the Ministry of War Transport, told them that the convoys were to continue and would be much bigger. The government was of the opinion that better air support for them was 'Naval Priority Number One'. He went on to say:

> We know what this convoy cost us. But I want to tell you that, whatever the cost, it was well worth it. The material which you have taken to Russia may be the deciding factor in bringing Hitler to his doom. This last convoy took the greatest quantity of arms, tanks and aircraft, which Russia has ever received. Very soon the Axis powers will have to fight great battles in every quarter of the globe. This year the great battle has been in Russia, where the Russian resistance has destroyed Hitler's hopes. Without the work of you seamen, our power would be in vain. Without your aid we could not reach the fighting forces which will eventually destroy Hitler, Mussolini and the Japanese. Of all the convoys, the one to Russia was the most important. Stalingrad may be the tombstone to the hopes of the Nazi gang.

* * *

Rear-Admiral Bob Burnett went on to have an illustrious wartime career. He was promoted to Vice-Admiral in December 1943, and whilst flying his flag in HMS *Belfast* played a decisive part in the Battle of the North Cape later that year, when the German battleship *Scharnhorst* was sunk in the Barents Sea. He retired in 1950 after forty-eight years of service in the Royal Navy.

Rear-Admiral Edye Boddam-Whetham, the convoy commodore, was awarded the CBE for the part he played in getting the merchant ships to Archangelsk. Not long after docking in Russia, Boddam-Whetham was given a rapturous reception at an event organized by the city's mayor, when the appreciation of those who had sailed with him was evident. However, the loss of so many ships and merchant sailors weighed heavily upon him, and he fell ill with smallpox whilst in Russia. Never having fully recovered, he died in Gibraltar in March 1944 whilst still on active service.

For his part overseeing Operation Orator and the aerial protection of PQ18, Group Captain Frank Hopps was awarded the Order of Kutuzov (3rd Class) by the Soviet Union, a medal given to senior officers. From 1943 to 1945 he commanded No.16 Group of RAF Coastal Command, and after the war he was appointed Air Officer in Charge of Administration for the RAF in Germany. Finishing his career as the commander of No.19 Group, he retired from the RAF in March 1950 after achieving the rank of Air Vice-Marshal. He died in Brighton in 1976 at the age of eighty-one.

Alan Scott-Moncrieff, the captain of HMS *Faulknor* who successfully sank the U-boat *U-88* on 11 September 1942 and took command of QP14's escorts when Bob Burnett left the convoy, went on to have a fine career in the Royal Navy. In 1950 he was appointed Chairman of the Naval Advisory Committee for NATO, and during the Korean War he was Commander of the Commonwealth Naval Forces. He ended his career as Commander-in-Chief of the Far East Fleet and retired in 1958 after forty-one years service. He died in Henley-on-Thames in 1980 at the age of eighty.

For his part in the sinking of the *U-589* on 14 September, Harold 'Beaky' Armstrong, captain of HMS *Onslow*, was awarded the Distinguished Service Order (DSO) to add to the Distinguished Service Cross (DSC) he had won for the part he played in the sinking of the *Bismarck* the year before. He won a bar to his DSO in 1944 and was posthumously mentioned in dispatches after successfully sinking the *U-223* in the Mediterranean the same year, whilst captain of the destroyer HMS *Laforey*. During the same action, *U-223* was able to fire off three torpedoes at the destroyer, resulting in her sinking. Armstrong was one of the 182 sailors killed when the *Laforey* was lost.

For his action on 18 September, in single-handedly breaking up the torpedo-bomber attack on PQ18 in the White Sea, Flying Officer Arthur Burr was awarded the Distinguished Flying Cross. His citation reads:

> Flying Officer Arthur Henry BURR (66513), Royal Air Force Volunteer Reserve. In September, 1942, 15 enemy aircraft attempted an attack on a convoy voyaging in the Arctic Ocean. Flying Officer Burr, whose aircraft was launched by catapult from the deck of one of the ships, engaged the enemy force with great skill and daring. Despite the odds, he destroyed one of the attackers and drove the others off. After ensuring that the enemy had abandoned their attack, Flying Officer Burr set course for land and reached an aerodrome with only a few gallons of petrol left in the tanks. This officer, who has always completed his tasks with similar determination, displayed great courage and devotion to duty throughout.

He was killed on 25 March 1945 after the plane he was test-flying crashed in Norfolk. He is buried in Heston (St Leonard) churchyard in Middlesex.

Charlie Erswell went on to sail on a total of eight Arctic convoys on the destroyers HMS *Milne* and HMS *Savage*. As well as the Arctic convoys, Charlie saw action in the Mediterranean (Operation Torch), the Battle of the Atlantic, on D-Day and in the liberation of Norway. He also took part in the repatriation of the Norwegian royal family at the end of the war. Leaving the Royal Navy in 1946, he joined the merchant navy where he enjoyed sunnier climes, seeing service in the Mediterranean and New Zealand before eventually returning to dry land two years later. After a number of engineering jobs he eventually found a position making artificial limbs for Roehampton Hospital. He died after a short illness in October 2021, just two months short of his ninety-eighth birthday, not before completing his wartime memoir (*Surviving the Arctic Convoys – The Wartime Memoir of Leading Seaman Charlie Erswell*, Pen & Sword).

Robert Hughes went on to serve with distinction on HMS *Scylla*, and in 1956 he published his war memoirs (*Through The Waters: A Gunnery Officer in HMS Scylla 1942–43*), giving a first-hand account of the actions of the *Scylla* and Rear-Admiral Burnett during PQ18. The foreword was written by Bob Burnett himself. He retired from the Royal Navy after the war and became head teacher at Whitchurch C of E Junior School, Shropshire until his retirement in 1977. He later served as Mayor of Whitchurch.

James Arthur Reeves, the Chief Officer of the *Atheltemplar*, who rescued two sailors from the flooded engine room during its sinking on 14 September 1942, received the Albert Medal for his bravery. His citation reads:

> The ship was torpedoed and was being abandoned when two men were seen floating in the oily water which flooded the engine room to a depth of 25 feet. Both were helpless, one being badly injured and the other overcome by oil fumes. All the engine-room ladders had been destroyed, but using a boat ladder, Chief Officer Reeves descended into the engine-room and secured lines about both men. While being hauled to safety, one of the men slipped back into the oily water. Mr. Reeves again descended into the engine room which was rapidly filling with surging oil and water, and secured another rope about the injured man who was then brought on deck. In descending into the darkened and flooded engine-room, Mr Reeves showed great bravery and complete disregard of his personal safety. His work was rendered doubly dangerous by the heavy oil fumes which had accumulated.

For rescuing Colin Maud, the captain of HMS *Somali*, from freezing waters during a storm, Leading Seaman William Goad was also awarded the Albert Medal. His citation reads:

Leading Seaman Goad went over his ship's side, on a line, in water well below freezing point, and rescued an unconscious man. It was blowing a full gale and there was very great risk that he would either be washed away by the breaking seas, or swept under the bilge keel of his ship, which was rolling heavily.

(NB The Albert Medal has since been replaced by the George Cross.)

Anatoly Sakharov, the captain of the SS *Stalingrad*, the first ship to be sunk on PQ18, returned to Russia and was immediately arrested for losing his ship. He was saved from punishment (probably execution) by the British High Command awarding him the Distinguished Service Cross for assisting with piloting some of the ships into port. Records show he died in October 1954 while serving on the ship *Kirovograd*.

On 13 August 1943, Werner Klümper led a successful air operation against an Allied convoy in the Mediterranean, off the coast of North Africa, in which twelve merchant and four warships were sunk; he personally sank an Allied tanker. At the war's end he was taken prisoner and afterwards continued his career with the West German Navy. He retired in 1969 and died in October 1989 at the age of seventy-eight.

Reinhard von Hymmen, skipper of *U-408*, the U-boat that survived the torpedo attack from the British submarine *P614* on 20 September and sank the SS *Stalingrad* and SS *Oliver Ellsworth* in the early hours of 13 September before finishing off the heavily damaged *Atheltemplar* the following day, was killed less than two months later in the Greenland Sea. On only its third patrol, the *U-408* was sunk with all hands following a depth-charge attack by a Catalina of Coastal Command.

The captain of *U-435*, Siegfried Strelow, was one of the Kriegsmarine's most successful U-boat commanders. In total, he was responsible for sinking thirteen Allied ships, including HMS *Leda* and three merchantmen (*Bellingham*, *Ocean Voice* and *Gray Ranger*) on QP14. He died along with all of his crew on 9 July 1943 in the North Atlantic, after coming under attack by a Wellington bomber off the coast of Portugal.

Reinhart Reche, the captain of *U-255*, the U-boat that sank the SS *Silver Sword* (QP14) on 22 September, already had a number of kills to his credit. Having been responsible for the sinking of four of the ships of PQ17 in July 1942, he went on to sink a total of ten Allied ships in the war as a whole. In June 1943 Reche moved to shore-based activities and in 1956 he joined the *Bundesmarine* (West German Navy). He retired in 1974 with the rank of Kapitän zur See and died in Bad Godesberg in 1993.

Epilogue

Heinz Bielfeld, captain of *U-703*, the U-boat that severely damaged HMS *Somali*, leading to her eventual sinking in a storm, took command of the Type IXC/40 U-boat *U-1222* in September 1943. The following July, *U-1222* was sunk in the Bay of Biscay, when its snorkel was spotted by a patrolling Sunderland aircraft of 201 Squadron, RAF, which carried out a successful depth-charge run. The submarine was lost with all hands, fifty-six men, including Bielfeld.

With regard to the sinking of *U-457* by HMS *Impulsive* in the early hours of 16 September, the ship's captain, Lieutenant-Commander Edward Roper, was never sure that he had sunk a U-boat and made no mention of the *Empire Baffin* ramming it in his report. Those on the *Empire Baffin* were convinced they had struck a U-boat after the *Impulsive*'s depth-charge run. The Kriegsmarine, however, confirmed its sinking at the location reported by Roper, and so HMS *Impulsive* is credited with its kill.

And finally, I can find no record of any punishment being given to William Mullender, skipper of the trawler HMS *Northern Gem*, for telling the captain of a destroyer to 'fuck off' after being told to halt his rescue operations after HMS *Leda* was struck by a torpedo on 20 September 1942 west of Spitzbergen. Maybe the destroyer captain saw sense and decided not to proceed with his threat. After all, if any situation justified the use of such a profanity, then this was surely it.

Appendix I

List of Merchant Ships on PQ18 (with pennant numbers and casualties)

Ship	Flag	Fate (no. of casualties)
Africander (94)	Panama	Sunk by aircraft, 13 September 1942 (0 killed)
Andre Marti (14)	Russia	Survived convoy
Campfire (63)	USA	Survived convoy
Charles R McCormick (13)	USA	Survived convoy
Dan-y-Bryn (81)	Britain	Survived convoy
Empire Baffin (11)	Britain	Survived convoy
Empire Beaumont (41)	Britain	Sunk by aircraft, 13 September (5 killed)
Empire Morn (53)	Britain	Survived convoy (CAM)
Empire Snow (31)	Britain	Survived convoy
Empire Stevenson (91)	Britain	Sunk by aircraft, 13 September (40 killed)
Empire Tristram (51)	Britain	Survived convoy
Esek Hopkins (43)	USA	Survived convoy
Exford (33)	USA	Survived convoy
Goolistan (74)	Britain	Survived convoy
Hollywood (34)	USA	Survived convoy
John Penn (73)	USA	Sunk by aircraft, 13 September (3 killed)
Kentucky (12)	USA	Sunk by aircraft, 18 September (0 killed)
Komiles (21)	Russia	Survived convoy
Lafayette (62)	USA	Survived convoy
Macbeth (102)	Panama	Sunk by aircraft, 13 September (0 killed)
Mary Luckenbach (93)	USA	Sunk by aircraft, 14 September (65 killed)
Meanticut (44)	USA	Survived convoy
Nathanael Greene (72)	USA	Survived convoy (1 killed*)
Ocean Faith (71)	Britain	Survived convoy
Oliver Ellsworth (105)	USA	Sunk by *U–408*, 13 September (1 killed)
Oregonian (101)	USA	Sunk by aircraft, 13 September (28 killed)
Patrick Henry (42)	USA	Survived convoy
Petrovski (22)	Russia	Survived convoy
Sahale (52)	USA	Survived convoy
Schoharie (64)	USA	Survived convoy
Stalingrad (103)	Russia	Sunk by *U–408*, 13 September (21 killed)
St Olaf (32)	USA	Survived convoy

Sukhona (104)	Russia	Sunk by aircraft, 13 September
Tblisi (75)	Russia	Survived convoy
Temple Arch (61)	Britain	Survived convoy
Virginia Dare (82)	USA	Survived convoy
Wacosta (92)	USA	Sunk by aircraft, 13 September (0 killed)
White Clover (23)	Panama	Survived convoy
William Moultrie (83)	USA	Survived convoy

Fleet oilers

Atheltemplar (45)	Britain	Sunk by *U-457*, 14 September 1942 (19 killed**)
Black Ranger (54)	Britain	Survived convoy
Gray Ranger (65)	Britain	Survived convoy
Oligarch (55)	Britain	Survived convoy

Rescue Ship

Copeland (15)	Britain	Survived convoy

* *Nathanael Greene* – one killed by debris from *Mary Luckenbach* explosion
** *Atheltemplar* – three were killed immediately, sixteen died later from wounds

HMS *Avenger* lost four Sea Hurricanes, with the loss of one pilot. A fifth plane was washed overboard.

Appendix II

Allied Naval losses QP14

HMS *Leda*	Sunk by *U-435* 20 September 1942 (47 killed)
HMS *Somali*	Torpedoed by *U-703* 20 September 1942 and broke up in a storm five days later whilst under tow (82 killed)
Silver Sword	Sunk by *U-255* 20 September 1942 (1 killed)
Bellingham	Sunk by *U-435* 22 September 1942 (0 killed)
Ocean Voice	Sunk by *U-435* 22 September 1942 (0 killed)
Gray Ranger	Sunk by *U-435* 22 September 1942 (6 killed)

German losses PQ18/QP14

U-88	Sunk by HMS *Faulknor*, 12 September 1942 (46 killed)
U-589	Sunk by HMS *Onslow*, 14 September 1942 (48 killed, including four airmen rescued the day before)
U-457	Sunk by HMS *Impulsive*, 16 September 1942 (45 killed)
U-253	Sunk by Catalina U/210 of Coastal Command, 23 September 1942 (45 killed)

German aircraft losses are reported to have been between forty and fifty, mainly He-111s and Ju-88 torpedo-bombers.

Bibliography

In the production of this book I have consulted many historians and experts and read as much as I could about PQ18, including contemporary accounts from sailors and airmen involved in the convoy. I have consulted records at the National Archives at Kew and discovered one or two new facts that I have included in the book. I have tried to dramatize events as much as possible, to try and bring history to life. Of course, we can never know what went on in the U-boats, since they were sunk by destroyers and Catalinas, so some dramatic licence has been taken in a few of those scenes.

Some of the books that have assisted me are:

Blond, Georges, *Ordeal below Zero: The Heroic Story of the Arctic Convoys in World War II*
Brown, Peter C., *Voices from the Arctic Convoys*
Campbell, Ian and Macintyre, Donald, *The Kola Run*
Edwards, Bernard, *The Road to Russia: Arctic Convoys 1942*
Gill, Paul, *Armageddon in the Arctic Ocean*
Grossmith Mason, Alfred and Grossmith Deltrice, Julie, *Arctic Warriors: A Personal Account of Convoy PQ18*
Hughes, Robert, *Through the Waters, A Gunnery Officer in HMS* Scylla *1942–43*
Mallmann Showell, Jak P., *U-boat Commanders and Crews 1935–45*
Schofiels, Ernest and Conyers Nesbit, Roy, *Arctic Airmen*
Smith, Peter C., *Convoy PQ18 Arctic Victory*
Thomas, Leona J., *Through Ice and Fire – A Russian Arctic Convoy Diary*
Walling, Michael G., *Forgotten Sacrifice: The Arctic Convoys of World War II*

Index

1PRU, 30, 39, 86, 89, 100, 126, 157
11th Flotilla, 26
20 Sqn (RFC), 85
144 Sqn, 29, 30, 86
210 Sqn, 29, 30, 86, 117, 153, 154, 157
330 Sqn, 144
422 Sqn, 30
455 Sqn, 29, 30, 86
802 Sqn, 18, 73
822 Sqn, 18
825 Sqn, 18, 28

Adam, Capt. Charles, 69, 92, 143
Admiral Hipper, 7, 21, 39
Admiral Scheer, 7, 39
Africander, SS, 6, 63, 72, 101
Afrikanda, 29, 40, 87
Akureyri, 144
Allied Supplies Executive, 70
Altenfjord, 7, 29, 30, 39, 40, 86, 100, 157
Archangelsk, 1, 3, 9, 10, 13, 14, 16, 17, 35, 42, 44, 55, 75–7, 79, 91, 93, 100, 101, 111, 113, 114, 116–19, 124–9, 139, 143, 148–51, 158, 160, 161
Armstrong, Harold 'Beaky', 89–92, 162
Asdic, 14, 20–3, 27–9, 31, 35–9, 45, 52, 56, 75, 90, 91, 108, 109, 137, 144
Atheltemplar, MV, 6, 20, 79, 81, 83, 84, 87, 167
Attlee, Clement, 70
Aultbea, 1, 2

B-Dienst, 23, 24, 35, 45, 133
Bailey, John Arthur, 81, 82

Bakharitsa, 16, 142, 149
Banak airbase, 5, 17, 42
Bardufoss airbase, 17, 42, 67, 75, 76, 98, 111
Bear Island, 5, 22, 34, 35, 42, 68, 79, 104, 129
Beckley, Lt Denis, 133–5
Bellingham, SS, 151, 164
Bergen, 24, 26
Bielfeld, Kapitänleutnant Heinz, 140, 165
Billefjord airbase, 77
Bismarck, 90, 159, 162
Black Ranger, RFA, 6, 79, 167
Bloedorn, Major, 94
Blue Ranger, RFA, 26, 35
Boddam-Whetham, Edye Kington, 4, 8, 18, 42, 56, 61–3, 68, 69, 93, 95, 125–7, 142, 161
Bohmann, Heino, 26, 27, 35–8
Bonham-Carter, Vice-Admiral Stuart, 8, 39, 41
Brandenburg, Karl, 83, 108–10
Broadbent, Asst Engineer *Atheltemplar*, 80–2
Burnett, Rear-Admiral Robert, 4, 8, 22, 30, 34, 42, 50, 56, 59, 62, 63, 68, 69, 84, 87, 89, 100, 107, 112, 113, 130, 133, 137–40, 143, 144, 149, 150, 158, 159, 161–3
Burr, Flying Officer Arthur, 93, 115, 121–4, 162

Campbell, Lt Cdr Ian, 58, 59, 137, 138
Campfire, SS, 78
Cape Gorodetski, 125

Carrique, Lt, 123, 124
Charles McCormack, SS, 110
Chatham Barracks, 61
Churchill, Winston, 3, 12, 55, 70, 102, 157, 160
Coastal Command, 8, 10, 17, 18, 24, 25, 29, 31, 32, 134, 137, 139, 144, 149, 152, 154, 157, 162, 164, 168
Colthurst, Cdr A.P., 18, 57, 69, 95, 98
Crombie, John Harvey-Forbes, 76, 113
Cruiser Covering Force (CCF), 8, 39, 41, 87, 159

Dan-y-Bryn, SS, 68
Dartau, Valentin, 43, 46, 47, 49, 50
Devons, Per, 146, 147
Distant Covering Force, 7, 39, 87, 159
Dowding, John (Jack), 76, 151
Dvina River, 1, 16, 116, 124–8, 139, 142

Effingham, SS, 129
Eisenhower, General Dwight D., 70, 160
Ekonomia, 16, 142, 149
El Occidonte, SS, 129
Empire Baffin, SS, 102, 111, 165
Empire Beaumont, SS, 6, 66, 72, 101
Empire Morn, SS, 13–15, 93, 112, 115, 120–2
Erswell, Charlie, 19, 32, 34, 42, 57, 58, 61, 64, 71, 92, 103, 138, 144, 149, 163
Exford, SS, 127

Fairhurst, Flt Lt Edward (Tim), 39, 86
Faxa Bay, 1, 15, 18
Federov, Alexander, 17, 53
Force A, 34
Force B, 20, 34, 42, 137, 158
Force P, 25, 26, 34, 130, 157
Fraser, Vice-Admiral Bruce, 7, 15, 40
Freeman, 60, 61

Friedrichs, Kapitänleutnant Adolf, 152, 154
Furniss, Flying Officer Donald, 39–41, 86

Gill, Paul, 96
Gneisenau, 21
Goad, Leading Seaman William, 156, 163, 164
Golden Comb (*Goldene Zange*), 59, 64, 69, 71, 74, 75, 78, 88, 92, 95, 99, 111, 118, 130, 158, 159
Göring, Hermann, 67, 75, 92, 93, 99, 111
Grasnaya, 30, 86, 126, 157
Gray Ranger, RFA, 20, 79, 151, 164
Greenwood, Sgt (RAF), 40
Gremyashchi, 116
Grossmith-Mason, Alfred, 110

Healy, Tim, 157
Hermann, Capt. Hajo, 118
Hill, Second Officer, MV *Atheltemplar*, 80, 81, 82
HMS *Alynbank*, 17, 20, 33, 69, 105, 113
HMS *Anson*, 7
HMS *Ashanti*, 139–41, 143, 152, 155, 156
HMS *Avenger*, 13, 18–21, 25, 28–30, 57–59, 66, 69, 71, 73, 78, 89, 92–5, 98, 105, 106, 112, 113, 121, 129, 130, 133, 137, 139, 140, 144, 153, 159
HMS *Berwick*, 12
HMS *Bramble*, 76, 113
HMS *Britomart*, 142
HMS *Cape Argona*, 13, 14, 127
HMS *Cape Mariato*, 120
HMS *Copeland*, 20, 49, 50, 52, 72, 101, 116
HMS *Cowdray*, 25
HMS *Cumberland*, 41
HMS *Daneman*, 128
HMS *Duke of York*, 7

HMS *Eclipse*, 41
HMS *Edinburgh*, 22
HMS *Faulknor*, 36, 38, 39, 43, 149, 151, 162
HMS *Fury*, 130, 139
HMS *Ganges*, 61
HMS *Glasgow*, 12
HMS *Harrier*, 72, 81, 84, 100–102, 127, 142
HMS *Hood*, 7
HMS *Impulsive*, 20, 21, 109–11, 130, 152, 165
HMS *Jamaica*, 7
HMS *Laforey*, 162
HMS *Leda*, 131, 132, 150, 164, 165
HMS *Lord Middleton*, 140, 152
HMS *Malcolm*, 113, 116
HMS *Maori*, 90
HMS *Marne*, 20, 21, 34, 148
HMS *Martin*, 34
HMS *Meteor*, 34
HMS *Milne*, 4, 19, 20, 32–4, 42, 57, 58, 61, 64, 65, 71, 92, 104, 137–40, 144, 149, 150, 163
HMS *Northern Gem*, 131, 132, 165
HMS *Oakley*, 26
HMS *Offa*, 112
HMS *Onslow*, 74, 89–92, 130, 162
HMS *Opportune*, 108, 109, 112, 133
HMS *Rathin*, 137
HMS *Savage*, 163
HMS *Scylla*, 4–6, 8, 9, 16, 18, 20–2, 30, 33, 34, 42, 50, 56, 59–63, 69, 77, 84, 89, 93–5, 97, 100–102, 112–14, 129, 133, 136–40, 149, 158, 163
HMS *Seagull*, 151
HMS *Sharpshooter*, 68, 72, 84, 100, 102, 120
HMS *Sheffield*, 41
HMS *Somali*, 140, 143, 144, 149, 152, 155–7, 163, 165
HMS *St Kenan*, 50, 52, 53, 127
HMS *Tartar*, 84, 85

HMS *Trinidad*, 22
HMS *Ulster Queen*, 17, 20, 33, 69, 92, 105, 113, 117, 118, 123, 128, 142, 143
HMS *Wheatland*, 139
HMS *Wilton*, 139
HMS *Windsor*, 25
HMS *Worcester*, 152
Hope Island, 5, 102
Hopps, Group Captain Frank, 29, 30, 40, 85, 99, 100, 114, 161
Horrer, Hans-Joachim, 73, 88–91
Hughes, Robert, 5, 6, 8, 9, 22, 33, 42, 56, 60, 61, 77, 78, 93, 94, 97, 101, 114, 136, 138, 140, 163
Hvalfjödur, 1, 9, 15, 41
Hymmen, Reinhard von, 44–6, 48, 133–5, 164

I/903, 77
I/KG26, 58, 59, 120
III/KG26, 92, 94
III/KG30, 118, 120

Jan Mayen Island, 5, 34, 41, 144, 146, 149
Jay, Commander Alan, 81, 84
Jennings, Second Engineer, MV *Atheltemplar*, 80, 81, 84
John Penn, SS, 66, 72

Kandalaksha, 30
Keg Ostrov airbase, 124
Kentucky, SS, 110, 120
Khromov, Russian diplomat, 16, 53
Klumper, Major Werner, 58, 59, 64, 66, 72, 75, 76, 92, 94, 95, 98, 99, 111, 118–20, 164
Kola Inlet, 1, 9, 18, 29, 30, 35, 77, 85, 93, 100, 102, 112, 129, 133
Köln, German cruiser, 7, 39
Krasny Quay, 142
Kuibyshev, 70

Lake Lakhta, 30
Langdon, Sgt, 153
Langfjord, 40
Lend-Lease, 20
Lerwick, 133
Lewin, Sub-Lt Terence, 141
Listenev, Soviet destroyer, 117
Loch Ewe, 1, 2, 4, 5, 12
Lofoten Islands, 7, 9
Lowe Sound, 26, 34, 42, 84
Luzhkov, Soviet destroyer, 117

Manley, Cdr Lawrence, 108
Mary Luckenbach, SS, 68, 69, 95–8, 102, 104
Maud, Lt Cdr Colin, 140, 155, 156, 163
MacIntyre, Capt. Ian, 8, 22, 42, 59, 95, 100
Meanticut, SS, 6
MMS203, 72
MMS212, 72
MMS90, 72
Mortensen, Soren, 151
Mudyugskiy, 149
Mullender, Skipper Lt William, 131, 132, 165
Murmansk, 1, 10, 29, 30, 32, 55, 85, 100, 161

Nancarrow, Fred, 11
Narvik, 7, 24, 73, 87, 100, 159
Nathanael Greene, SS, 68, 75, 95–7
Navarino, SS, 132
Nocken, Klaus, 92–4
Noel-Baker, Philip, 161

Ocean Freedom, SS, 151
Ocean Voice, SS, 76, 151, 164
Oligarch, RFA, 26, 35, 79, 130
Oliver Ellsworth, SS, 48, 50, 53, 54, 68, 101, 164
Operation EVY, 8, 41
Operation Gearbox II, 41

Operation Orator, 29, 77, 87, 100, 112, 114, 117, 126, 130, 139, 157, 159, 161
Operation Torch, 70, 157
Oregonian, SS, 63, 72, 101, 166
Ornoya, 40

P614, 20, 133–5, 164
P615, 20, 133
Palomares, 17
Payne, Leading Seaman, 141
Polyarny, 85
Poolewe, 1, 2, 4
Pozarica, 17
PQ17, 3–5, 7, 9, 21, 24, 26, 29, 56, 68, 69, 71, 77, 86, 113, 129, 132, 150, 158, 159, 164
PQ19, 70, 71, 160
PQ20, 70, 71, 160

QP10, 129
QP14, 8, 9, 29, 35, 76, 93, 100, 112–14, 116, 129, 131–3, 136, 137, 139, 141, 143, 144, 145, 148–50, 153, 155–7, 161, 162, 164

RAF Cranwell, 85
RAF Eastchurch, 85
Rathin, SS, 137
Ray, Master Carl, 79, 80
Reche, Reinhardt, 137, 164
Reeves, James Arthur, 81–4, 163
Ridgewell, Harry, 80–4
River Afton, SS, 132
RNAS Hatston, 18
Roberts, Ernest, 80, 81
Roosevelt, Franklin D., 20, 70
Roper, Lt Cdr Edward, 109, 111, 165
Royal Flying Corps, 85
Russell, Cdr Archibald, 113, 116, 118, 126

Sakharov, Anatoly, 15–17, 43, 44, 46, 47, 49–53, 116, 128, 142, 164

Scapa Flow, 5, 6, 156, 157
Scharnhorst, 21, 161
Scott-Moncrieff, Alan, 37–9, 149, 151, 152, 155, 162
Sea Hurricanes, 13, 14, 18, 19, 21, 25, 30, 31, 57–9, 64, 66, 67, 69–71, 73, 78, 92–5, 98, 99, 105–107, 111, 112, 115, 120–4, 137, 159
Semmens, Flt Sgt J., 153, 154
Seydisfjördur, 18, 19, 149
Shmakov, USSR diplomat, 16, 53
Silver Sword, SS, 136, 164
Simpson, Lt Robert, 53
Skomenfjord, 45, 46
Sorfjord, 40
Sorushitelni, Soviet destroyer, 116
Spitzbergen, 25, 34, 35, 41, 79, 84, 129, 130, 157, 158, 165
Stalin, Joseph, 54, 55, 70, 102, 160
Stalingrad, Battle of, 4, 21, 111, 149, 158, 160, 161
Stalingrad, SS, 15, 16, 43, 44, 46–50, 52–4, 68, 101, 116, 128, 142, 164
Stansberg, Lt Carl, 144–8
Strelkov, SS *Stalingrad*, 49, 53
Strelow, Siegfried, 129, 131, 150, 151, 164
Sturges, Robert, 12
Sukhona, SS, 6, 16, 63, 72, 101
Sullom Voe, 30, 137, 153
Swordfish, 7, 18, 21, 24, 28, 29, 36, 56, 88–90, 112, 117, 130, 133, 137, 139, 140, 144, 153, 159

Taylor, Lt (802 Sqn), 73
Temple Arch, SS, 4, 6, 8, 18, 56, 61, 62
Tirpitz, 3–5, 7, 8, 21, 29, 41, 85–7, 100, 102, 159, 160
Torsvaag, 40
Tournaig, 2

Trägertod, wolf-pack, 26, 44, 73
Troubadour, SS, 130
Tuscaloosa, USNS, 30, 85

U-1222, 165
U-223, 162
U-253, 152, 154, 155
U-255, 137, 164
U-408, 44, 45, 48, 133–5, 164
U-435, 129, 131, 150, 164
U-457, 83, 108–12, 133, 165
U-586, 145
U-589, 73, 75, 88–92, 162
U-606, 145, 147, 148
U-703, 140, 165
U-88, 26, 27, 35–8, 45, 162
U/210, 153, 154
US Navy Armed Guard, 9, 96

Vaenga, 30, 39, 40
Vickers, Capt., 95–7
Virginia Dare, SS, 68
Von der Esch, Dietrich, 145–8

Wacosta, SS, 63, 72
Wager, Sqn Ldr Lawrence, 40
Walker, Capt., Ocean Freedom, 151, 152
Walker, Pilot Officer Gavin, 100, 157
War Cabinet, 70
Western Approaches, 1, 5, 9, 12, 139
Wightman, Les, 14
Winston Salem, SS, 130
Wylie, Leading Seaman, 141

Yermilov, First Lt, 43, 46, 49

Z/330, 144–6, 148
Zamalek, SS, 137, 151